◆ 浙江省高等学校课程思政教学研究项目"留学生'中国概况'课程思政教学内容融入研究"最终成果
◆ 宁波大学历史学国家一流本科专业建设点阶段性成果
◆ 宁波大学本科线上一流课程项目"中国概况"配套教材
◆ 浙江省哲学社会科学重点研究基地宁波大学浙东文化研究院资助项目

中国概况

（汉英对照）

主编　白　斌　罗　娜
编著　杨桂珍　刘颖男
　　　宋佳睿　芦王菲
翻译　罗　娜

浙江大学出版社
·杭州·

图书在版编目（CIP）数据

中国概况：汉英对照 / 白斌，罗娜主编. —杭州：浙江大学出版社，2023.11
 ISBN 978-7-308-24347-6

Ⅰ. ①中… Ⅱ. ①白… ②罗… Ⅲ. ①汉语－对外汉语教学－教材②中国－概况－汉、英 Ⅳ. ①H195.4 ②K92

中国国家版本馆CIP数据核字(2023)第207155号

中国概况（汉英对照）
白 斌 罗 娜 主编

策划编辑	吴伟伟
责任编辑	马一萍　宁　檬
责任校对	陈逸行
封面设计	周　灵
出版发行	浙江大学出版社
	（杭州市天目山路148号　邮政编码310007）
	（网址：http://www.zjupress.com）
排　　版	杭州林智广告有限公司
印　　刷	广东虎彩云印刷有限公司绍兴分公司
开　　本	710mm×1000mm　1/16
印　　张	21.5
字　　数	510千
版 印 次	2023年11月第1版　2023年11月第1次印刷
书　　号	ISBN 978-7-308-24347-6
定　　价	98.00元

版权所有　侵权必究　　印装差错　负责调换

浙江大学出版社市场运营中心联系方式：0571-88925591；http://zjdxcbs.tmall.com

序

21世纪以来，随着国家综合实力的提升和国际地位的提高，中国与世界各国的交流与合作也愈发紧密。在中国人走出国门向世界学习的同时，大量其他国家的居民也来到中国学习和生活。

"中国概况"课程是面向留学生设置的高校国际学生学历教育的必修课。"中国概况"是一门让留学生系统、全面、客观地了解中国政治、经济、文化等各方面基本情况的基础课程，便于留学生认识中国、了解中国，也有助于提升他们学习汉语的兴趣。

"中国概况"课程实行线上与线下的混合教学。在这种教学方式下，任课教师以线上直播或录播的形式进行课堂讲解，学生以自主学习的方式完成"中国概况"课程的学习。这种教学方式将学生的学习由传统的计时定点教学转为学生可以自由选择时间地点的多维度学习。一方面，线上教学极大地扩充了教师可以使用的教学资源，增加了教学趣味性；另一方面，线上教学不仅对学生的学习自觉性要求高，而且对教师课堂教学设计也提出了更高的要求。在无法实现线上教学的区域，特别是非洲等地区不具备线上教学条件的孔子学院和中文教学点，教师和学生仍使用传统的教学模式，对教材的依赖性依旧存在。在教材编写过程中有效平衡两者之间的需求，是我们对"中国概况"课程教材编撰的新要求。

"中国概况"课程一般设置为一个学期17周，其中正常教学课时为15周。因此，本教材设置15个章节，可执行每周一章的教学计划。本教材为宁波大学本科线上一流课程"中国概况"的配套教材。线上课程将与教材同步推出。

相比以往的同类教材，本教材在内容上有大幅增加。本教材在每一章都设计了6个主题，每个主题之间是并列的关系。从事线下教学的任课教师可以根据自己的授课风格及学生的文化背景与兴趣，自由选择适合的主题进行课堂教学。每个主题由两篇文章组成，其中必读课文为学生在课堂上需要重点掌握的内容，而拓展知识则供学生线下自主学习使用。

本教材由宁波大学白斌、罗娜、杨桂珍、刘颖男、宋佳睿、芦王菲共同编写。其中，白斌承担全书各章节的策划和统稿工作，并承担教材第一章至第六章的编写工作；罗娜承担全书的校稿与英文翻译工作，并承担教材第十章至第十二章的编写工作；杨桂珍承担教材第十三章至第十五章的编写工作；刘颖男承担教材第七章至第九章的编写工作；宋佳睿和芦王菲承担全书相关资料、数据的搜集与各主题讨论题的编写工作。在本教材的编写过程中，华东师范大学丁安琪教授提出了诸多宝贵意见，在此深表感谢。除此之外，本教材的编写还得到宁波大学教务处、国际处、浙东文化研究院、人文与传媒学院、教师教育学院，以及马达加斯加塔马塔夫大学孔子学院、冰岛大学北极光孔子学院领导与同事的大力支持，谨此一并致谢！

因编者水平有限，难免存在疏漏和不足，希望使用本教材的老师和同学们能提出宝贵的意见和建议。

白斌　罗娜

2023 年 3 月

目 录

- 导 论 | 001
- **地理变迁篇**
  - 第一章　自然地理 | 004
  - 第二章　人文地理 | 015
  - 第三章　人与环境 | 025
- **历史演进篇**
  - 第四章　古代中国（一） | 038
  - 第五章　古代中国（二） | 048
  - 第六章　近代以来 | 058
- **经济发展篇**
  - 第七章　经济转型 | 070
  - 第八章　文化产业 | 080
  - 第九章　合作共赢 | 091

● **科技创新篇**

第 十 章　信息网络　　　　　　　　　　| 102

第十一章　人工智能　　　　　　　　　| 112

第十二章　航空航天　　　　　　　　　| 122

● **文化传承篇**

第十三章　传统文化　　　　　　　　　| 134

第十四章　饮食文化　　　　　　　　　| 144

第十五章　中外差异　　　　　　　　　| 154

CONTENTS

Introduction | 165

Geographical Variations

Chapter 1 Physical Geography | 168
Chapter 2 Human Geography | 179
Chapter 3 People and Environment | 190

Historical Evolution

Chapter 4 Ancient China (I) | 202
Chapter 5 Ancient China (II) | 213
Chapter 6 Modern Times | 224

Economic Development

Chapter 7 Economic Transformation | 238
Chapter 8 Cultural Industry | 249
Chapter 9 Win-Win Cooperation | 259

Science and Technology Innovation

Chapter 10 Information Network | 272
Chapter 11 Artificial Intelligence | 282
Chapter 12 Aerospace | 292

Cultural Heritage

Chapter 13 Traditional Culture | 304
Chapter 14 Food Culture | 315
Chapter 15 Differences Between China and Foreign Countries | 327

>>>>
导 论

中国，位于亚洲东部、太平洋的西岸。中国领土辽阔，陆地总面积约960万平方千米，海域总面积约470万平方千米。中国地势西高东低，大致呈阶梯状分布。气温和降水的不同形成了中国多种多样的气候。中国省级行政单位共有34个，包括23个省、5个自治区、4个直辖市和2个特别行政区。中国人口基数大，民族众多。中国资源丰富，但人均资源占有量相对较少。

中国，是世界上历史最悠久的国家之一。史前时期的有巢氏、燧人氏、伏羲氏、神农氏、轩辕氏被尊为中华人文始祖。夏商周时期是中国的奴隶制社会时期。秦朝至清朝是中国的封建社会时期。辛亥革命后，中国确立了共和政体。1949年，中华人民共和国成立。

中华人民共和国成立后，中国通过有计划的大规模建设，取得了举世瞩目的成就，为国民经济的发展打下了坚实基础，逐步从一个传统的农业国向现代化的工业强国迈进。改革开放以来，中国经济得到前所未有的快速增长。进入21世纪，中国经济继续保持稳步高速增长。目前，中国已成为世界第二大经济体，是世界上最具发展潜力的经济大国之一。

中华人民共和国成立后，中国的科学技术水平得到了很大提高，在计算机、航空航天、生物工程、新能源、新材料、激光技术等领域都取得了重大科技成果。20世纪80年代至90年代，中国先后推出了"863计划"和"科教兴国战略"，大大促进了中国科技的发展和进步。中国设有众多公立的科研机构，每年有大量的成果产出，国际科技竞争力迅速提升。

中华文明是当代中国文化的根基，起源于史前时期。汉唐时期，中国儒释道思想以及文字、绘画、建筑、雕刻等已经非常繁荣。中国文化不仅对日本和朝鲜半岛产生了重要影响，还传播至越南等东南亚国家，形成了以中国文化为枢纽的东亚文化圈。明清以来，随着东西方文化交流日益频繁，中国文化走向世界，并在世界文化体系内占有重要地位。

中国作为一个历史悠久的文明古国，巍然屹立于世界东方。

地理变迁篇

第一章

自然地理

一 海洋

必读课文

中国海域

中国海域，由中国大陆边缘的渤海、黄海、东海和南海组成，横跨温带、亚热带和热带。东部和南部大陆海岸线 1.8 万千米。内海和边海的水域面积约为 470 万平方千米。

渤海是中国最北端的海域，三面环陆，位于辽宁、河北、山东和天津之间。渤海盛产对虾、蟹和黄花鱼。黄海位于中国大陆与朝鲜半岛之间，北起鸭绿江口，南以长江口北岸启东角到韩国济州岛西南角连线与东海分界。黄海长期受黄河等河流大量黄褐色泥沙注入的影响，含沙量较大，近岸海水呈黄色，黄海也因此而得名。东海是中国三大边缘海之一，也是中国大陆架最宽的边缘海。东海盛产黄鱼、带鱼、墨鱼等。东海海底石油和天然气资源丰富。南海，因位于中国南部而得名。南海自然资源丰富，有种类繁多的动植物资源和丰富的矿产资源。

拓展知识

南　海

南海，位于中国的南方，中国三大边缘海之一，为中国近海中面积最大、水最深的海区。南海东南至菲律宾群岛，西南至越南和马来半岛，最南边的曾母暗沙靠近加里曼丹岛。南海通过巴士海峡、苏禄海和马六甲海峡等，与太平洋和印度洋相连。

南海有超过 200 个岛屿和岩礁，通称为南海诸岛。南海诸岛包括东沙群岛、西沙群岛、中沙群岛和南沙群岛。南海诸岛在古代即为中国人所利用和开发，是中国领土不可分割的一部分。1988 年海南省设立后，南海诸岛成为海南省的一部分。2012 年，中国设立海南省三沙市，管辖西沙群岛、中沙群岛、南沙群岛及海域。

南海和南海诸岛全部在北回归线以南，接近赤道，属赤道带、热带海洋性季风气候，终年高温高湿，四时皆夏。南海是全球台风活动的主要区域之一，每月都有可能生成台风。南海是中国联系东南亚、南亚、西亚、非洲的必经之地，也是西欧至远东最重要的海上航线之一。

讨论

从中国到你的国家有海上航线吗？分别经过哪些海域？

（二） 高原

必读课文

中国高原

高原，指海拔在 500 米以上、顶面比较平缓的高地。中国的四大高原分别是青藏高原、云贵高原、内蒙古高原、黄土高原。

青藏高原，是中国最大、世界海拔最高的高原，号称"世界屋脊"。青藏高原位于中国西部及西南部，面积约 250 万平方千米，平均海拔 4000 米以上，为东亚、东南亚和南亚许多大河的发源地。

云贵高原，位于中国西南部，西与青藏高原相接。云贵高原是世界上喀斯特地貌发育最完整、最典型的地区之一，拥有丰富多样的自然环境。云贵高原是长江、西江和元江三大水系的分水岭。

内蒙古高原，中国第二大高原，为蒙古高原的一部分。内蒙古高原主要以低缓的丘陵和宽浅的盆地为主。东部为草原，是中国的重要畜牧业基地；西部气候干燥，为干草原、荒漠草原与荒漠。

黄土高原，在秦岭及渭河平原以北、长城以南、太行山以西、洮河及乌鞘岭以东。黄土高原土质疏松，地形破碎，水土流失严重。经过多年的综合治理，黄土高原的水土流失已得到一定控制。黄土高原富藏煤炭、石油、铝土等。

拓展知识

帕米尔高原

帕米尔高原，位于中国新疆维吾尔自治区西南部、塔吉克斯坦东南部和阿富汗东北部一带。帕米尔高原是天山、昆仑山、喀喇昆仑山和兴都库什山等交会而成的大山结。帕米尔高原海拔 4000 米～7700 米，拥有多座高峰。中国境内的公格尔峰为 7649 米，慕士塔格峰为 7509 米。

帕米尔高原属高寒气候，自然景观垂直变化明显。帕米尔高原冰川广布，是世界上最大的山地冰川之一。山地冰川使一些荒漠、河流得到水源。帕米尔高原西北角的菲德钦科冰川长达71.2千米，为世界上最长的高山冰川之一。帕米尔高原东部是山羊和盘羊的主要繁育地。中部地势起伏和缓，有宽广的谷地。帕米尔高原河谷地带有灌溉条件的地方可栽培葡萄等水果。

帕米尔高原，为中国习称"葱岭"的一部分，历史上著名的陆上"丝绸之路"在穿越帕米尔高原后才能到达中亚及地中海各国。

讨论

> 在地图上找一找，古代从中国西安到意大利罗马的陆上丝绸之路要经过哪些高原？

三　平原

必读课文

中国平原

平原，指海拔高度小于200米的宽广低平地区。按成因分为冲积平原、侵蚀平原、湖成平原等。中国有三大平原，分别是东北平原、华北平原和长江中下游平原，分布在中国东部地势第三级阶梯上。

东北平原是中国面积最大的平原，位于大、小兴安岭，长白山和燕山之间，主要由辽河、松花江、嫩江冲积而成。东北平原夏季短促而温暖多雨；冬季漫长而寒冷少雪。东北平原土层深厚，土壤肥沃，富含有机质，是中国重要的粮食基地。

华北平原是中国第二大平原，位于黄河下游，面积约31万平方千米。华北平原是典型的冲积平原。华北平原地势平坦，一望无际；河湖众多，交通便利。华北平原是中国的政治、经济、文化和交通中心。

长江中下游平原指中国长江三峡以东的中下游沿岸带状平原，由长江及其支流冲积形成。长江中下游平原，地势平坦，湖泊众多，沃野千里。长江中下游平原是中国著名的"鱼米之乡"，也是中国水资源异常丰富的地区。

拓展知识

关中平原

关中平原，又称"渭河平原"或"关中盆地"，在陕西省中部，秦岭与陕北高原之间，是一个三面环山向东敞开的河谷盆地。关中平原西起宝鸡，东至潼关，南接秦岭，北抵陕北高原。关中平原东西长300多千米；东宽西窄，海拔400米左右，关中平原地势平坦，土壤肥沃，气候温和，水源丰富，灌溉便利。关中平原自然、经济条件优越，是中国历史上农业最富庶的地区之一。目前，关中平原仍是中国工业、农业和文化发达地区之一，也是中国重要的小麦和棉花产区。

因交通便利，四周有山河之险，故从西周开始，先后有秦、西汉、隋、唐等10个王朝建都于关中平原，历时千余年。作为古代王朝的政治、经济和文化中心，关中平原因为东有函谷关、西有大散关、南有武关、北有萧关，居四关之内，故称"关中"。

关中平原拥有非常丰厚的历史文化底蕴，春秋战国时期为秦国故地。战国末期，秦国从此东出统一全国，建立了中国第一个封建王朝——秦朝，所以关中平原又被称为"秦川"或"八百里秦川"。

讨论

中国还有哪些平原属于冲积平原？你的国家也有类似的冲积平原吗？

（四）盆地

必读课文

中国盆地

盆地，是指地球表面四周高、中部低的地区。中国盆地主要有塔里木盆地、准噶尔盆地、柴达木盆地和四川盆地。它们多分布在地势的第二级阶梯上，由于所处位置不同，其特点也不同。

塔里木盆地，位于中国新疆南部，是中国面积最大的内陆盆地。塔里木盆地处于天山、昆仑山和阿尔金山之间，西起帕米尔高原，东至罗布泊洼地，面积约53万平方千米。塔里木盆地边缘是戈壁，塔里木河以南的中部是沙漠与盐湖。盆地边缘和沙漠间是冲积扇和冲积平原，并有绿洲分布。盆地气候干旱少雨，昼夜温差很大。盆地中蕴藏着丰富的石油和天然气资源。

准噶尔盆地，位于新疆北部，天山、阿尔泰山及西部诸山间，呈不等边三角形。准噶尔盆地为半封闭的内陆型盆地，地势东高西低。盆地边缘为山麓绿洲，栽培作物多为一年一熟，盛产棉花、小麦。盆地中部为广阔草原和沙漠，部分被灌木及草本植物覆盖。盆地南部是新疆农业、工业、能源、文化、科教的重要示范基地。

柴达木盆地，位于青海省北部，阿尔金山、祁连山、昆仑山之间，平均海拔2600米~3000米。柴达木盆地是中国地势最高的巨型内陆盆地。盆地地势自西北向东南倾斜，从边缘至中心依次为戈壁、丘陵、平原、湖泊等。盆地气候干旱，降水稀少。盆地矿产资源丰富。

拓展知识

四川盆地

四川盆地，位于中国四川省东部、长江上游，南部为云贵高原，西部为青藏高原，北部为大巴山。按地理差异，四川盆地自西向东可分为成都平原、川中丘陵和川东平行岭谷三部分。四川盆地的土壤呈紫色，是中国最肥沃的自然土壤之一，因此又被称为"紫色盆地"。

四川盆地气候温和、雨量充沛，特别是自战国时期修建了都江堰水利工程之后，成都平原成为中国历史上农业和手工业都十分发达的地区，成为中央王朝的主要粮食供给基地和赋税的主要来源，号称"天府之国"。四川盆地人口稠密，经济繁荣，文化昌盛。盆地中的主要城市有成都、重庆、绵阳等。

四川盆地是中国动物种类最多、最齐全的地区之一，其中属于国家一级保护动物的有大熊猫、川金丝猴等。四川盆地有煤、盐、天然气、石油等矿产资源。四川盆地水陆交通方便，除公路网外，有成渝、成昆、宝成等铁路干线和以川江为主的水运网。

讨论

中国或你的国家还有哪些盆地？是否也盛产石油？

(五) 沙漠

必读课文

中国沙漠

沙漠，地面完全为沙所覆盖，缺乏流水，气候干燥，植物稀少的地区。中国西北干旱地区是中国沙漠最为集中的地区。中国的主要沙漠有塔克拉玛干沙漠、古尔班通古特沙漠和巴丹吉林沙漠。

塔克拉玛干沙漠，位于新疆塔里木盆地的中部，是中国最大的沙漠，世界著名大沙漠之一。受风的影响，沙漠沙丘时常移动。西部受西北风影响，沙丘向东南移动，东部受东北风影响，沙丘向西南移动。沙漠里的植物较少，以胡杨、红柳等为主。塔克拉玛干有着辉煌的历史文化，古丝绸之路就途经沙漠南端。

古尔班通古特沙漠，位于新疆准噶尔盆地中央，是中国第二大沙漠。沙漠内部绝大部分为固定和半固定沙丘。在西北风和西风影响下，沙漠形成西北—东南走向的大沙垄带。该沙漠水源较多，植物种类较丰富，有白梭梭、蒿属等沙生植物，为优良的冬季牧场。沙漠西北部有大型盐矿。

巴丹吉林沙漠，位于内蒙古自治区阿拉善右旗西部和额济纳旗东部一带。沙漠气候干旱，降水少，光照强。高耸的沙山、神秘的鸣沙和宁静的湖泊构成了巴丹吉林沙漠独特的迷人景观，吸引着众多的国内外游客。

拓展知识

乌兰布和沙漠

乌兰布和沙漠，地处内蒙古自治区中部偏西，北至狼山，东北与河套平原相邻，东至黄河，南至贺兰山北侧，西至吉兰泰盐池。

乌兰布和沙漠地势由东南向西北倾斜，南部多流沙，中部多垄岗形沙丘，北部多固定和半固定沙丘。乌兰布和沙漠北部是古黄河冲积平原，沙丘之间有大面积土质平地，进行土地平整后就可开发利用，发展农业具有潜在优势，目前已开辟多处农场。乌兰布和沙漠地势平坦，由黄河岸向西缓缓倾斜，可以引黄河水自流灌溉。沙漠西部及西南部的半固定、固定沙丘地区分布有不少天然草场，其中红砂、梭梭柴、白刺等沙生、旱生、盐生类植物对当地环境有极强的适应性。

乌兰布和沙漠形成的主要原因是干旱和风，加上人们滥伐树木，破坏草原，周边自然环境一度十分恶劣。随着国家的大规模治理，西部地区注意保持牧业经济，乌兰布和沙漠的生态环境渐渐好转。

讨论

你去过沙漠吗？沙漠中有哪些风景？

六 山脉

必读课文

中国山脉

山脉，是沿一定方向作线状延伸的山体，常由多条山体组成。中国的山脉按走向可分为东西走向、东北—西南走向、西北—东南走向、南北走向和弧形山脉五种，具有代表性的山脉有喜马拉雅山脉、昆仑山山脉和横断山脉。

喜马拉雅山脉，为弧形山脉，位于青藏高原南部，是世界上海拔最高的山脉。喜马拉雅山脉南北两侧气候迥异，南坡气候暖湿，北坡气候干燥，南北两坡的地形、水文、生物、土壤及农业生产差异较大。山脉主峰是世界最高峰珠穆朗玛峰，位于喜马拉雅山脉的中段。

昆仑山脉，又称"亚洲脊柱"，为东西走向山脉。昆仑山脉位于亚洲中部，西起帕米尔高原东部，横贯新疆、西藏两个自治区，向东延伸至青海省境内。昆仑山脉西高东低，按地势可分为西、中、东三段，每段都有几座海拔在6000米以上的山峰。

横断山脉，是中国最长、最宽和最典型的南北走向山脉。横断山脉位于青藏高原东南部，通常为四川、云南两省西部和西藏自治区东部南北走向山脉的总称。因山脉"横断"东西交通，故名"横断山脉"。横断山脉气候垂直变化明显，森林资源和水能资源丰富。

拓展知识

五 岳

五岳，是中国传统文化对五大名山的统称，分别是东岳泰山、西岳华山、中岳嵩山、南岳衡山和北岳恒山。

泰山，位于山东省中部，是世界自然与文化双重遗产。在"盘古开天"神话中，盘古死后，头变成泰山，腹变成嵩山，左臂变成衡山，右臂变成恒山，两脚变成华山。因此，泰山被称为"天下第一山"，是五岳之首。

华山，位于陕西省东部，秦岭山脉以北。华山是道教名山，元朝时为全真道华山派发源地。华山险阻，有"华山自古一条路"的说法。山上的西岳庙，建于汉武帝时期，为历代帝王祭祀西岳神的祠庙。

嵩山，位于河南省登封市北部，由太室山和少室山组成。嵩山是中国佛教禅宗的发源地和道教圣地，也是中国功夫之源少林寺的所在地。嵩山为世界地质公园国家级风景名胜区。

衡山，位于湖南省中部，是中国最著名的佛教、道教圣地。衡山著名山峰有72座，其中以祝融、天柱、芙蓉、紫盖、石廪五峰最为高大。衡山绿化面积大，处处古木参天，奇花异草繁多，有"五岳独秀"之称。

　　恒山，位于山西省北部和河北省西北部，是道教圣地之一。传说，"八仙"之一的张果老就是在恒山隐居后修炼成仙的。

讨论

在地图上找一找，中国除了"五岳"外，还有哪些名山？

第二章

人文地理

一 人口

必读课文

中国人口

人口，指生活在特定社会制度、特定区域内的人的总和。历史上，中国人口一直占据着世界人口的较大比例。近代时期，由于战乱等原因，中国人口增长缓慢。1949年以后，由于生产发展和人均寿命延长，中国人口增长迅速。

根据2020年第七次全国人口普查结果，中国人口超过14亿。数据显示，中国人口十年来继续保持低速增长态势。受中国人口流动和年轻人婚后独立居住等因素影响，中国家庭户人口规模继续缩小，平均每个家庭户人口不到3人。从中国人口的地区分布看，东部地区约占40%，中部地区约占26%，西部地区约占27%，东北地区约占7%。与2010年相比，东部和西部地区人口比重上升，中部和东北地区下降，人口向经济发达区域、城市群进一步集聚。从性别构成看，男女性别比例与2010年基本持平。从年龄构成看，人口老龄化程度进一步加深。从城乡人口构成看，城镇人口超过9亿，城镇人口比重进一步上升。

拓展知识

人口政策

人口政策是指国家为实现一定的人口目标而制定、采取的旨在调节或影响人口的数量、素质、构成、分布等状况的政策。不同国家的人口政策会根据本国人口发展的实际情况而进行调整。

中国古代的人口政策与婚姻政策关系密切。一些朝代在经历长期战争后，人口大量减少。为解决这一问题，政府通过鼓励早婚的方式，推动人口增长。如春秋时期的越国，规定男子 20 岁和女子 17 岁为最迟结婚年龄。如果男女超过这个年龄没有结婚，其父母要受到处罚。

20 世纪 80 年代，中国将计划生育作为一项基本国策，即按人口政策有计划地进行生育。计划生育政策提倡晚婚、晚育、少生、优生，一对夫妇只生育一个孩子。其目的是有计划地控制人口增长，促进人口长期均衡发展。

21 世纪初，计划生育政策在中国经济发达的地区有一定的调整。2016 年，中国全面实施二孩政策。2021 年，中国进一步优化生育政策，实施一对夫妻可以生育三个子女政策。

讨论

你的国家有哪些人口政策？和中国的人口政策有哪些异同？

(二) 民族

必读课文

中国的民族

民族，指历史上形成的、处于不同社会发展阶段的各种人的共同体。一个国家可以有不同的民族，一个民族可以生活在不同的国家。中国是一个统一的多民族国家，有汉族、壮族、回族、满族、维吾尔族等 56 个民族。汉族是中国的主体民族，其他 55 个民族统称为"少数民族"。

汉族，由古代华夏族和其他民族长期融合而成。无论在社会科学领域，还是在自然科学领域，汉族都创造了辉煌的成就。汉族是一个历史悠久的民族，是世界上人口最多的民族。汉族遍布全国，主要聚居于黄河、长江、珠江三大流域和松辽平原。除中国外，汉族还分布在东南亚、北美洲和西欧。

壮族，是中国人口最多的一个少数民族，民族语言为壮语。壮族由中国古代百越的一支发展而来。壮族主要分布在中国南方，广西壮族自治区是壮族的主要分布区。除中国外，壮族还分布在越南北部与中国相邻的地区。

回族，是中国人口较多的一个少数民族。回族以 13 世纪迁入中国的中亚人、波斯人和阿拉伯人为主，在长期发展中吸收汉、蒙古、维吾尔等民族成分逐渐形成。回族主要分布在中国西北地区，宁夏回族自治区是回族的主要分布区。

拓展知识

满 族

满族，是中国人口较多的一个少数民族，民族语言为满语、汉语。满族主要分布在中国北方，辽宁、河北、黑龙江和吉林等省是满族的主要分布区。

东北地区的"白山黑水"是满族的故乡和发源地。满族的起源，可以追溯到

2000多年前的"肃慎"及后来的"女真"。辽朝时，女真建立金国（前金）。随后，金朝与北宋联合消灭辽国。蒙古崛起后，金朝被元朝取代。明朝中后期，女真再次建立金国，史称后金，后改为"大清"。1644年，清军入关，并逐步统一中国。1911年，辛亥革命爆发，清朝统治彻底瓦解。

满族，以农业为主，兼事捕鱼、畜牧、养殖业等。满族儿歌和民谣中有很多狩猎生活的痕迹。满族传统服饰的代表是男子身穿马褂、女子身穿旗袍。满族食品极具特色，最能代表满、汉饮食文化融合的当属"满汉全席"。在中国古代，满族流行娶"大媳妇"，即女方比男方年龄大为好，有"女大三，抱金砖"的说法。清朝以来，满族教育与文化有很大发展，代表人物有曹雪芹和老舍。

讨论

你属于哪个民族？你的民族有哪些特征？

三 省份

必读课文

中国省份

中国的省级行政区共计34个，包括23个省、5个自治区、4个直辖市和2个特别行政区，简称分别是：

华北地区：北京市，"京"；天津市，"津"；河北省，"冀"；山西省，"晋"；内蒙古自治区，"内蒙古"。

东北地区：辽宁省，"辽"；吉林省，"吉"；黑龙江省，"黑"。

华东地区：上海市，"沪"；江苏省，"苏"；浙江省，"浙"；安徽省，"皖"；福建省，"闽"；江西省，"赣"；山东省，"鲁"；台湾省，"台"。

华中地区：河南省，"豫"；湖北省，"鄂"；湖南省，"湘"。

华南地区：广东省，"粤"；广西壮族自治区，"桂"；海南省，"琼"；香港特别行政区，"港"；澳门特别行政区，"澳"。

西南地区：重庆市，"渝"；四川省，"川""蜀"；贵州省，"贵""黔"；云南省，"云""滇"；西藏自治区，"藏"。

西北地区：陕西省，"陕""秦"；甘肃省，"甘""陇"；青海省，"青"；宁夏回族自治区，"宁"；新疆维吾尔自治区，"新"。

拓展知识

浙江省

浙江，省会为杭州。浙江下辖11个地级市，其中杭州、宁波为副省级城市，舟山市是浙江省唯一的海岛城市。

浙江位于中国东南沿海，东临东海，南接福建，西与安徽、江西相连，北与上海、江苏接壤。浙江境内最大的河流为钱塘江，又称"浙江"。浙江四季分明，气温适中，光照较多，雨量充沛，是中国降水较丰富的地区之一。

浙江省是中国省内经济发展程度差异最小的省份之一，其中杭州和宁波的经济实力长期居中国前20位。浙江省有"鱼米之乡"之称，海洋渔业捕捞量居全国首位。浙江沿海主要港口有宁波舟山港。杭州萧山国际机场为中国十大机场之一。

浙江著名的自然景观有西湖、千岛湖、东钱湖、钱塘江潮、四明山、天台山、雁荡山，人文景观有宋城、西塘古镇、鲁迅故里、横店影视城、象山影视城。浙江的代表人物有思想家王守仁、文学家鲁迅和科学家屠呦呦。

讨论

你去过或了解中国哪些省份？谈一谈你对这些省份的印象。

（四）城市

必读课文

中国城市

城市，是具有一定的人口密度和建筑密度、第二及第三产业高度集聚、以非农业人口为主的居民点。中国的主要城市有北京、香港、上海、台北、广州、深圳、杭州、南京、成都和武汉等。

北京，古称"燕京""北平"，是中国的首都，也是中国的政治中心、文化中心、国际交往和科技创新中心，现代化国际大都市，全国交通中心，铁路、公路和航空运输的总枢纽。

香港，全称"中华人民共和国香港特别行政区"，是一座高度繁荣的自由港和国际大都市，为粤港澳大湾区中心城市。香港是重要的国际金融、贸易、航运旅游和信息中心，也是国际公认的最自由开放的经济体。

上海，是全球第三大城市、国家中心城市之一。上海是中国的国际经济、金融、贸易、科技及航运中心之一，是长江经济带和长三角城市群核心城市。上海港集装箱吞吐量位居世界第一。

台北，是台湾省省会，也是其政治、经济、文化和交通中心。台北市是台湾省最大的城市，金融、贸易、批发、旅游等第三产业发达，工业以电机及电器制造为主。

拓展知识

广　州

广州，简称"穗"，又称"羊城""花城"。广州是广东省省会、副省级城市、超大城市。广州是国家中心城市之一，为粤港澳大湾区及珠三角城市群中心城市，华南地区经济、文化、交通中心。广州是中国首批沿海开放城市，是中国通往世界的南大门，是"一带一路"的枢纽城市。

秦汉至明清时期，广州一直是中国对外贸易的重要港口城市，是中国古代海上"丝绸之路"的发源地之一。唐宋时期，广州成为世界著名的东方大港，并设立了中国管理外贸事务的机构——市舶司。明清时期，广州在较长一段时间内是中国唯一的对外贸易港口城市。1840年鸦片战争后，广州是中国五个被迫开放的通商口岸之一。

广州自然条件优越，物产资源丰富，是中国果树资源最丰富的地区之一，有荔枝、香蕉、菠萝等众多品种。广州旅游资源丰富，著名的自然与人文景观有越秀山、广州塔、白云山、中山纪念堂、黄埔军校等。

讨论

你在中国的哪个城市学习或工作过？这个城市有哪些特点？

(五) 港口

必读课文

中国港口

港口，是位于江、河、湖、海和水库沿岸，可供船舶安全进出和停泊的水陆运输枢纽。中国的主要港口有上海港、天津港和广州港。

上海港，中国上海市港口，中国沿海的主要枢纽港，成形于隋朝。晚清时期，上海港是中国最早开放的五个通商口岸之一，是中国对外贸易的主要港口。上海港港区主要由长江口港区、杭州湾港区、黄浦江港区和洋山港区组成，是中国第一大港、世界集装箱第一大港。

天津港，中国天津市港口，中国北方最大的综合性港口，是世界航道等级最高的人工深水港。成形于唐朝。1860年，天津港成为对外通商口岸。天津港位于海河下游及其入海口，地处渤海湾西端，是京津冀城市群和环渤海湾经济圈的交汇点。

广州港，中国广东省广州市港口，成型于秦汉时期。清朝时，广州港是中国对外通商口岸和对外贸易港口。广州港由海港和内河港组成，是中国综合运输体系的重要枢纽和华南地区对外贸易的重要口岸。

拓展知识

宁波舟山港

宁波舟山港，是中国浙江省宁波市和舟山市港口，由宁波港和舟山港合并重组而来，自2009年起，宁波舟山港是全球货物吞吐量第一大港。

宁波港的历史可追溯至史前时期。唐朝明州建立后，明州港迅速发展成为中国远洋和近海贸易的主要港口。明朝初期，明州改为宁波。明朝前中期，宁波港成为中国对日贸易的唯一港口。明朝后期，宁波港被禁止从事对外贸易，成为中国南北货物的转口贸易港。1842年,宁波港再次对外开放。

舟山港历史悠久,唐宋时期曾为中国南北航运和国际航运的避风港与中转港。民国时期,定海、沈家门两港建木质码头9座。1987年,舟山港正式对外开放。全港有定海、沈家门、老塘山、高亭、衢山、泗礁、绿华山、洋山8个港区。

目前,宁波舟山港共有19个港区,其中主要港区有北仑、洋山、六横、衢山、穿山、金塘、大榭、岑港、梅山等9个。

讨论

中国沿海还有哪些港口是你所熟知的?举例说明其特点。

(六) 铁路

必读课文

中国铁路

铁路,是一种陆上运输方式。中国第一条铁路建于上海。中国的铁路总长度居世界第二位。中国主要的铁路类型有国家干线铁路、区际干线铁路和城市轨道交通。

国家干线铁路,是全国区域内拥有关键的经济、政治、文化和国防效益的铁路。2004年,中国公布《中长期铁路网规划》。至2005年,中国的国家干线铁路有11条,其中南北走向铁路线有6条,分别是京哈—京沪线、京九线、京广线、焦柳线、宝成—成昆线和成渝—川黔线;东西走向铁路线有5条,分别是京包—包兰线、陇海—兰新线、沪昆线、襄渝线和南昆线。

区际干线铁路，是连接一定距离范围内的不同城市群、城市带或省级行政区的铁路系统。中国比较有代表性的区际干线铁路线有广州至汕头铁路、金华至宁波铁路等。

城市轨道交通，服务于城市客运交通，通常以电力为动力。城市轨道交通具有速度快、安全准时、成本低、节约能源等特点，常被称为"绿色交通"。中国较早开通城市轨道交通的城市有香港、北京、天津、台北、上海、广州等。

拓展知识

中国高速铁路

中国高速铁路，简称"中国高铁"，是中国境内建成使用的高速铁路。中国高速铁路营运里程超过4万公里，为世界第一。中国高速铁路列车分为高速动车组旅行列车、城际动车组旅行列车和动车组旅行列车，车次分别用"G""C""D"三个字母开头。2016年，中国公布新的《中长期铁路网规划》，其中高速铁路主通道由8条纵向高速铁路和8条横向高速铁路组成。

8条纵向高速铁路：大连至北海高速铁路、北京至上海高速铁路、北京至香港高速铁路、哈尔滨至香港高速铁路、呼和浩特至南宁高速铁路、北京至昆明高速铁路、包头至海口高速铁路、兰州至广州高速铁路。

8条横向高速铁路：绥芬河至满洲里高速铁路、北京至兰州高速铁路、青岛至银川高速铁路、连云港至乌鲁木齐高速铁路、上海至成都高速铁路、上海至昆明高速铁路、厦门至重庆高速铁路、广州至昆明高速铁路。

讨论

你所在的中国城市有哪些类型的铁路？你乘坐过其中哪些铁路？

第三章

人与环境

一 森林

必读课文

中国森林

森林，通常指大片生长的树木；林业上指在相当广阔的土地上生长的很多树木，连同在这块土地上的动物以及其他植物所构成的整体。森林有丰富的物种、复杂的结构和多种多样的功能，被誉为"地球之肺"。森林资源是自然资源的重要组成部分，人类的发展离不开对森林资源的利用。

中国森林资源数量少，地区分布不均。中国森林植物和森林类型丰富多样。中国森林资源可分为东北、西南和南方三个区域。东北地区的森林为中国的主要天然林区。在经过采伐和人工改造后，东北森林中人工林的比重逐渐增加。西南地区的森林为中国第二重要天然林区，主要位于青藏高原的东南部。南方山区面积大，气候条件好，具有林业生产潜力，中国的很多特有树种都产于南方地区。

中国对森林资源的利用有悠久的历史。在农业社会，人们砍伐树木作为能源，木材是修建房屋和制作各种物品的原材料。目前，中国通过植树造林的方式积极应对北方地区的沙漠化并已取得一定成效。

拓展知识

"三北"防护林工程

"三北"防护林工程，指中国在西北、华北北部和东北西部地区建设的大型人工林业生态工程。"三北"防护林体系东起黑龙江，西至新疆，覆盖新疆、青海、甘肃、宁夏、内蒙古、陕西、山西、河北、辽宁、吉林、黑龙江、北京和天津等13个省（区、市）。

"三北"地区分布着沙漠、沙地和广阔的戈壁。"三北"地区降水稀少，干旱等自然灾害十分严重。因此，建设"三北"防护林是中国改善生态环境、减少自然灾害和维护生存空间的需要。工程自1978年启动，规划2050年结束，分三个阶段八期进行，具有防风固沙、保持水土、调节气候、改善环境的作用。目前，"三北"防护林工程已建成一批防护林体系，初步遏制"三北"地区生态恶化的趋势，促进区域农村产业结构调整和经济发展。

"三北"防护林工程建设规模大、速度快、效益高，被誉为"绿色万里长城"。2003年，"三北"防护林工程获得世界上"最大的植树造林工程"吉尼斯证书。

讨论

你所在的城市周围有森林公园吗？能描述一下吗？

(二) 畜牧

必读课文

中国畜牧

畜牧，是指饲养禽兽和放养牲畜。畜牧业是中国农业的重要组成部分，与种植业并列为农业生产的两大支柱。畜牧既为人们提供肉、奶、蛋、脂肪等动物性食品，也为轻工业提供毛、皮、羽、骨等原料。在古代，牛、马和驴是中国农业和交通运输业的重要畜力。

中国的畜牧业有悠久的历史。原始社会时期，中国古人就已人工饲养马、牛、羊、鸡、狗、猪等"六畜"，在黄河流域，人们已经开始圈养鸟兽和驯养牛马。夏商周时期，中国已经出现了兽医和养马的官员。《史记》中记载了夏商周时期人们养殖和放牧的活动。春秋时期，牛成为农耕的主要畜力。"田忌赛马""伯乐相马"和"千军万马"等成语表明马已成为中国人生活的一部分。

当代，中国农村家庭饲养的动物有猪、牛、羊、马、鸡、鸭、鹅、兔等。中国驯养的经济动物有鹿、狐、貂等。中国畜牧分为人工饲养和野生放养两种。中国畜牧的主要生产形式有奶业生产、生猪生产、牛羊生产和蛋肉鸡生产。

拓展知识

四大牧区

牧区，是指有大量草原资源，且以草原畜牧业为主要生产方式的经济类型区域。中国的牧区主要分布在西部和西北部，中国的四大牧区分别是内蒙古牧区、新疆牧区、西藏牧区和青海牧区。

内蒙古牧区，是中国最大的天然草场牧区，东起大兴安岭，西至额济纳戈壁。内蒙古牧区的草场面积居全国第一位，畜牧品种以三河牛、三河马、草原红牛、内蒙古细毛羊、乌珠穆沁肥羊、内蒙古白绒山羊、双峰驼为主。牧区的羊毛、羊绒、毛线、毛料、毛毯等主要畜产品在全国占有重要地位。

新疆牧区，是山地牧区，主要分布在天山以北的北疆和南疆西部山区。新疆牧区草场类型多样，牧草种类繁多，为多种畜类发展提供了有利条件。新疆牧区的主要畜牧品种有细毛羊、羔皮羊、伊犁马、塔城牛等。

西藏牧区，是独具特色的高寒草原畜牧区。近年来，西藏牧区开始人工种植牧草，扩大草场。西藏牧区的主要畜牧品种有牦牛、藏绵羊、藏山羊、黄牛等，其中又以藏绵羊、牦牛数量最多。

青海牧区，主要分布在青南高原、祁连山地和柴达木盆地，畜牧业历史悠久。

讨论

你在中国吃过哪些肉类美食？和你所在国家的肉类美食有哪些异同？

三 渔业

必读课文

中国渔业

渔业，又称"水产业"，是以栖息、繁殖在海洋和内陆水域中的水产经济动植物为开发对象，进行合理采捕、人工增殖与养殖及水产品贮藏与加工利用等的生产事业。渔业是中国农业的重要组成部分，既为人们提供种类丰富的食物，也为医药、化工工业提供重要原料。渔业一般分为海洋渔业和淡水渔业。

中国渔业生产有十分悠久的历史。鱼类是中国原始先民的主要食物之一。

《山海经》中就记载，中国古人可以单手在水中捉鱼。夏商周时期，贝壳成为货币的重要形式之一。国家认识到渔业的重要性，禁止人们在特定时间捕鱼。春秋战国时期，中国有一个叫范蠡的人，总结了养鱼的技术，并在东南沿海推广。同时期中国也出现了管理渔业的官员。

秦汉时期以后，中国的海洋渔业和淡水渔业同时发展。随着船只越来越大，航行距离越来越远，中国沿海渔民逐渐到近海进行捕鱼。一些渔民在捕鱼的同时，还从事人员和货物的运输。政府对渔业的管理也延伸到对渔民、渔船和渔业区域的管控。至此，渔业已经成为中国沿海居民重要的谋生方式之一。

拓展知识

舟山渔场

渔场，指鱼类等水产经济动物栖息分布高度集中、适合捕捞作业，并可获得一定产量的水域。中国沿海渔民在长期的捕捞活动中发现了很多近海渔场，其中最大的是舟山渔场。

舟山渔场，位于浙江东北部的东海。舟山渔场是江苏省、浙江省、福建省和上海市渔民的传统捕捞区域。舟山渔场的捕捞历史可以上溯到夏商周时期，长期以来因渔业资源丰富而闻名。明清时期，舟山渔场成为中国重要的渔场之一，一年四季都有鱼汛。舟山渔场的主要产品有大黄鱼、小黄鱼、带鱼和墨鱼。舟山渔场可分为大戢、嵊山、浪岗、黄泽、岱衢、中街山、洋鞍和金塘等 8 个渔场。

近代以来，随着渔船数量的增加和沿海工业建设的发展，舟山渔场海洋渔业出现过度捕捞和海洋污染的现象。舟山渔场的产品产量出现大幅下降。20 世纪 80 年代后，舟山渔场已经无法自然形成鱼汛。对此，政府在中国沿海各个渔场实行禁渔期。在禁渔期，沿海渔船不能下海捕捞。

讨论

你见过或吃过哪些中国水产品？和你所在国家的水产品有哪些异同？

（四）矿产

必读课文

中国矿产

矿产，指一切埋藏在地下可供人类利用的天然矿物或岩石资源。中国是世界上开发和利用矿产资源历史较为悠久的国家之一。

原始人类时期，石器的制作和使用是区分旧石器时代和新石器时代的主要标志。夏商周时期，中国由石器时代进入到青铜器时代，代表性的青铜器有后母戊鼎。春秋战国时期，中国由青铜器时代进入到铁器时代。秦汉时期，中国对铁器的使用已经非常普遍。此外，金已成为主要的流通物。北宋时期，金、银、铜、铁、铅、锡、水银等矿产的产量都达到了历史上前所未有的水平，矿税甚至成为国家重要的财政收入。中国古代对矿产的利用既推动了中国生产力的发展，也推动了政治、经济、文化的发展和社会进步。

目前，中国的矿产资源种类多、储量大，部分矿产储量居世界前茅，但人均占有量却低于世界平均水平。中国矿产资源贫矿多富矿少，共（伴）生矿多、独立矿少。中国的矿产资源分布不均衡，表现为分布广泛但储量特别集中，如东北、华北多煤、稀土，南方多有色金属和磷。

拓展知识

矿产分布

中国主要的矿产资源有金、银、铜、铁、钨等。

金矿，分布在胶东、小秦岭（含豫西）、黑龙江、华北、陕甘川交界—祁连山区、长江中下游、黔桂滇交界区。

银矿，在中国分布十分广泛，主要分布在赣北、陕南鄂西北、豫南、华北—吉西、南岭、江浙。中国是世界上发现和利用银矿最早的国家之一。

铜矿，资源比较丰富，主要分布在华东和西南地区，具体省份有江西、云南、湖北、上海、江苏、甘肃、安徽、山西、辽宁等。

铁矿，分布非常广泛，资源储量丰富，但富铁矿比重很小，主要分布在北京、山西、内蒙古、山东、河北、湖北、云南、安徽等省（区、市）。

钨矿，是中国优势矿产资源。中国钨矿资源丰富，储量、产量和出口量居世界第一。中国钨矿主要分布在湖南、江西、广西、广东、云南等省（区）。

讨论

> 分类说明中国进口的矿产资源主要来自哪些国家。

（五）能源

必读课文

中国能源

能源，是指能产生机械能、热能、光能、电磁能、化学能等各种能量的自然资源。中国的主要能源有煤炭、石油、天然气、水电和风电等。

煤炭：中国煤炭资源丰富，储量居世界前列。中国煤炭资源的地理分布不平衡，北多南少，西多东少。中国北方煤炭资源集中在山西、陕西、内蒙古、河南、新疆；南方煤炭资源集中在四川、云南和贵州。

石油：中国石油资源总量比较丰富，但地理分布不均，东西部多，中部少。中国陆地石油资源集中分布在松辽、塔里木、准噶尔、华北、四川和鄂尔多斯等盆地。中国海上石油资源主要分布在渤海湾。

天然气：中国天然气资源以煤成气为主，主要分布在渤海湾、准噶尔、塔里木、四川、鄂尔多斯、柴达木、松辽等地。

水电能：属于可再生能源。中国是世界上水电能资源较为丰富的国家之一。中国水电能资源分布不均匀，主要集中在西南、西北、中南三个地区。

风能：属于可再生能源。中国风能资源比较丰富，较为集中的地区为东南沿海及其岛屿、新疆北部、内蒙古、甘肃北部。

拓展知识

"三桶油"

"三桶油"是中国石油天然气集团有限公司、中国石油化工集团有限公司和中国海洋石油集团有限公司三家石油企业的简称，这三家石油企业是中国最主要的石油企业。

中国石油天然气集团有限公司，简称"中国石油"。"中国石油"的总部在北京，有大庆油田、辽河油田、长庆油田、新疆油田、大港油田、华北油田、西南油田等 15 家下属油气田企业。中石油成立于 1998 年，是综合性国际能源公司、世界五百强企业。

中国石油化工集团有限公司，简称"中国石化"。"中国石化"成立于 1983 年，是中国最大的成品油和石化产品供应商，是世界第一大炼油公司、世界五百强企业。

中国海洋石油集团有限公司，简称"中国海油"。"中国海油"的总部在北京，共有 5 家控股境内外上市公司。"中国海油"成立于 1982 年，是中国最大的海上油气生产运营商、世界五百强企业。

讨论

中国的石油主要从哪些国家进口？通过哪些线路运到中国？

（六）保护区

必读课文

自然保护区

自然保护区，指国家用法律形式确定的长期保护和基本上任其自然变化的自然生态系统和自然景观地域。

中国古代就有朴素的自然保护思想。《逸周书》记载："春三月，山林不登斧，以成草木之长；夏三月，川泽不入网罟，以成鱼鳖之长。"说明当时的官方有封山禁渔以保护资源的措施。民众也经常自发地划定一些不准樵采的地域，并制定若干乡规民约加以约束，有些已具有自然保护区的雏形。

中华人民共和国成立后，中国在建立自然保护区方面得到发展。1956年，中国在广东建立了中国第一个自然保护区——鼎湖山国家级自然保护区。20世纪70年代以后，中国的自然保护事业发展迅速。目前，中国加入世界生物圈保护区网的自然保护区有长白山、鼎湖山、卧龙等34个。

吉林长白山国家级自然保护区，位于吉林省安图县、抚松县、长白朝鲜族自治县三县交界处，主要保护火山地貌景观和森林生态系统。保护区建立于1960年，总面积19万公顷，其中绝对保护区13万公顷，一般保护区6万公顷。本区冬季严寒而漫长、夏季温暖而潮湿，是亚洲东部大陆上唯一具有高山冻原的山地。

拓展知识

海洋自然保护区

海洋自然保护区是以海洋自然环境和资源保护为目的，依法把包括保护对象在内的一定面积的海岸、河口、岛屿、湿地或海域划分出来，进行特殊保护和管理的区域。建立海洋自然保护区是保护海洋生物多样性和防止海洋生态环境恶化行之有效的手段之一。1988年底，国家海洋局制定颁布了《建立海洋自然保护区工作纲要》。

1990年9月，中国有五处海洋自然保护区被列为首批国家级海洋自然保护区，分别是河北省昌黎黄金海岸自然保护区，主要保护对象是海岸自然景观及海区生态环境；广西山口红树林生态自然保护区，主要保护对象是红树林生态系统；海南大洲岛海洋生态自然保护区，主要保护对象是金丝燕及其生活的海岸生态环境；海南省三亚珊瑚礁自然保护区，主要保护对象是珊瑚礁及其生态系统；浙江省南麂列岛贝藻类自然保护区，主要保护对象是贝、藻类及其生态环境。

1993年，天津古海岸与湿地国家级自然保护区等5个海洋自然保护区加入世界生物圈保护区网。1995年，国家海洋局颁布了《海洋自然保护区管理办法》，开始对海洋自然保护区进行依法规划和管理。

讨论

你了解中国的哪些自然保护区？简单介绍一下。

历史演进篇

第四章

古代中国（一）

一、夏朝

必读课文

夏　朝

夏朝，是中国历史上第一个奴隶制王朝，是中国史书中记载的第一个世袭制朝代。夏朝的建立者为禹。夏朝一共有17位君王，延续400多年，最后被商汤所灭。

舜将部落首领之位禅让给禹是夏朝的开端。禹死后，将王位传给儿子启，此时世袭制正式取代禅让制，这段历史被看作是中国历史上"家天下"的开始。夏朝的领土范围在现在相当于西起河南省西部、山西省南部，东至河南省与山东省交界处，南达湖北省北部，北及河北省南部。王朝建立后，夏朝的各个部落与中央王室在血缘上是宗法关系，政治上是分封关系，经济上是贡赋关系。夏朝的统治并不稳定，先后经历了太康失国、少康中兴等变故。夏朝末期的暴政直接导致商部落首领成汤的起义，最后在鸣条之战中灭亡。

拓展知识

大禹治水

大禹治水，是中国古代神话传说，也是著名的上古大洪水传说之一。

尧舜时期，中国的中原地区洪水泛滥，淹没了庄稼和山陵，也淹没了民众的房屋，人们流离失所，只得背井离乡。在这种情况之下，尧决心要消灭水患，于是开始寻访能治理洪水的人。起初禹的父亲被推举治水，但治水数年并无成效。等到舜担任部落联盟首领后，他向大臣们寻求治水人才，看谁能治理水患。大臣们推荐禹来治理洪水。当时，大禹刚刚结婚才四天。为了治水，大禹只好将妻子留在家中，数年中三次经过家门却没有回家。治水期间，禹带领着伯益、后稷和一批助手到处奔走，考察地理环境，设计治水方案。禹吸取了父亲堵截治水的教训，采用疏导的办法，和百姓一起开通了很多条河道，最终顺利将洪水引到了海里。

经过十三年的努力，大禹终于成功治理了水患。人们重建了家园，不再受到洪水的威胁。农业生产也逐渐恢复，百姓过上了太平的日子。

讨论

你的国家有治水的传说吗？和中国的治水传说有何异同？

（二）商朝

必读课文

商　朝

商朝，是中国历史上第二个王朝。从公元前 1600 年至公元前 1046 年，商朝共有 31 位君王，前后存续 500 余年。

商的先世商族是兴起于黄河中下游的一个部落，传说它的始祖是与禹同时期的契。夏朝末期，商国君主商汤在鸣条之战中灭夏，以"商"为国号，在亳建立商朝。商朝初期，国都频繁迁移。自盘庚迁殷以后，商朝的国都才逐渐固定下来，因此商朝又被后世称为"殷"或"殷商"。由于商朝最后一代君主帝辛昏庸无道，周起兵伐商，并在牧野一战中大败商朝军队。最终，商被周所取代。

商朝处于中国奴隶制社会的鼎盛时期，初步确立了国家权力，奴隶制的社会秩序已经稳固。商朝的青铜冶炼技术达到鼎盛，青铜器种类繁多，主要用于占卜和祭祀。商朝青铜器的代表是后母戊鼎，它是青铜铸造史上的杰出之作。另外，商朝已经出现了甲骨文，它是中国最早的成熟文字，用以记载商朝的占卜记录和卜辞。

拓展知识

盘庚迁殷

盘庚迁殷，是发生在商朝中后期的一次历史事件，指盘庚为挽救政治危机决定将都城迁至殷地的历史事件。

商朝建立初期，国都定在亳。之后的 300 年间，商朝的都城先后搬迁过 5 次。国君盘庚继位之初，黄河以北面临水灾的威胁，王族内部政治危机频发。因此，盘庚决定迁都到殷地。由于前代商朝君主频繁迁都，百姓苦不堪言，不愿再迁；同时，贵族贪图安逸，也不愿意迁都。盘庚迁都的决定几乎遭到举国上下的反对。但是，盘庚仍坚持迁都。他一面劝诫贵族随自己迁都，一面严厉镇压反对的百姓。最后，盘庚挫败了反抗势力，带领人民顺利渡过黄河，将都城搬迁至殷地。

自盘庚迁殷以后，商朝的都城终于固定在殷地，人民不必再承受频繁迁都的苦难。商朝的政局因此稳定，政治、经济、文化都繁荣发展，衰落的商朝再次出现了复兴的景象。在商代后期的250多年间，殷成为全国政治、经济和文化发展的中心。

讨论

> 你见过哪些中国青铜器？谈一谈你所知道的青铜器。

三 周朝

必读课文

周　朝

周朝，是中国历史上继商朝之后的第三个奴隶制王朝。周王朝继承了夏商两朝的国家制度，是中国古代奴隶社会发展到极盛和开始衰落的转折时期。

周，原是居于今陕西中部和甘肃东部黄土高原地区的古老部族。商朝时期，周为其诸侯国之一。周文王担任周国首领时，周国国力强盛。公元前1046年，周文王的儿子周武王率兵与商朝军队大战于牧野。牧野之战推翻了商王朝的统治，周军大胜，建立了周朝。周朝分为西周和东周两个时期。公元前771年，西周灭亡。公元前770年，周平王东迁，重新建立周朝，史称"东周"。东周以"三家分晋"事件为节点，又分为春秋和战国两个时期。公元前249年，秦灭东周。

周武王建立周朝后，政治上，实行分封制，大封皇族及功臣；经济上，实行井田制，促进了小农经济的发展，推动生产力的提高；文化上，实行了礼乐制度，调节了贵族内部关系，维护了封建统治。

拓展知识

百家争鸣

百家争鸣，指战国时期学术界互相辩争的局面和风气。战国时期是社会大变革的时代，各种社会矛盾错综复杂。激烈的政治斗争和经济文化繁荣，对当时社会的各个阶层产生了深远影响，人们对当时社会大变革中的许多问题，表明自己的态度，提出主张、愿望和要求。战国时期的各个学派著书立说，议论政治，对当时的社会变革及文化发展起了促进作用。

百家争鸣中影响最大的莫过于儒、法、道、墨四家。儒家创始人是孔丘。他周游列国，提出"为政以德""克己复礼""有教无类"等思想主张。孔子晚年著书立说，致力于教学。孟子和荀子继承并发扬了孔子的儒家思想。在诸子百家中，儒家对中国的影响最为深远。法家的代表人物是韩非。韩非是先秦法家思想的集大成者，主张严刑峻法。道家的创始人是老子。庄子继承和发扬了老子的思想，是战国时期道家的代表人物。墨家的创始人是墨翟，提出"兼爱""非攻""兼相爱，交相利"等理论。

这一时期形成的各种学术思想，成为以后中国思想、文化的主要源头。

讨论

列举一个周朝的成语故事并简单说明一下其历史背景。

（四）秦朝

必读课文

秦　朝

秦朝，是中国历史上第一个统一的封建王朝。公元前359年，秦孝公重用商鞅推行变法，使秦国的经济得到发展，成为战国后期最富强的诸侯国。秦王嬴政先后消灭韩、魏、楚、燕、赵、齐六国，完成统一。公元前221年，嬴政称帝，史称"秦始皇"。

秦朝废除分封制，设立郡县制，管理全国各地。秦朝还统一书写文字、车辆宽度和计量单位。对外，秦朝北征匈奴，南伐百越，修筑长城抵抗北方外敌入侵。对内，秦朝修筑驰道，改善全国交通。驰道是中国历史上最早的国道，以秦朝首都咸阳为中心，通往全国各地。公元前210年，秦始皇病逝，其子胡亥即位。公元前209年，陈胜、吴广发动农民起义。公元前206年，秦朝灭亡。

秦朝结束了自春秋战国以来500余年诸侯分裂的局面，成为中国历史上第一个中央集权制国家，奠定了中国大一统王朝的统治基础，对中国历史产生了深远影响。

拓展知识

秦灭六国之战

秦灭六国之战，又称"秦国统一战争"，指中国战国末期的秦国消灭其他六个诸侯国，完成中国统一的战争。公元前238年，秦王嬴政在李斯、尉缭等人的辅佐下，采取远交近攻的外交政策，笼络燕国和齐国，稳住魏国和楚国，消灭韩国和赵国。

秦国自商鞅变法后，经济发展迅速，军队战斗力强。秦王嬴政即位后，秦国越来越强，而其他六国已经衰败。公元前230年，秦国消灭韩国。公元前

228年，秦国攻下邯郸，俘赵王迁。赵公子嘉奔代，自称代王。公元前226年，秦国攻入燕都蓟、燕王喜迁都辽东。公元前225年，秦国攻下大梁，魏国灭亡。公元前223年，秦国消灭楚国。公元前222年，秦国消灭燕国，俘代王嘉，赵亡。公元前221年，秦国消灭齐国。至此，秦国消灭六国，统一了中国。

秦灭六国之战中，燕国曾派荆轲刺杀秦王，史称"荆轲刺秦王"。1998年，中国导演陈凯歌拍摄的电影《荆轲刺秦王》讲的就是这个故事。此外，2002年，中国导演张艺谋拍摄的电影《英雄》也是以此故事为历史背景的。

讨论

> 你知道哪些以秦朝为背景的中国电影和小说？

(五) 汉朝

必读课文

汉　朝

汉朝，是中国继秦朝之后的又一个大一统王朝。汉朝分为西汉和东汉两个时期，共有29位皇帝，前后存续400余年。汉朝是当时世界上最先进的文明及最强大帝国。

在秦末农民起义中，刘邦推翻秦朝后被封为汉王。楚汉争霸时，刘邦战胜了项羽。公元前202年，刘邦称帝，建立汉朝，定都长安，史称"西汉"。西汉初年，基本上沿袭了秦朝的政治制度。汉高祖刘邦组织军队复员、招抚流亡，安定人民生活，恢复和发展生产。之后，汉文帝和汉景帝推行休养生息的国策，开创了"文景之治"。西汉第四个皇帝——汉武帝即位后,加强中央集权,派张骞出使西域开辟丝绸之路,向北击败匈奴,开创了大一统的繁荣局面。汉宣帝时期,西汉国力达到顶峰,西域被纳入中国版图,史称"昭宣中兴"。公元8年,西汉灭亡。

公元25年,刘秀重建汉朝,定都洛阳,史称"东汉"。刘秀统一天下后,安置流民,轻徭薄赋,休养生息,政治、经济得以发展。汉和帝即位后,派遣班超经营西域,丝绸之路延伸至欧洲。公元166年,罗马帝国派遣使者来到中国。公元190年,汉朝各地起义频发,天下大乱。公元220年,汉朝灭亡。

拓展知识

王莽改制

王莽改制,是新朝皇帝王莽为缓和西汉末年日益加剧的社会矛盾而采取的一系列新措施。王莽,是新朝开国皇帝、政治改革家。公元前45年,王莽出生。公元前8年,王莽担任大司马,为西汉最高军事长官。公元8年,王莽自立为帝,改国号为"新"。

新朝建立后,王莽开始进行全面的社会改革,包括土地、商业和币制改革。公元9年,针对西汉时期最突出的土地问题,王莽发布法令废除土地私有制,实行土地国有制,私人不得买卖。公元10年,王莽在长安及全国五大城市任命官员管理市场物价。酒、盐和铁由国家专卖,私人不得经营。货币由国家专营,私人不得铸造货币。

王莽的土地国有政策遭到大地主和大商人的强烈反对,一部分人甚至举兵反抗。王莽的商业政策加强了中央集权,是汉武帝时期经济政策的延续,但后来成为贵族官员谋利的工具。货币改革实质上剥削了普通民众的财富,成为新朝迅速灭亡的原因之一。

讨论

你还知道中国汉朝的哪些故事？

（六）晋朝

必读课文

晋　朝

晋朝，三国时期后的统一王朝。东汉灭亡后，中国进入魏、蜀、吴三国时期。之后，晋朝统一中国。晋朝分为西晋和东晋两个时期，其中西晋为大一统王朝，东晋属于中国南方的六个王朝之一。晋朝共有15位皇帝，存续了155年。

265年，司马炎夺取魏国政权，建立晋朝，定都洛阳，史称"西晋"。司马炎就是晋朝的第一个皇帝，史称晋武帝。280年，西晋消灭吴国，完成统一。晋武帝在致力于统一全国时，颁行了许多重大政治、经济措施，收到一些效果，史称"太康之治"。316年，西晋灭亡。第二年，西晋皇室成员司马睿在中国南方延续晋朝，史称"东晋"。420年，刘裕建立宋朝，史称"南朝宋"，东晋至此灭亡，中国历史进入南北朝时期。

两晋时期，中华文化在文学、艺术、史学和科技方面有新的发展，代表作品有陶渊明的《桃花源记》、王羲之的《兰亭集序》和刘徽的《海岛算经》等。西晋末期，中国北方社会动荡，大量人口南迁，中国的经济重心逐渐由北方向南方转移。

拓展知识

淝水之战

淝水之战，发生于 383 年，是中国历史上著名的以少胜多的战争。

西晋灭亡后，中国北方各少数民族政权先后建立。357 年，前秦国大将军苻坚控制了国家。他重用王猛，增强了国家实力。到 376 年，前秦国先后灭掉前燕、前凉、代等国家，统一了中国北方。

373 年，苻坚攻下东晋的梁、益二州。此后，经过一年的艰苦战斗，前秦国夺取了东晋的军事重镇襄阳、彭城。为统一全国，苻坚不顾众人的反对，发起对东晋的进攻。383 年，大将军苻坚亲自率领军队攻打东晋。东晋派遣将军谢石、谢玄等北上迎敌。双方在淝水遭遇。面对没有全部抵达的前秦军队，谢石决定改变防守，立即发起进攻。前秦军队退后防守，想等东晋军队过河后再发起进攻。结果在移动过程中，前秦军队的后方发生混乱。于是，东晋抓住机会，发起进攻。最终，前秦军队战败。

拥有绝对优势的前秦战败后，逐渐衰败，走向分裂。东晋的胜利，使南方避免了一场大的混乱和破坏，经济文化得以继续发展。东晋将领谢玄、谢安和谢石等人也因此战被载入史册。

讨论

> 中国还有哪些以少胜多的战役？你的国家有类似的战役吗？

第五章

古代中国（二）

(一) 隋朝

必读课文

隋　朝

　　隋朝，晋朝之后的又一个大统一王朝，一共有2位皇帝，存续了37年。隋朝的第一个皇帝是杨坚，史称"隋文帝"。杨坚在位期间，在政治、经济等制度方面进行了一系列的改革：实行三省六部制，巩固中央集权；多次减轻赋税，促进国家农业生产，稳定经济发展。604年，杨坚去世后，其子杨广继位，史称"隋炀帝"。杨广在位期间，在洛阳周边修建国家粮仓；开凿大运河，沟通了南方经济地区、中原政治地区和北方军事地区；修建驰道和长城，整体上促进了社会经济的发展。618年，隋朝灭亡。

　　隋灭陈统一全国后，疆域东起辽河、北抵大漠、西至敦煌、南据交趾。隋朝时期，中国的科学技术取得一系列成就。李春设计和主持建造的赵州桥，是当时世界桥梁工程的最先进水平，比欧洲早700多年。刘焯在制定《皇极历》时，最早提出了"等间距二次内插法"的公式。由陆法言执笔编写完成的《切韵》为音韵学奠定了基础。

拓展知识

三省六部制

三省六部制，是中国古代封建社会的中央官制。三省六部制确立于隋朝，一直延续到清朝末年。

三省，指中书省、门下省和尚书省。中书省，是发布政令的机构，最早是在三国时期的魏国设置。宋朝时，中书省与门下省合并。明朝初期，中书省被撤销。门下省，与中书省共同掌管行政事务，负责审查和签署法令，最早设置于东汉时期。门下省原为皇帝的顾问机构，后来逐渐成为中央政权机构的中心。尚书省，是国家最高行政机构，从汉朝皇帝的秘书机构发展而来。尚书省的组织机构在隋朝定型，下辖六部，负责执行诏令。

六部，指尚书省下属的吏部、户部、礼部、兵部、刑部和工部。吏部，掌管全国官员的任免、考核、升降和调动等。户部，掌管全国户籍、土地、赋税。礼部，主管礼仪之制，如礼乐、学校、衣冠、册命等。兵部，掌管全国军官、士兵、军事装备和军事命令等。刑部，掌管全国各种法律，审查各地案件。工部，掌管全国各项工程、工匠和水利等。

讨论

你知道中国历史上有哪些水利工程？简单描述一下。

（二）唐朝

必读课文

唐　朝

唐朝，隋朝之后的又一个大一统王朝。唐朝共有 21 位皇帝，前后 289 年。唐朝是当时世界上最强盛的国家之一，与亚洲、欧洲国家均有往来。唐朝以后，海外多称中国人为"唐人"，现在中国人在海外的聚居区被称为"唐人街"。

隋朝末年，天下大乱。618 年，隋朝灭亡，李渊称帝，建立唐朝，定都长安。626 年，李世民成为唐朝的第二个皇帝，史称"唐太宗"。628 年，唐朝统一全国。李世民厉行节约，完善了三省六部制、科举制等一系列政治制度，使社会出现了较为安定的局面。此外，他还积极抵御外敌入侵，促进民族融合，稳定了边疆。此历史时期被称为"贞观之治"。

712 年，李隆基继位，史称"唐玄宗"。唐玄宗时期，唐朝的国力空前强盛，被称为"开元之治"。755 年，唐朝将领安禄山发动叛乱，唐朝由盛转衰。907 年，唐朝灭亡。

拓展知识

武则天

武则天，并州文水（山西人文水县）人，生于 624 年。武则天是中国历史上唯一的女皇帝。武则天于 67 岁称帝，82 岁去世。

635 年，武则天的父亲病逝，她随母亲搬至长安居住。637 年，14 岁的武则天被选入皇宫。655 年，武则天成为皇后。660 年，皇帝李治因病不能处理国家大事，武则天参与管理国家事务，并逐渐形成了李治与武则天共掌朝政的"二圣"格局。李治去世后，武则天作为皇太后执掌国家。690 年，武则天称帝，建立武周，定都洛阳。

武则天在位期间，打击既得利益的保守力量，为社会进步和经济发展创造了良好的条件。武则天重视人才的选拔，进一步完善了科举制度；加强对官员的管理，整顿吏治，严惩贪污；重视发展农业，减轻农民赋税，推广先进的农业生产经验和生产技术。

705 年，宰相张柬之等人发动政变，恢复唐朝。同年，武则天病逝。

讨论

你看过哪些有关中国唐朝的影视作品？简单谈一谈你的体会。

三 宋朝

必读课文

宋 朝

宋朝，分北宋和南宋两个阶段，共有 18 位皇帝，一共存续了 319 年。宋朝是中国历史上商品经济、文化教育和科技创新高度繁荣的时代。

960 年，赵匡胤建立宋朝，史称"北宋"。赵匡胤为北宋第一个皇帝，被称为"宋太祖"。赵匡胤加强中央集权，剥夺武将兵权。赵匡胤的弟弟——赵光义在位期间统一了全国。1004 年，北宋与辽朝签订了盟约，避免了战争。之后，社会趋于稳定，经济逐渐繁荣。宋神宗时期，著名的改革家王安石进行朝政改革，史称"王安石变法"。1120 年，北宋与金朝结盟，共同攻打辽朝。1125 年，金朝消灭辽朝。1127 年，金朝南侵，北宋灭亡。

1127 年，赵构在今天的江苏南京重新建立宋朝，史称"南宋"。1141 年，南宋与金朝议和，结束战争。1234年，南宋联合蒙古国消灭金朝。1276年，元朝攻占南宋首都临安，南宋灭亡。

● 拓展知识

王安石变法

王安石变法，是北宋时期王安石主持的一场政治改革运动。王安石变法以发展生产、富国强兵、挽救北宋政治危机为目的。变法内容涉及政治、经济、军事、社会、文化等各个方面。王安石变法是中国古代史上继商鞅变法后又一次规模巨大的政治改革运动。

王安石，出生于1021年，是中国北宋时期的政治家、文学家、思想家和改革家。1047年，27岁的王安石担任鄞县县令。四年任期中，王安石兴修水利，扩办学校。1059年，王安石系统地提出了变法的主张。王安石总结自己多年担任地方官员的经历，指出国家面临的经济、社会和国防等诸多问题。1068年，宋神宗任命王安石主持变法。第二年，王安石在全国开始大规模的改革运动，颁布一系列法令。这些法令主要涉及财政和军事。

王安石变法触犯了保守派的利益，遭到他们的反对。1085年，宋神宗去世，宋哲宗即位，王安石变法被停止。通过变法，政府的财政收入大幅提高，国力有所增强。

● 讨论

列举一位中国宋朝时期的历史人物并简单谈一谈他的事迹。

（四）元朝

必读课文

元　朝

元朝，中国历史上首个由少数民族建立的大一统王朝，存续时间自 1271 年至 1368 年。

1206 年，铁木真统一蒙古，建立大蒙古国。蒙古国先后消灭西辽、西夏、金朝等政权。1260 年，忽必烈继承汗位，是为元世祖。1271 年，忽必烈建立元朝。1276 年，元朝消灭南宋，统一中国。之后，元朝持续对外扩张。到了中后期，元朝政治腐败严重，民族矛盾加剧。1368 年，朱元璋建立明朝。元朝皇室退居北方，史称"北元"。1402 年，北元灭亡。

元朝时期，中国的国土面积超过历代王朝，领土东至日本海，南至南海，西至天山，北至贝加尔湖。元朝在地方实行行省制度，影响了现代中国的行政体制。为维护蒙古贵族的专制统治权，元朝实行等级制度，将中国人分为四等，其中蒙古人为第一等。元朝商品经济和海外贸易繁荣，与各国外交往来频繁。元朝是中国历史上第一个完全以纸币为流通货币的朝代。

拓展知识

大蒙古国

大蒙古国，指 13 世纪由蒙古族铁木真建立的蒙古政权。孛儿只斤·铁木真（Genghis Khan）是世界史上杰出的军事家和政治家，1162 年出生。1189 年，铁木真被推举为首领。1206 年，铁木真建立了大蒙古国，尊号成吉思汗。1227 年，铁木真病逝，终年 66 岁。

大蒙古国建立后屡次对外扩张，先后占据东亚、中亚、西亚和东欧在内的辽阔地域。1218年，大蒙古国灭西辽，向西一直打到伏尔加河流域。1227年，大蒙古国灭西夏。1234年，大蒙古国消灭金朝。1237年，大蒙古国占领莫斯科。1241年，大蒙古国分兵两路入侵波兰、匈牙利、斯洛伐克、捷克等国，抵达奥地利维也纳附近。1253年，大蒙古国灭大理国。1258年，大蒙古国占领阿拉伯帝国首都巴格达。1259年后，大蒙古国逐渐分裂为元朝和其他4个国家。

大蒙古国的建立加速了东西方的文化和技术的传播，促进了多民族的文化交流。

讨论

你知道哪些外国人在古代曾来到过中国？他们有哪些事迹？

（五）明朝

必读课文

明　朝

明朝，元朝之后的统一王朝。明朝共有16位皇帝，存续了276年。明朝初期定都南京，后迁都北京。

1364年，朱元璋建立西吴政权。1368年，朱元璋称帝，建立明朝，定都南京。之后，经过数次战争，明朝统一中国。1421年，明成祖朱棣迁都北京。明朝初期，政治清明，国力强盛，社会经济得以恢复和发展。1449年，土木之变后，明朝由盛转衰。万历年间，随着张居正改革的实施，明朝的国力再次强大。晚明时期，政治腐败、自然灾害和外敌入侵导致国家实力衰退。1644年，李自成攻入北京，明朝灭亡。之后，中国南方建立了多个明朝政权，史称"南明"。1662年，南明覆灭。

明朝时期，中央集权制度得以强化，多民族国家进一步统一和巩固。明朝手工业和商品经济繁荣，大量商业资本转化为产业资本，出现商业市镇和资本主义萌芽。明朝文化艺术呈现世俗化趋势，《西游记》《水浒传》《三国演义》等小说均在这一时期被创作。

拓展知识

明朝小说

明朝小说，是中国文学创作的一种题材，是在宋元时期说话艺术的基础上发展起来的。明朝时期，出现了小说空前繁荣的局面，充分显示出它的社会作用和文学价值。在中国文学史上，明朝小说取得了与唐诗、宋词、元曲相提并论的地位。明朝著名的小说有《西游记》《水浒传》《三国演义》等。

《西游记》，作者吴承恩。小说主要描写了孙悟空出世及大闹天宫后，遇见了唐僧、猪八戒、沙僧和白龙马，决定一起西行取经，一路上历经艰险，最终到达西天见到如来佛祖的故事。该小说以"唐僧取经"这一历史事件为蓝本。

《水浒传》，作者施耐庵。小说主要描写的是北宋末年，以宋江为首的108位好汉在山东梁山泊聚义的故事。该小说以"宋江起义"这一历史事件为背景。

《三国演义》，作者罗贯中。小说大致分为黄巾起义、董卓之乱、群雄逐鹿、三国鼎立、三国归晋等五个部分，描写了从东汉末年到西晋初年近百年的历史风云。

讨论

中国是在什么时候开始和你的国家交往的？简单说明一下。

六　清朝

必读课文

清　朝

　　清朝，中国历史上最后一个封建王朝，第二个由少数民族建立的大一统王朝。清朝的统治者为女真族，又称"满族"。1616 年，女真族建立后金政权。1636 年，皇太极称帝，建立清朝。1644 年，明朝将领吴三桂投降清朝，清兵定都北京。至此，清朝成为统治中国的中央王朝。随后，清朝消灭各地政权，平定叛乱，收复台湾，统一中国。

　　清朝前期，中国传统社会取得前所未有的发展成就，国家综合国力强盛。清王朝奖励垦荒，减免赋税，因此全国土地开垦面积增加。清朝手工业以纺织和瓷器为主，尤其是以江西景德镇为瓷器中心。清朝商业发达，城市繁荣，形成了区域性的商业中心。随着商业的发展，全国形成了十大商帮，其中山西和安徽商人最为突出。

　　1840 年，清朝遭到西方国家的侵略，被迫签订了大量不平等条约。同时，面对内忧外患，清政府也积极进行了洋务运动和戊戌变法等近代化的探索和改革。1912 年，清朝最后一位皇帝溥仪宣布退位，清朝结束。

拓展知识

《四库全书》

　　《四库全书》，全称《钦定四库全书》，是清朝乾隆年间编修的大型丛书。《四库全书》是中国古代最大的文化工程，对中国古典文化进行了一次系统、全面的总结。该书呈现了中国古典文化的知识体系。

　　《四库全书》是由乾隆皇帝主持，360 多位官员和学者参与编修，耗时 13 年完成的。该丛书分为经、史、子、集等四部，故名"四库"，收录图书3503种，79337卷，装订成36000余册。为存放《四库全书》，乾隆皇帝效仿宁波藏书楼"天一阁"的形制建造藏书阁。《四库全书》总计誊抄了7套，其中4套存放于中国北方，另外3套存放于南方的扬州、镇江和杭州。

《四库全书》完成至今200余年间，多套毁于战火。现藏于台北故宫博物院的《四库全书》是保存较为完好的一部。《四库全书》保存了中国历代大量文献，对当时和以后的文化发展都有巨大的影响，是中国传统文化宝库中的珍品。

讨论

你的国家有和中国《四库全书》类似的文献丛书吗？简单介绍一下。

第六章

近代以来

一、鸦片战争

必读课文

鸦片战争

鸦片战争，指1840年至1842年英国对中国发动的侵略战争。鸦片战争是中国近代史的开端。

19世纪初，英国成为世界资本主义最强大的国家，建立了"日不落"帝国。同一时期，中国清朝仍是一个独立的封建国家，自给自足的自然经济占据中国社会经济的主导地位。在中英贸易中，中国占据优势地位。为改变这种局面，英国向中国大量走私鸦片。中国政府派遣林则徐在广州禁烟的行为成为中英战争的起因。

1839年8月，林则徐禁烟的消息传到伦敦后，英国政府开始策划侵华战争。1840年4月，英国国会通过了发动对华战争的决议。6月，英国舰队抵达珠江口外，封锁海口，断绝中国对外贸易。随后，英军攻占浙江舟山岛作为前进基地。1841年1月，英军占领香港。10月，英军占领浙江宁波。1842年6月，英军攻占吴淞，并计划攻占南京。8月，清政府与英国议和，签订中国近代史上第一个不平等条约——《南京条约》。

拓展知识

虎门销烟

虎门销烟，指 1839 年林则徐在广东虎门集中销毁鸦片的历史事件。虎门销烟是鸦片战争的导火线。

为改变与中国贸易中的不利地位，英国向中国大量走私鸦片，导致中国鸦片泛滥。大量鸦片输入中国，不仅导致中国的财富外流，还影响民众的身心健康。因此，清朝道光皇帝在 1838 年任命林则徐负责全国禁烟。

1839 年 3 月，林则徐抵达广东。他与邓廷桢等官员合作，发起声势浩大的禁烟运动。他发布禁令，逮捕鸦片贩子，收缴大量鸦片和烟具。他发布谕令，要求烟商在三天内交出全部鸦片，并声明以后不准贩卖鸦片。英美鸦片商人极力抗拒林则徐的命令。3 月下旬，林则徐下令包围商馆，停止中英贸易，断绝广州与澳门间的交通。面对强大压力，各国鸦片商人陆续向中国政府缴交鸦片。6 月，林则徐将收缴的鸦片在虎门公开销毁。

虎门销烟在一定程度上遏制了鸦片在中国的泛滥，但并没有彻底解决中国的鸦片问题。这次禁烟运动增加了中国民众对于鸦片危害的认识，负责虎门销烟的林则徐成为中国的民族英雄。

讨论

简述你所在的国家历史上遭遇的一次入侵，并讨论其与中国鸦片战争的异同。

(二) 洋务运动

必读课文

洋务运动

洋务运动，又称"同光新政""自强新政""自强运动"。洋务运动是19世纪60年代到90年代晚清政府进行的与资本主义有密切联系的军事、政治、经济、文化教育、外交等方面的活动。

鸦片战争后，中国一批具有改革意识的中上层官僚，发起以学习外国工业制造技术为主要内容，以自强求富、挽救清朝危机为宗旨的洋务运动。清政府引进西方先进的生产技术，创办新式军事工业，训练新式陆军，建成北洋海军等近代海军。江南机器制造总局、金陵机器局和福州船政局是这一时期中国创办的主要军事工业企业。清政府兴办轮船、铁路、电报、邮政、采矿、纺织等各种新式民用工业，推动了近代中国民族工业的发展。轮船招商局是上海创办的最大的民用企业。此外，清政府建设新式军队，在天津训练新式陆军。同时，清政府通过外购和自建的方式组建新式海军。1862年，在北京创办的京师同文馆是第一个培养洋务人才和介绍洋务知识的文化教育机构。

1894年，甲午战争中中国所建新式陆军和海军受到毁灭性的打击，洋务运动遂告失败。洋务运动，客观上刺激了中国资本主义的发展，在一定程度上抵制了外国资本主义的经济输入，但并没有使中国走上富强道路。

拓展知识

江南机器制造总局

江南机器制造总局，清末官办军事工厂。1865年，李鸿章在上海虹口购买美商旗记铁工厂，并入原有两个制炮局，拨给曾国藩派容闳从美国购来的机器，建成该局。1867年，该局迁高昌庙，扩充为清政府规模最大的军事工厂，主要制造枪炮和修造轮船。

1867年，江南机器制造总局有泥船坞一座。1868年，成立翻译馆，由徐寿、华蘅芳主持。同年，该局建成第一艘轮船"恬吉"。次年，该局建成第二艘轮船"操江"。1883年，设立军械所。1885年后，造船长期停顿，专门修理南、北洋各省船舰。1905年，造船部分单独设厂，称江南船坞。从此，江南机器制造总局分为江南制造局和江南船坞两部分，前者成为专门制造军火的兵工厂。

辛亥革命后，江南船坞改称江南造船所，归北洋政府海军部管辖；江南机器制造总局改名上海制造局，隶属于陆军部。1914年，上海制造局改称上海兵工厂。1927年后，江南造船所由国民政府海军管理。1932年淞沪抗战后，上海兵工厂停办，后场地并入江南造船所。1949年5月，江南造船所改称江南造船厂。

讨论

> 你的国家在近代有哪些经济发展措施？比较一下其与中国洋务运动的异同。

三　戊戌变法

必读课文

戊戌变法

戊戌变法，亦称"戊戌维新"，清末政治改革运动。1895年中日甲午战争中中国惨败，民族危机空前严重。康有为等在北京发动各省应试举人1300余人上书光绪帝，反对签订《马关条约》，以"变法图强"为号召，组织强学会，掀起维新变法运动。

　　康有为、梁启超、谭嗣同、严复等人在各地组织学会，设立学堂和报馆，宣传变法维新，影响及于全国。以康有为为首的资产阶级改良派政治力量，得到军机大臣翁同龢和湖南巡抚陈宝箴等的支持。1897年冬，德国强占胶州湾，帝国主义阴谋瓜分中国日亟，康有为又赶到北京上书，请求变法。1898年4月，康有为等以保国、保种、保教为宗旨，倡设保国会于北京。光绪帝接受变法主张，引用维新人士。6月11日，光绪帝颁发"明定国是"诏，宣布变法自强。此后103天内，连续颁发维新法令，从政治、经济、军事、文教等方面推行新政。

　　以慈禧太后为首的守旧派操纵军政实权，坚决反对变法维新。9月21日，慈禧太后发动政变，幽禁光绪帝，杀害谭嗣同等六人，变法运动失败。

拓展知识

甲午战争

　　甲午战争，亦称"中日甲午战争"，指1894年至1895年发生的中日战争。这次战争导致中国国际地位的急剧下降，给中华民族带来空前严重的民族危机。

　　1868年，日本通过明治维新，开始走上资本主义道路，国力日渐强盛。同时，中国处于清朝晚期，清政府发起洋务运动，向西方学习先进科学技术。1872年，日本侵略中国附属国琉球。1874年，日本侵略中国台湾。1879年，日本吞并琉球王国，改为冲绳县。到1887年，日本已制定了侵略中国的计划，叫作"征讨清国策"。

　　1890年，日本爆发经济危机。1894年初，朝鲜发生内乱，日本趁机出兵朝鲜。7月下旬，日军突袭中国海陆军。8月1日，中日双方正式宣战。在平壤战役中，清军战败，随后日军控制朝鲜全境。平壤陷落后，中日舰队在鸭绿江口附近爆发黄海海战，日军夺取黄海制海权。10月，日军分陆海两路入侵中国辽东半岛和山东半岛。1895年4月，清政府与日本签订《马关条约》。

讨论

你的国家在近代有哪些政治改革措施？比较一下其与中国戊戌变法的异同？

（四）辛亥革命

必读课文

辛亥革命

辛亥革命，指 1911 年中国爆发的资产阶级民主主义革命。

1905 年，孙中山等人在日本东京成立中国同盟会，以"驱除鞑虏，恢复中华，创立民国，平均地权"为纲领。之后，中国的革命派多次发动武装起义，冲击了清王朝的统治，扩大了革命影响。1911 年 6 月，为对抗清政府发布的铁路国有法令，四川、湖南、湖北、广东等省爆发保路运动。10 月 10 日，湖北武昌革命党人发动武昌起义，成立湖北军政府。武昌起义胜利后两个月内，陕西、湖南、江西、安徽等 14 个省相继宣布独立。1912 年 1 月，孙中山就任中华民国临时大总统。2 月，清朝皇帝宣布退位。

辛亥革命是一场资产阶级领导的以反对封建君主专制制度、建立资产阶级共和国为目的的革命，开创了完全意义上的近代民族民主革命。辛亥革命打开了近代中国历史进步的闸门，开启了中国前所未有的社会变革，为中华民族发展进步探索了道路，具有伟大的历史意义。

拓展知识

五四运动

五四运动，指1919年5月4日爆发的中国人民反帝反封建的爱国运动。

第一次世界大战结束后，英、法、美等国于1919年1月在巴黎召开对德和会，中国政府向和会提出希望列强放弃在华特权、要求取消"二十一条"和收回被日本夺取的原德国在山东的权利，遭到与会帝国主义国家拒绝，北洋政府准备在和约上签字。中国在外交上失败的消息传出，举国愤怒。5月4日下午，北京学生3000余人在天安门前集会。会后，学生举行游行示威，遭到使馆巡捕的阻拦。政府派军警镇压，逮捕30多名学生。6月3日起，政府实行特别戒严，激起全国人民更大愤怒。5日起，上海工人罢工、商人罢市、学生罢课。全国150多个城市相继卷入，运动中心也由北京移到上海。10日，北洋政府被迫释放被捕学生。28日，中国代表团拒绝在《凡尔赛和约》上签字。

五四运动是彻底的不妥协的反帝反封建的爱国运动，中国工人阶级由此登上政治舞台，为中国共产党的成立在思想上和干部上做了准备，标志着新民主主义革命的开端。

讨论

第一次世界大战对中国及你的国家有哪些影响？

（五）中国人民抗日战争

必读课文

中国人民抗日战争

中国人民抗日战争（简称抗日战争），指中国人民于20世纪三四十年代进行的抗击日本侵略的正义战争。抗日战争的时间从1931年9月至1945年9月，共计14年。

1931年9月18日，日军发动九一八事变，相继侵占中国东北三省，中国局部抗战开始。1932年1月，日军进攻上海，中日军队进行了第一次全面对抗和较量。1937年7月7日，日军向北平（今北京）西南卢沟桥发起进攻，开始全面侵华战争，中国军队奋起抵抗，从此开始全国性抗日战争。8月，上海淞沪会战爆发。12月，南京沦陷。1938年10月，日军侵占广州、武汉后，被迫停止战略进攻，战争进入战略相持阶段。1941年12月7日，日本发动太平洋战争。1945年8月15日，日本无条件投降。9月2日，日本在投降书上签字。中国抗日战争胜利结束。

中国人民的抗日战争是第二次世界大战的重要组成部分，对世界反法西斯战争的胜利作出了巨大牺牲和不可磨灭的历史贡献。中国人民抗日战争，是中国近代以来抗击外敌入侵第一次取得完全胜利的民族解放战争，成为中华民族由衰败走向振兴的历史转折点。

拓展知识

中华人民共和国成立

1949年10月1日，中华人民共和国中央人民政府成立。10月1日，成为中华人民共和国的国庆日。

抗日战争胜利后，中国进入解放战争时期。面对国民党发动的全面内战，中国共产党领导的中国人民解放军先后打赢辽沈、淮海、平津三大战役和渡江战役，并向中南、西北、西南进军。最终，由中国共产党领导的人民力量推翻了国民党政权，建立了中华人民共和国。

1949年9月21日，由中国各界代表组成的中国人民政治协商会议第一届全体会议在北平（今北京）召开。会议通过了具有临时宪法作用的《中国人民政治协商会议共同纲领》。10月1日下午2时，中央人民政府委员会举行第一次会议，宣布就职。下午3时，首都30万军民在天安门广场举行隆重的开国大典，第一面五星红旗冉冉升起，毛泽东宣告中华人民共和国中央人民政府成立。

中华人民共和国的成立，标志着中国新民主主义革命已经取得伟大胜利，标志着中国人民受奴役受压迫的半殖民地半封建时代已经过去，中国已成为一个新民主主义国家。

讨论

第二次世界大战对中国及你的国家有哪些影响？

（六）抗美援朝

必读课文

抗美援朝战争

抗美援朝战争，是中华人民共和国成立初期，中国人民组成志愿军，为援助朝鲜人民抵抗美国侵略、保卫中国安全而进行的战争。

1950年6月25日，朝鲜内战爆发。27日，美国总统杜鲁门公开宣布对朝鲜进行武装干涉，并令美国海军第七舰队侵入台湾海峡。10月上旬，中共中央根据朝鲜政府的请求和中国人民的意愿，做出"抗美援朝，保家卫国"的战略决策，组成中国人民志愿军。10月19日，中国人民志愿军开赴朝鲜战场。25日，揭开抗美援朝战争序幕。抗美援朝战争历时两年零九个月，分两个作战阶段。第一阶段，中国人民志愿军和朝鲜人民军以运动战为主要作战形式实施战略反攻。第二阶段，中国人民志愿军和朝鲜人民军以阵地战为主要作战形式。1953年7月27日，战争双方在朝鲜停战协定上签字，抗美援朝战争随之结束。

抗美援朝战争伟大胜利，对中国和世界都有着重大而深远的意义。经此一战，奠定了中华人民共和国在亚洲和国际事务中的重要地位。

拓展知识

"一五"计划

"一五"计划，是中华人民共和国第一个五年计划的简称。编制与实施"一五"计划是对中国实现工业化具有重大意义的关键一步。

中华人民共和国从1951年着手编制第一个五年计划。"一五"计划是一边执行实施，一边修改补充。1954年3月，"一五"计划的编制进入最后阶段。1955年7月，第一届全国人大第二次会议正式通过第一个五年计划，并向全国颁布执行。

1953年，中国开始执行第一个五年计划，全国人民以极高的政治觉悟和生产热情投身"一五"计划建设。冶金工业是整个工业的基础，发展冶金工业的重点是对鞍山钢铁公司进行大规模的改扩建。煤炭工业是能源建设的重点，石油工业、化学工业、兵器工业也都获得长足发展。这一时期，国家还集中力量重点建设航空和电子两个新兴工业部门。"一五"计划后期，中国开始创建核工业和航天工业两个新兴尖端行业。截至1957年，第一个五年计划的各项任务均超额提前完成，为我国全面开始社会主义建设奠定了良好的基础。

讨论

你的国家是什么时候和中国建立外交关系的?简单谈一谈这一过程。

经济发展篇

第七章

经济转型

一、农业转型

必读课文

农业转型

农业，是利用植物、动物和微生物的生活机能，通过人工培育以取得农产品的社会生产部门。农业是国民经济的基础，为人们提供粮食、副产品和工业原料。广义的农业包括种植业、林业、畜牧业、渔业、副业五种产业形式。中华人民共和国成立以来，伴随着国家的现代化进程，农业现代化也取得了重大进展。当前，随着经济发展从高速增长向高质量发展转变，中国农业发展也随之转型。

从中华人民共和国成立到20世纪70年代，中国农业处于农村集体所有制制度下探索农业现代化的阶段。中国在农村实行农村土地集体所有、农产品统购统销和农业户籍制度。20世纪70年代末至90年代，中国农业处于以农村改革与结构变革为主导的农业现代化阶段。家庭联产承包责任制的确立与制度化，使农户成为农业发展的主人。20世纪90年代以来，中国农业处于农民离开土地和农村向城镇转移的农业现代化阶段。机械化投入大幅度增加，农业劳动生产率快速提升。中国农业现代化正在朝着以提高劳动生产率为主的模式转型。

拓展知识

家庭联产承包责任制

家庭联产承包责任制，是农户以家庭为单位向集体，组织承包土地等生产资料和生产任务的农业生产责任制形式。家庭联产承包责任制是中国现阶段农村的一项基本经济制度。

中华人民共和国成立后，中国的农业经济实行集体统一经营。1978年秋，中国安徽、四川部分地区因遭受灾害，农民自发恢复了20世纪60年代初期曾经出现过的包产到组、包产到户等生产责任制形式。1980年5月，邓小平在一次重要谈话中公开肯定小岗村"大包干"的做法。1982年1月1日，中国共产党历史上第一个关于农村工作的"一号文件"正式出台。1982年9月，党的十二大对以包产到户为主要形式的农村生产责任制给予充分肯定，强调必须长期坚持下去并逐步加以完善。之后，中国大多数农户实行了各种形式的联产承包责任制，其中实行最多的是大包干。

中国政府不断稳固和完善家庭联产承包责任制，鼓励农民发展多种经营，推动广大农村地区逐步走上富裕的道路。

讨论

简述一下你所在的国家的农业政策。谈一谈其与中国农业政策的异同。

(二) 金融体制

必读课文

金融体制

　　金融体制，指银行等金融机构利用各种信用活动组织、调节货币流通与资金运动的形式和管理制度的总和，包括银行体制、货币发行体制、借贷资本管理体制和利率管理体制等方面。根据中国共产党第十一届中央委员会第三次全体会议关于实行经济体制改革和对外开放的方针，从 1979 年起，中国开始对金融体制进行一系列重大改革。

　　1948 年中国人民银行成立后，中国实行计划管理的"大一统"金融体制。1949 年以后，中国按照建立社会主义所有制的要求没收官僚资本银行，改造私营银行和钱庄，同时大力发展农村信用合作社，实行高度集中的计划经济模式。1979 年以后，中国金融体制改革的总方向是逐步建立适应社会主义市场经济运行机制的金融体制。

　　目前，中国建立了以中国人民银行为核心，以国家专业银行为主体，多种金融机构并存的金融组织体系。中国人民银行专门行使中央银行职能。

拓展知识

四大银行

　　四大银行，指由国家直接管控的四家大型国有银行，包括：中国工商银行、中国农业银行、中国银行和中国建设银行。

　　中国工商银行，成立于 1984 年，总部位于北京，是中央管理的大型国有银行。中国工商银行拥有优质的客户基础，是中国最大的商业银行，也是世界五百强企业之一。

中国农业银行，成立于 1951 年，总部位于北京，是中央管理的大型国有银行。中国农业银行是中国金融体系的重要组成部分，是世界五百强企业之一。

中国银行，成立于 1912 年，总部位于北京，是中央管理的大型国有银行。中国银行香港、澳门分行为当地的发钞行，业务范围涵盖投资银行、保险、基金和飞机租赁。中国银行在全球范围内为个人和公司客户提供金融服务。

中国建设银行，成立于 1954 年，总部位于北京，是中央管理的大型国有银行。中国建设银行拥有广泛的客户基础，与多个大型企业集团及中国经济战略性行业的主导企业保持银行业务联系。

讨论

你了解中国的哪些银行？你在银行都办理过哪些业务？

三 东部发展

必读课文

东部发展

东部发展，是中华人民共和国为充分发挥东部地区沿海的地理优势，鼓励中国东部地区率先发展的一项政策。东部、东北、中部和西部是中国四大经济区，其中中国东部地区包括辽宁省、河北省、山东省、江苏省、浙江省、福建省、台湾省、广东省、海南省、北京市、天津市、上海市、香港特别行政区、澳门特别行政区。

20 世纪 80 年代，中国相继设立了深圳、珠海、汕头、厦门和海南 5 个经济特区，以及大连、秦皇岛等 14 个经济技术开发区，之后又相继把长江三角洲、珠江三角洲、闽南厦漳泉三地等开辟为沿海经济开放区。进入 21 世纪，国务院先后批准上海浦东新区和天津滨海新区为全国综合配套改革试验区，先行试验一些重大的改革开放措施。

东部的率先发展承担着为全国引路、试验的任务，所以东部在发展、转型、改革、转轨方面走在前面，能够为全面深化改革起到先行先试、搭桥铺路的作用。

拓展知识

长江三角洲地区

自然地理意义上的长江三角洲，北起通扬运河，南抵杭州湾，西至镇江，东到海边，是长江中下游平原的一部分。经济地理意义上的长江三角洲地区包括上海，江苏省的南京、无锡、常州、苏州、南通、扬州、镇江、泰州，浙江省的杭州、宁波、嘉兴、湖州、绍兴、舟山在内的 15 个城市。长江三角洲地区是中国经济最发达，开放程度最高的地区之一。

长江三角洲地区有着悠久的文化历史，在中国封建社会的中后期就已经初步形成了一个可观的城市群。明清时期，长江三角洲地区出现了较大的商业与手工业城市。近代以来，上海成为整个长江三角洲乃至中国的贸易中心、金融中心和工业中心。改革开放后，长江三角洲地区的城市功能分化重组，上海以其优越的地理区位重新成为国际性大都市。进入 21 世纪，中国明确了长江三角洲地区发展的战略定位，即亚太地区重要的国际门户、全球重要的现代服务业和先进制造业中心、具有较强国际竞争力的世界级城市群。

讨论

你的国家有哪些大的城市或城市群？简单描述一下。

（四）东北振兴

必读课文

东北振兴

东北振兴，指中华人民共和国促进东北地区等老工业区转型振兴的一项政策。2004年8月，国务院总理温家宝提出"振兴东北"的战略。2018年9月，国家主席习近平明确提出新时代东北振兴，是全面振兴、全方位振兴。

东北地区是中华人民共和国工业的摇篮。在中国特色社会主义工业化初期，东北地区为建立独立、完善的国民经济体系，推动中国工业化和城市化进程做出了历史性重大贡献。东北地区是中国重工业的重要基地，也是重要的农副产品生产基地。20世纪90年代以来，由于体制、机制等多种原因，东北地区在全面融入市场经济的过程中面临重重障碍，亟待解决。

东北振兴具体包括巩固发展现代农业、完善现代产业体系、推动产业集聚发展、促进资源型城市可持续发展、改善基础设施条件、强化资源节约和节能减排、采取多种措施增加就业岗位、继续深化国有企业改革、全面提升对外开放水平等诸多内容。

拓展知识

东北地区

中国的东北地区包括辽宁、吉林、黑龙江三省及内蒙古自治区东部，简称"东北"。

辽宁，省会沈阳，南临黄海、渤海，西南与河北接壤，西北与内蒙古自治区相连，东北与吉林为邻，东南以鸭绿江为界与朝鲜隔江相望。辽宁省地势大致为自北向南、自东西两侧向中部倾斜。中华人民共和国成立后，辽宁是中国工业的摇篮，被誉为"共和国长子"。

吉林，省会长春，与辽宁、内蒙古、黑龙江相连，并与俄罗斯、朝鲜接壤，地处东北亚地理中心位置。吉林省地势由东南向西北倾斜，呈现出东南高、西北低的特征。吉林省是近代东北亚政治军事冲突完整历程的见证地，是中国重要的工业基地和商品粮生产基地。

黑龙江，省会哈尔滨，北部、东部与俄罗斯隔江相望，西部与内蒙古相邻，南部与吉林省接壤，是中国最北端以及陆地最东端的省级行政区。黑龙江省位于东北亚区域腹地，是亚洲与太平洋地区陆路通往俄罗斯和欧洲大陆的重要通道、中国沿边开放的重要窗口。

讨论

简单描述一下你所知道的中国东北地区的城市。

(五) 中部崛起

必读课文

中部崛起

中部崛起，是中华人民共和国促进中部六省共同崛起的一项政策。2004年3月，国务院总理温家宝在政府工作报告中首次明确提出。2006年，中国明确了中部地区全国重要粮食生产基地、能源原材料基地、现代装备制造及高技术产业基地和综合交通运输枢纽的定位。

中国的中部地区包括山西、安徽、江西、河南、湖北、湖南六省。随着"中部崛起"政策的实施，中部地区承东启西、连南接北，交通网络发达、生产要素密集、人力资源丰富、产业门类齐全等优势得到进一步发挥。目前，中部地区的战略定位是中国的重要先进制造业中心、中国新型城镇化重点区、中国现代农业发展核心区和中国生态文明建设示范区。

中部地区在中国经济社会发展全局中占有重要地位，长期以来为全国经济社会发展做出了重大贡献。中部地区是中国新一轮工业化、城镇化、信息化和农业现代化的重点区域，是扩大内需、提升开放水平最具潜力的区域，也是支撑中国经济保持中高速增长的重要区域。

拓展知识

中部地区

中国的中部地区包括山西、安徽、江西、河南、湖北和湖南六省。

山西，省会太原，东与河北为邻，西与陕西相望，南与河南接壤，北与内蒙古自治区毗连。山西是典型的被黄土覆盖的山地高原，地势东北高西南低。山西省地处中纬度地带的内陆，属温带大陆性季风气候。

安徽，省会合肥，东连江苏，西接河南、湖北，东南接浙江，南邻江西，北靠山东。安徽省是长江三角洲地区的重要组成部分，经济、文化和长江三角洲其他地区有着历史和天然的联系。

江西，省会南昌，东邻浙江、福建，南连广东，西接湖南，北靠湖北、安徽。

河南，省会郑州，东接安徽、山东，北靠河北、山西，西连陕西，南临湖北。河南地处沿海开放地区与中西部地区的接合部，是中国重要的综合交通枢纽和人流物流信息流中心。

湖北，省会武汉，东邻安徽，西连重庆，西北与陕西接壤，南接江西、湖南，北与河南毗邻。

湖南，省会长沙，东临江西，西接重庆、贵州，南毗广东、广西，北连湖北。

讨论

你了解中国中部的哪些城市？简单描述一下你的印象。

（六）西部开发

必读课文

西部大开发

西部大开发，是中国提高西部地区经济和社会发展水平的一项政策。实施西部大开发战略，是中国面向新世纪做出的重大决策。1999年9月，中国提出西部大开发战略。2000年10月，中国把实施西部大开发、促进地区协调发展作为一项战略任务。西部大开发，是对中国经济发展布局进行的一次重大战略调整。

西部大开发的范围包括四川省、陕西省、甘肃省、青海省、云南省、贵州省、重庆市、广西壮族自治区、内蒙古自治区、宁夏回族自治区、新疆维吾尔自治区、西藏自治区、湖北省恩施土家族苗族自治州、湖南省湘西土家族苗族自治州、吉林省延边朝鲜族自治州。

实施西部大开发以来，中央投入力度不断加大，西部地区经济社会发展加快，交通、水利、电网和通信等基础设施条件得到明显改善。2000年以来，国家在西部地区相继启动实施了一批重点生态建设工程，取得了明显的生态效益、社会效益和较好的经济效益。

拓展知识

西北五省

西北五省，包括陕西省、甘肃省、青海省、宁夏回族自治区、新疆维吾尔自治区。西北五省是基于中华人民共和国成立初期行政区划的概念，与自然地理区划中的西北地区不同。

陕西省，省会西安，位于中国内陆的腹地，属于黄河中游和长江上游。陕西省是连接中国东、中部地区和西北、西南地区的重要枢纽。

甘肃省，省会兰州，东通陕西，西达新疆，南临四川、青海，北靠宁夏、内蒙古，西北端与蒙古国接壤。

青海省，省会西宁，因境内有全国最大的内陆咸水湖——青海湖而得名。青海是中国长江、黄河、澜沧江的发源地，被誉为"中华水塔"。

宁夏回族自治区，省会银川，东邻陕西，西、北接内蒙古，南连甘肃。

新疆维吾尔自治区，省会乌鲁木齐，位于亚欧大陆中部。新疆是中国陆地面积最大、陆地边境线最长、毗邻国家最多的省区。新疆沙漠广布，石油、天然气丰富，是中国西气东输的起点、西部大开发的主要阵地。

讨论

你了解中国西部的哪些城市和景点？简单描述一下。

第八章

文化产业

一 流行音乐

必读课文

流行音乐

　　流行音乐，亦称"通俗音乐"，是相对于严肃音乐、古典音乐而言的一种结构短小、内容通俗、形式活泼，为广大群众所喜爱、广泛传唱的器乐曲和歌曲。流行音乐是商业性的音乐消遣娱乐，以市场为导向。流行音乐起源于19世纪末至20世纪初的美国。

　　中国的流行音乐出现于20世纪30年代。1949年以后，港台地区的流行音乐也逐渐发展。进入21世纪，华语流行音乐形成了东南亚和中国互相融合、渗透、影响的状态，主要流行于中国、马来西亚、新加坡以及其他通用华语的社区。华语流行音乐在华人社区外如韩国、日本等地也有一定影响力。

　　上海是华语流行音乐的中心。黎锦晖被誉为"中国流行音乐之父"，他是华语流行音乐体裁的创始者。他于20世纪20年代创作的作品《毛毛雨》被视为最早的中文流行音乐。华语流行音乐在发展中催生了许多具有国际影响力的华语流行音乐明星，如邓丽君。

拓展知识

邓丽君

邓丽君在中国的流行音乐乐坛中享有极高的地位。1953年，邓丽君出生于中国台湾，祖籍是中国河北。她是一位在全球华人社会极具影响力的台湾歌唱家，也是20世纪后半叶最负盛名的日本歌坛巨星之一。1967年，邓丽君推出首张唱片《邓丽君之歌第一集·凤阳花鼓》，开始了演唱生涯。1969年，邓丽君因演唱台湾电视连续剧《晶晶》主题曲而成名。1974年，邓丽君以一曲《空港》奠定了其日本演艺事业的基础。1980年，邓丽君当选台湾电视最高荣誉金钟奖"最佳女歌星奖"。20世纪80年代初期，邓丽君先后受邀于美国纽约林肯中心、洛杉矶音乐中心和拉斯维加斯"凯撒皇宫"举行个人演唱会。

邓丽君的演艺足迹遍及中国、日本、东南亚、美国的许多地区，演唱了汉语、日语、英语、粤语、闽南语、印尼语等歌曲1000余首，对华语乐坛，尤其是大陆流行乐坛的启蒙与发展产生了深远影响，也为亚洲不同流行音乐文化间的相互交流做出了重要贡献。

讨论

你听过中国的哪些流行音乐？简单谈一谈你的体会。

二 电影电视

必读课文

电影电视

电影电视，是电影和电视视觉艺术的统称。1905年，任庆泰拍摄的《定军山》是中国第一部电影，标志着中国电影的诞生。1958年，北京电视台拍摄播出的《一口菜饼子》是中国的第一部电视剧。在20世纪中后期的中国电影电视发展史上，台湾和香港拍摄的电影电视在世界各国具有极大的影响力。

台湾电影，特色在于强调导演风格、注重台湾历史，并崇尚以电影作为宣传工作。除了侯孝贤与杨德昌外，台湾出生的李安也是世界瞩目的电影导演。台湾的电视剧擅长讲浪漫的爱情故事，古装剧有《新白娘子传奇》《戏说乾隆》《包青天》等，偶像剧有《16个夏天》《王子变青蛙》《流星花园》等，家族剧有《再见阿郎》《意难忘》等。

香港电视剧的热潮开始于20世纪80年代的《上海滩》《霍元甲》。1999年拍摄的《创世纪》达到了香港商战剧的顶峰。香港的电影有很多种类型，如功夫片、喜剧片、警匪片等。香港也有许多优秀的电影演员，如张国荣、梁朝伟、成龙、周星驰等。

拓展知识

香港电影

香港电影，根据内容可分为功夫片、喜剧片、警匪片等不同类型。

功夫片是香港最大的特色，也是香港影坛最高的成就。香港功夫片让全世界都知道了中国功夫。在李小龙成名之前，香港影坛就有关德兴、石坚等人出演的《黄飞鸿》系列电影。继李小龙之后，香港功夫片的影星有成龙、李连杰、甄子丹等。

喜剧片是香港电影所擅长的。香港著名的喜剧之王有两个，一个是许冠文，另一个是周星驰。香港喜剧电影既有《八星报喜》《家有喜事》这样的普通喜剧片，也有《赌圣》《功夫》这样的多类型喜剧片，后者融合了功夫片、赌片等各类元素，使喜剧的表现形式更为丰富。

警匪片突出的是警察的神勇，在香港电影最辉煌的 20 世纪八九十年代，警匪片也同样发展到了顶峰。吴宇森的《喋血双雄》、黄志强的《重案组》、刘伟强的《无间道》系列都是警匪片的经典之作。

讨论

你看过哪些香港电影？简单谈一谈你的体会。

三 动画影片

必读课文

动画影片

动画影片，是用人工或电脑绘制出的图画表现艺术形象的一种美术电影。动画最早发源于 19 世纪上半叶的英国，兴盛于美国。

中国的动画事业起步较早。在 20 世纪 20 年代，中国的动画艺术家就已经创作了《过年》《狗请客》等作品。1941 年，万氏兄弟拍摄了亚洲第一部动画长片《铁扇公主》，其艺术魅力可以和当时迪士尼的《白雪公主和七个小矮人》平分秋色。中华人民共和国成立后，上海美术电影制片厂在艺术创作上达到了很高的水准，先后拍摄出《神笔》《小蝌蚪找妈妈》《大闹天宫》《牧笛》《哪吒闹海》等精美的动画影片。

进入 21 世纪，在国家政策的支持与鼓励下，中国动画的制作单位不断增多、从业队伍不断壮大、动画产品的创作水准有所提高，动漫产业园区建设同样取得了可喜的成绩，中国动画进入快速发展的新阶段。这一时期，中国代表性的原创动画有《喜羊羊和灰太狼》系列、《熊出没》系列、《秦时明月》系列、《画江湖》系列、《那年那兔那些事儿》系列等。

拓展知识

《西游记之大圣归来》

《西游记之大圣归来》是根据中国传统神话故事《西游记》进行拓展和演绎的 3D 动画电影。《西游记之大圣归来》动画电影由北京燕城十月文化传播有限公司、横店影视制作有限公司、北京微影时代科技有限公司等单位联合出品，田晓鹏导演，2015 年 7 月上映。

影片借用《西游记》中的主要角色重新架构内容，讲述了已于五行山下寂寞沉潜 500 年的孙悟空被儿时的唐僧——俗名江流儿的小和尚——误打误撞地解除封印后，在相互陪伴的冒险之旅中找回初心，完成自我救赎的故事。影片依托好莱坞经典叙事模式，故事架构较为完备，制作技术水平达到了国际水准。《西游记之大圣归来》最为成功的当属营销策略，为此后动画电影的宣传提供了可资借鉴的范本。

影片于 2015 年在中国公映后，立即以优秀的口碑引发众多观众的追捧和媒体的广泛报道。2015 年，该片获得第 30 届中国电影金鸡奖最佳美术片奖和第 16 届中国电影华表奖优秀故事影片奖。

讨论

你看过中国的哪些动画片？简单谈一谈你的体会。

（四）体育赛事

必读课文

体育赛事

体育赛事，一般指有规模、有级别的体育竞技活动。中国承办过多个世界级的体育赛事，如奥运会、亚运会和各类世界锦标赛。中国国内的主要体育赛事有中国男子篮球职业联赛、中国足球协会超级联赛和中国乒乓球俱乐部超级联赛等。

中国男子篮球职业联赛，简称"中职篮"，开始于1995年，是由中国篮球协会主办的跨年度主客场制篮球联赛。中国男子篮球职业联赛是中国最高等级的篮球联赛，其中诞生了姚明、王治郅、易建联、朱芳雨等著名运动员。

中国足球协会超级联赛，简称"中超"，开始于2004年，是由中国足球协会组织的中国大陆地区最高级别的职业足球联赛。中国足球协会超级联赛的下级联赛分别是中国足球协会甲级联赛、中国足球协会乙级联赛及中国足球协会会员协会冠军联赛。

中国乒乓球俱乐部超级联赛，开始于1999年，是由中国乒乓球协会与中央电视台联合主办的精品赛事。中国乒乓球俱乐部超级联赛每年举行一届，比赛项目有男子团体、女子团体。

拓展知识

中国女排

中国女排，是中国国家女子排球队的简称，隶属于中国排球协会。中国女排是中国各体育团队中成绩突出的体育团队之一，代表运动员为郎平。

中国女排曾在1981年和1985年世界杯、1982年和1986年世锦赛、1984年洛杉矶奥运会上夺得冠军，成为世界上第一个"五连冠"。中国女排在2003年世界杯、2004年奥运会、2015年世界杯、2016年奥运会、2019年世界杯五度夺冠，共十次成为世界冠军。2020年，陈可辛执导的电影《夺冠》讲述的就是中国女排夺冠的故事。

郎平，女，1960年出生于中国天津。1973年，郎平进入少年体校练习排球。1978年，郎平入选国家集训队。1981年、1982年和1984年，郎平随中国女排实现三连冠。1985年，郎平退役。2002年10月，郎平正式入选排球名人堂，成为亚洲获此殊荣的第一人。2016年，郎平以主教练身份率领中国女排获得奥运会冠军。

讨论

你在中国看过什么体育赛事？简单谈一谈你的看法。

（五）网络文学

必读课文

网络文学

网络文学，是在互联网上发表和阅读的一种文学样式。网络文学无须纸质印刷媒介和出版机构的中介和运作，运用电子超文本技术和网络进行创作并传播，具有最大限度的发表自由和个人创作空间。网络文学是随着互联网的普及而产生的。

与传统文学作品形式不同，网络文学具有多样性、互动性和知识产权保护困难的特点。相比传统文学创作，网络文学创作深受读者喜好的影响。利用互联网平台的互动性，网络文学的读者可以与作者和其他读者互动，随时评论分享，不断丰富阅读体验。

网络文学以小说为主，题材非常广泛。以百度小说为例，其面向男性的题材有都市、玄幻、奇幻、历史、科幻、军事、竞技、游戏、武侠和悬疑等，面向女性的题材有现代言情、古代言情、幻想言情、青春、游戏和悬疑等。

拓展知识

网络文学作品

目前，中国比较有影响力的网络文学作品有《斗破苍穹》《诛仙》和《盗墓笔记》等。

《斗破苍穹》，是一部连载于起点中文网的古装玄幻小说，作者是天蚕土豆。小说讲述了天才少年萧炎在创造了家族空前绝后的修炼纪录后突然成了废人，他经过艰苦修炼最终成就辉煌的故事。2010年，该小说被改编开发为网页游戏。2018年，该小说被改编成电视剧。

《诛仙》，是当代作家萧鼎创作的一部长篇小说。该小说讲述了青云山下普通少年张小凡的成长故事。整部小说构思巧妙、气势恢宏，开启了一个独具魅力的东方仙侠传奇架空世界。2007年，该小说被改编开发为网络游戏。2016年，该小说被改编成电视剧。

《盗墓笔记》，是以盗墓为题材的系列小说，作者是南派三叔。该系列小说讲述了吴邪、张起灵、吴三省等人进入古墓探险的故事。该系列小说于2006年开始在网上连载，2007年1月正式出版。2015年，该小说被改编成网络剧。

讨论

你看过哪些中国网络文学作品？简单谈一谈你的体会。

（六）图书出版

必读课文

图书出版

图书，是现代出版物的主要种类之一，是以纸张为载体、以印刷等方式复制图文信息形成的非连续出版物。图书出版指依照国家有关法规设立的图书出版法人实体的出版活动。在中国，图书出版执行许可证制度。图书由依法设立的图书出版单位出版。设立图书出版单位须经国家出版主管部门审批，取得图书出版许可证。

中国的图书出版首先是出版社编辑通过市场调研提出出版选题。经出版社内部论证通过后，选题报送省一级新闻出版局批准。选题经省一级新闻出版局批准后，出版业务进入编辑环节。编辑环节的主要工作有审稿和编辑加工，编辑加工是在审稿的基础上进行的。接着，图书进入装帧设计环节，装帧质量和图书体例格式直接影响图书的价值。最后，图书完成书稿发排、样稿校对、图书印刷等环节后，进入市场。

改革开放以来，中国图书出版行业取得快速发展，规模不断壮大。在国家严格控制新增出版社的背景下，中国图书出版从规模数量增长向优质高效发展转变。与此同时，大量中央各部门各单位出版社和地方出版社已经基本改制，成为公司制市场主体。

拓展知识

出版社

出版社，主要经营出版图书、音像制品或电子出版物的出版单位，有的也兼营报纸、期刊出版与网络出版业务。中国共有580多家出版社，从出版类别来看，中国的图书出版社可分为综合出版社和专业出版社。

商务印书馆，1897年成立于上海，是中国出版业中历史最悠久的出版机构。商务印书馆的创立标志着中国现代出版业的开始。商务印书馆成立不久就成立股份有限公司，开展以出版为中心的多种经营，实力迅速壮大。1954年，商务印书馆迁址北京。

中华书局，1912年1月1日成立于上海。中华书局是中国一家集编辑、印刷、出版、发行于一体的出版机构。中华书局创立之初，以出版中小学教科书为主，并印行古籍、科学、文艺著作和工具书等。1954年5月，中华书局总部迁址北京。

人民出版社，1921年9月1日成立于上海，是中国共产党创建时期创办的，是中国共产党创办的第一个出版社。中华人民共和国成立后，人民出版社于1950年12月在北京重建，毛泽东同志亲笔题写社名。

讨论

你还了解哪些中国的图书出版社？简单介绍一下。

第九章

合作共赢

一 沿海开放

必读课文

沿海开放城市

沿海开放城市，指中国沿海地区对外开放并在对外经济活动中实行经济特区的某些特殊政策的一系列港口城市。沿海开放城市是经济特区的延伸。

1984年5月，中国将大连、秦皇岛、天津、烟台、青岛、连云港、南通、上海、宁波、温州、福州、广州、湛江、北海等14个城市定为沿海开放城市。1985年和1988年，营口市和威海市先后被列入沿海开放城市。这些沿海开放城市交通方便，工业基础好，技术水平和管理水平比较高，科研文教事业比较发达，既有开展对外贸易的经验，又有进行对内协作的信息网络，经济效益较好，是中国经济比较发达的地区。

中国开放沿海城市的基本目的是发挥城市的自然资源优势与经济优势，进一步开展对外经济合作与技术交流，引进外资与先进技术，扩大出口和吸收外汇的能力，加速社会主义现代化的建设。

拓展知识

经济特区

　　经济特区，指在一个国家或地区内划出一定的范围实行特殊经济政策和经济体制的地区，一般设置在地理位置优越、交通方便的港口或边境城市。1979年4月，邓小平首次提出要开办"出口特区"。之后，"出口特区"改名为"经济特区"。经济特区的实质是世界自由港区的重要形式之一。经济特区以减免关税等优惠措施为手段，通过创造良好的投资环境，鼓励外商投资，引进先进技术和科学管理方法，以达到促进特区所在国经济技术发展的目的。中国的经济特区实行特殊的经济政策、灵活的经济措施和特殊的经济管理体制，并坚持以外向型经济为发展目标。

　　从1979年9月起，中国先后在广东省的深圳、珠海、汕头和福建省的厦门分别指定一定区域，设立了经济特区。1988年4月，中国设立海南经济特区。1992年中国加快改革开放后，将上海的浦东作为经济特区。2006年5月，中国将天津滨海新区作为全国综合配套改革试验区。2010年5月，中国在新疆霍尔果斯和喀什设立经济特区。

讨论

> 你了解中国的哪些对外开放城市？简单描述一下。

（二）中国加入世界贸易组织

必读课文

中国加入世界贸易组织

中国加入世界贸易组织，指中国于 2001 年 12 月 11 日正式加入世界贸易组织的社会事件。中国自改革开放以来，特别是 1992 年提出建设社会主义市场经济体制以来，经济实力明显增强，在诸多领域已具备参与国际分工与竞争的能力。

中国加入世界贸易组织的谈判经历了三个阶段：第一个阶段从 20 世纪 80 年代初到 1986 年，主要是准备阶段；第二个阶段从 1987 年到 1992 年，主要是审议中国经贸体制阶段；第三个阶段从 1992 年到 2001 年，进入实质性谈判阶段，即双边市场准入谈判和围绕起草中国入世法律文件的多边谈判。经过谈判，中国与所有世界贸易组织成员就中国加入世界贸易组织达成协议。2001 年 11 月 11 日，在卡塔尔首都多哈，中国签署加入世界贸易组织的议定书。

2001 年中国加入世界贸易组织，是中国深度参与经济全球化的里程碑，标志着中国改革开放进入历史新阶段。

拓展知识

中国加入亚太经济合作组织

亚太经济合作组织，简称"亚太经合组织"，是亚太地区重要的经济合作论坛，也是亚太地区最高级别的政府间经济合作机制。作为全球最大的地区性经济组织，亚太经济合作组织经济总量超过全球经济总量的一半；成员国富有多样性和代表性，既有美国、日本等发达国家，也有中国、墨西哥等新兴经济体。

1989 年 11 月 5 日至 7 日，亚太经济合作会议首届部长级会议举行，标志着亚太经济合作组织的成立。1991 年 11 月，在"一个中国"和"区别主权国家和地区经济体"原则的基础上，中国以主权国家身份，中国台北和中国香港以地区经济体名义正式加入亚太经合组织。

自中国加入亚太经合组织以来，亚太经合组织便成为中国与亚太地区其他经济体开展互利合作、多边外交以及展示中国国家形象的重要舞台。2001年10月，亚太经合组织第九次领导人非正式会议在中国上海成功举行。2014年11月，亚太经合组织第二十二次领导人非正式会议在中国北京成功举行。

讨论

> 你的国家加入了哪些国际性经济组织？简单描述一下。

三、上海合作组织

必读课文

上海合作组织

上海合作组织，为政府间国际组织，是世界上幅员最广、人口最多的综合性区域组织。其前身为"上海五国"会晤。

2001年6月14日至15日，中国、俄罗斯、哈萨克斯坦、吉尔吉斯斯坦、塔吉克斯坦等"上海五国"元首和乌兹别克斯坦元首在上海举行第六次会晤，乌兹别克斯坦以完全平等的身份加入"上海五国"。六国元首签署了《"上海合作组织"成立宣言》，宣布成立上海合作组织。2002年6月，上海合作组织成员国在圣彼得堡举行第二次峰会，六国元首签署了《上海合作组织宪章》。宪章对上海合作组织的宗旨、组织结构、运作形式、合作方向及对外交往原则等作了明确阐述。从 2004 年开始，上海合作组织启动了观察员机制。2017 年，印度和巴基斯坦加入上海合作组织。2022 年，伊朗加入上海合作组织。

上海合作组织的宗旨是，加强成员国之间的相互信任与睦邻友好；发展成员国在政治、经济、文化等各个领域的有效合作；维护和保障地区的和平、安全和稳定；推动建立民主、公正、合理的国际政治经济新秩序。

拓展知识

中非合作论坛

中非合作论坛，是中国和非洲国家之间在平等互利基础上的集体对话机制，成立于 2000 年。中非合作论坛的宗旨是平等磋商、增进了解、扩大共识、加强友谊、促进合作。中非合作论坛的成员包括中国、与中国建交的 53 个非洲国家以及非洲联盟委员会。中非合作论坛部长级会议每 3 年举行一届。部长级会议由外交部长和负责国际经济合作事务的部长参加。

2000 年 10 月，为进一步加强中国与非洲国家在新形势下的友好合作，共同应对经济全球化挑战，谋求共同发展，在中非双方共同倡议下，中非合作论坛——北京 2000 年部长级会议在北京召开，中非合作论坛正式成立。中非合作论坛第一届部长级会议通过了《中非合作论坛北京宣言》和《中非经济和社会发展合作纲领》，为中国与非洲国家发展长期稳定、平等互利的新型伙伴关系确定了方向。2000 年 11 月，中非合作论坛中方后续行动委员会成立，秘书处办公室设在外交部非洲司。2018 年 9 月，中非合作论坛北京峰会隆重举行。

讨论

目前中国和你的国家有哪些经济交往？简单描述一下？

(四) 中国—东盟自由贸易区

● 必读课文

中国—东盟自由贸易区

中国—东盟自由贸易区,指中国与东南亚国家联盟十国组建的自由贸易区,是世界三大区域经济合作区之一。2010年,中国—东盟自由贸易区正式全面启动。中国—东盟自由贸易区涵盖11个国家,是世界上人口最多的自由贸易区,也是由发展中国家组成的最大的自由贸易区。

中国与东南亚国家联盟的对话始于1991年。1996年,中国成为东南亚国家联盟的全面对话伙伴国。2000年11月,在第四次中国—东盟领导人会议上,中国首次提出建立中国—东盟自由贸易区的构想。2002年11月,在第六次中国—东盟领导人会议上,11个国家的领导人签署了《中国与东盟全面经济合作框架协议》,决定到2010年建成中国—东盟自由贸易区,标志着中国—东盟建立自由贸易区的进程正式启动。2004年11月,双方签署了自由贸易区《货物贸易协议》和《争端解决机制协议》。2007年1月,中国和东盟签署了自由贸易区《服务贸易协议》。2010年1月1日,中国—东盟自由贸易区正式建立。

● 拓展知识

中国—智利自由贸易区

中国—智利自由贸易区,指中国与智利组建的自由贸易区。随着经济全球化和区域经济一体化的发展,世界各国积极签订各种自由贸易协定,以达到提高成员方和世界整体的福利。智利是继东南亚国家联盟后第二个与中国签订自由贸易协定的国家,也是第一个与中国签订自由贸易协定的拉丁美洲国家。

自1970年中国与智利建立外交关系以来,两国经济和贸易关系进入正常发展阶段。在贸易方面，中国与智利贸易发展迅速，智利成为中国在拉丁美洲的重要贸易伙伴，中国也成为智利在全球的重要贸易伙伴。进入21世纪，中国和智利的双边贸易进入一个高速发展的阶段。2005年11月，经过谈判，中国与智利两国政府正式签订了《中华人民共和国政府和智利共和国政府自由贸易协定》。2006年10月1日，中国—智利自由贸易区正式建立。

中国—智利自由贸易区的建立，为两国经济与贸易关系的发展提供了一个广阔的平台。

讨论

> 你的国家加入了哪些自由贸易区？简单描述一下。

（五）中巴经济走廊

必读课文

中巴经济走廊

中巴经济走廊，是新时代中巴合作的标志性工程，也是"一带一路"建设的重大先行项目和样板工程。中巴经济走廊的建设有助于促进两国间资本、技术、信息、人才的跨国流动，实现互利双赢。

中巴经济走廊的设想最早是由巴基斯坦总统于2006年2月在接受《中国日报》专访时提出的。2013年5月，中国总理访问巴基斯坦期间，正式提出建设中巴经济走廊的合作倡议。随后，两国政府签署了《关于开展中巴经济走廊远景规划合作的谅解备忘录》。2013年底，随着中国"一带一路"倡议的提出，中巴经济走廊作为"一带一路"的有益补充，战略重要性进一步提升。2014年2月，巴基斯坦总统访华期间，中巴双方同意加速推进中巴经济走廊建设。2015年4月20日，中巴经济走廊项目正式启动。

中巴经济走廊起点在喀什，终点在巴基斯坦瓜达尔港，全长3000公里，北接"丝绸之路经济带"，南连"21世纪海上丝绸之路"，是贯通南北丝路的关键枢纽，是一条包括公路、铁路、油气和光缆通道在内的贸易走廊。

拓展知识

喀喇昆仑公路

喀喇昆仑公路，连接中国新疆喀什与巴基斯坦北部，穿越喀喇昆仑、喜马拉雅、兴都库什三大山脉和帕米尔高原，被世人称为"天路"。20世纪六七十年代，中国援助巴基斯坦建起这条该国北部地区唯一的对外经济生命线，因此这条公路也被称为"中巴友谊公路"。

1965年9月，巴基斯坦提出在中国与巴基斯坦之间修建一条现代公路的想法。1966年3月，中国和巴基斯坦签署《中巴两国政府关于修建喀喇昆仑公路的协定》。喀喇昆仑公路从1966年开始修筑，到1979年通车，前后历时14年。1983年5月，两国间正式开放了旅客班车。1986年5月中巴公路向第三国开放后，车流量大增，大大促进了中巴两国旅游和贸易。2010年，公路因大规模滑坡通行被中断。2015年9月，喀喇昆仑公路重新贯通。

喀喇昆仑公路是巴基斯坦通往其首都伊斯兰堡及南部沿海地区的交通要道，也是中国通往巴基斯坦及其南部港口卡拉奇、南亚次大陆、中东地区的唯一陆路通道。

讨论

中国和你的国家有哪些友好往来？简单描述一下？

(六) 《区域全面经济伙伴关系协定》

必读课文

《区域全面经济伙伴关系协定》

《区域全面经济伙伴关系协定》，是 2012 年由东南亚国家联盟发起，包括中国、日本、韩国、澳大利亚和新西兰等 15 个成员的自由贸易协定。

2020 年 11 月 15 日，第四次区域全面经济伙伴关系协定领导人会议以视频方式举行，会后东南亚国家联盟 10 国和中国、日本、韩国、澳大利亚、新西兰共 15 个亚太国家正式签署了《区域全面经济伙伴关系协定》。《区域全面经济伙伴关系协定》的签署，标志着当前世界上人口最多、经贸规模最大、最具发展潜力的自由贸易集团正式启航。

2021 年 4 月 15 日，中国向东南亚国家联盟秘书长正式交存《区域全面经济伙伴关系协定》核准书。11 月 2 日，《区域全面经济伙伴关系协定》保管机构东南亚国家联盟秘书处发布通知，宣布 6 个东盟成员国和 4 个非东盟成员国已向东盟秘书长正式提交核准书，达到协定生效门槛。2022 年 1 月 1 日，《区域全面经济伙伴关系协定》正式生效。

拓展知识

中韩自由贸易区

中韩自由贸易区，指中国和韩国组建的自由贸易区。

21 世纪以来，中国逐渐成为韩国最大贸易伙伴国、最大出口对象国和最大进口来源国，韩国逐渐成为中国第一大进口来源国和重要投资来源国之一。2012 年 5 月，中国和韩国正式启动中韩自由贸易区谈判。2014 年 11 月 10 日，中韩双方共同宣布中韩自由贸易区结束实质性谈判。2015 年 2 月 25 日，中韩自由贸易区谈判全部完成。6月1日，中韩自由贸易协定正式签署，标志着中韩自由贸易区建设进入实施阶段。12月9日，中韩双方共同确认《中华人民共和国政府与大韩民国政府自由贸易协定》于2015年12月20日正式生效并第一次降税，2016年1月1日第二次降税。

中韩自由贸易协定创新性引入地方经济合作条款，明确中国威海市和韩国仁川自由经济区作为地方经济合作示范区，发挥示范和引导作用。中韩自由贸易区给两国相关产业发展带来了极大的推动作用。

讨论

你的国家和中国都有哪些经济协定？简单描述一下。

科技创新篇

第十章

信息网络

一、通信网络

必读课文

第五代移动通信网络

移动通信网络,指的是将移动用户与固定点用户之间或移动用户之间的通信实现的通信介质。在现代通信领域中,移动通信与卫星通信、光通信并列为三大重要通信手段。目前,中国主要使用的是第五代移动通信网络。第五代移动通信网络,是由中国华为公司主持研发的一项通信网络科技。第五代移动通信网络给中国人带来更加便利快捷的信息生活方式。目前,中国的第五代移动通信网络正在普及当中。

相比第四代移动通信网络,第五代移动通信网络呈现很多创新点。首先,第五代移动通信网络的传输速率大大提高。在提高传输速度的同时,第五代移动通信网络的传输稳定性也得到提升。其次,第五代移动通信网络可以灵活支持不同的设备,例如手机、电脑、智能手表、智能家庭设备等。最后,第五代移动通信网络还可以延长设备的电池使用寿命。

第五代移动通信网络正在改变中国人的生活,也向世界展示了中国科技。

拓展知识

第五代移动通信基站

移动通信基站，指在一定的无线电覆盖区中，通过移动通信交换中心，与移动电话终端之间进行信息传递的无线电收发信电台。移动通信基站是移动设备接入互联网的接口设备，也是无线电台站的一种形式。随着移动通信网络业务向数据化、分组化方向发展，移动通信基站的发展趋势也必然是宽带化、大覆盖面建设。

第五代移动通信基站是第五代移动通信网络的核心与基础。第五代移动通信基站可以实现无线覆盖，完成有线通信网络与无线终端间的无线信号传输。第五代移动通信基站的架构和形态直接影响第五代移动通信网络的部署。由于移动通信网络存在频率越高，信号传播过程中的衰减也越大的问题，第五代移动通信网络的基站密度将更高。

中国的移动通信运营商正在大力建设第五代移动通信基站。目前，中国所有的地级市都已建成第五代移动通信基站。中国第五代移动通信基站的大量建成，使得中国第五代移动通信网络用户的数量在全世界遥遥领先。

讨论

> 你的国家使用的是第几代移动通信技术？简单谈一谈你的使用感受。

二 搜索引擎

必读课文

搜索引擎

搜索引擎，指根据用户需求与一定算法，运用特定策略从互联网检索出相关信息并反馈给用户的检索技术。搜索引擎可以提高人们的信息搜集能力，是人们普遍使用的检索技术。搜索引擎的特点是信息获取的效率高、速度快。从功能和原理上，搜索引擎大致被分为全文搜索引擎、元搜索引擎、垂直搜索引擎和目录搜索引擎四大类。

中国搜索引擎技术出现于21世纪初。在中国互联网刚开始发展时，搜狐、网易、新浪等网站就开始探究搜索引擎技术，他们推出的搜索引擎属于第一代目录式搜索引擎。1999年，随着雅虎中国网站的开通，中国互联网用户体验到更强大的搜索功能，用户可以检索到政治、经济、文化、体育等各方面的信息。2000年，李彦宏创建百度公司。百度作为第二代搜索引擎，实现了信息的自动获取，提高了检索效率。自此以后，各种搜索引擎陆续被推出。目前，中国用户普遍使用的搜索引擎有百度、360、网易、搜狗等。

拓展知识

中国的搜索引擎

中国的搜索引擎技术在过去20多年间发展迅速，目前中国典型的搜索引擎有百度、360、搜狗等。

百度搜索引擎，是百度公司研发和推广的中文搜索引擎。百度公司创立于2000年，创始人是李彦宏。"百度"二字，来自800多年前南宋词人辛弃疾的一句词："众里寻他千百度"。百度的出现，使中国成为全球仅有的4个拥有搜索引擎核心技术的国家之一。目前，百度是中国用户最常用的搜索引擎，成为网民获取中文信息的主要入口。

360 搜索引擎，是北京奇虎科技有限公司研发和推广的一种全文搜索引擎。北京奇虎科技有限公司创立于 2005 年 9 月，是中国领先的互联网安全软件与互联网服务公司。360 是第三代搜索引擎，包括新闻搜索、网页搜索、视频搜索等多种功能。

搜狗搜索引擎，是搜狐公司开发的第三代互动式搜索引擎。搜狗通过智能分析技术，在不同网站选择性抓取重要信息，确保最新的资讯及时被用户获得。

讨论

> 你平时都使用哪种搜索引擎？简单谈一谈你的体会。

三　通信平台

必读课文

通信平台

通信平台，指将现有的通信联络方式如移动电话、邮件、传真等，进行统一处理，在一个终端上实现通信联络的平台。通信平台核心内容是人们可以随时随地在任意一个设备上获得信息，实现通信自由。通信平台以企业组织结构为基础，结合即时通信、网络会议等系统，使得文字、语音、视频等多种沟通手段融合为一。中国实时通信平台有钉钉、腾讯会议等。

钉钉，是 2015 年阿里巴巴集团专为中国企业打造的免费沟通和协同的多端平台。钉钉平台的核心功能包括组织在线、企业沟通功能、企业团队办公协同功能。

腾讯会议，是2019年腾讯公司开发的一款音视频会议软件。腾讯会议具有300人在线会议、全平台一键接入、音视频智能降噪、美颜、背景虚化、锁定会议、屏幕水印等功能。腾讯会议软件能实时共享屏幕且支持在线文档协作。

钉钉、腾讯会议等通信平台软件开创了会议、办公的新模式，克服了地域限制，提高了工作效率。

拓展知识

即时通信软件

除了办公常用的实时会议通信平台，中国人普遍使用的通信软件还有腾讯QQ和微信。

腾讯QQ，是一款基于互联网的即时通信软件。1999年，腾讯QQ正式上线运营，至今仍是中国人最重要的交流工具。腾讯QQ支持在线聊天、视频通话、共享文件、接收邮件等多种功能，并可以和多种通信终端连接，形成庞大的通信网络。目前，腾讯QQ覆盖了几乎所有的主流智能操作平台。

微信，是腾讯公司于2011年推出的一个为智能终端提供即时通信服务的免费应用程序。微信支持跨通信运营商、跨操作系统平台通过网络快速发送免费语音短信、视频、图片和文字。微信还提供朋友圈、消息推送等服务，满足用户的娱乐需求。同时，微信也支持朋友转账、二维码付款功能，促进电子货币的流通，大大方便了人们的生活。

目前，即时通信软件已逐渐取代手机通信，成为中国年轻人主要的通信方式。

讨论

你使用过哪种通信软件？简单谈一谈你的体会。

（四）网上购物

必读课文

网上购物

网上购物，指买家通过互联网搜索商品并下单，卖家邮寄商品给买家，买家检验商品后完成交易的一种购物方式。

相比传统的实体店购物，网上购物具有很大的优势。消费者通过互联网检索可以获得全面的商品信息，并及时与卖家取得联系。网上购物不受时间、地点限制，消费者往往可以以更优惠的价格获得更好的商品，既省时又省力。网上购物扩大了消费市场，商家只需要在平台上发布相关商品信息即可，不需要租赁实体店，节约了经营成本。

1991年，中国开展了电子数据交换的应用。1996年，中国国际电子商务中心成立。1997年，网上书店、网上购物及中国商品订货系统开始出现。1998年7月，中国商品交易与市场网站正式运行，北京、上海启动了电子商务工程。1999年底，中国网上购物的用户规模不断上升。2014年3月15日《网络交易管理办法》施行。

目前，随着互联网的普及，网上购物日益成为中国消费者重要的购物形式。"双十一"购物狂欢节和京东"618"是有代表性的大型网购促销活动。

拓展知识

网上购物平台

目前，中国主要的网上购物平台有淘宝网、京东网和当当网。

淘宝网，是阿里巴巴集团于2003年创立的综合类网上购物平台。同年10月，阿里巴巴推出新型支付工具支付宝，健全了线上购物体系。淘宝网的出现，既节省人们购物的成本，又保证购物的安全性，是中国最为流行的购物方式。

随着淘宝网规模的扩大和用户数量的增加，淘宝也从单一的网络集市变成了包括分销、拍卖、直供、众筹、定制等多种电子商务模式在内的综合性零售商圈。

京东网，又称"京东商城"，是中国电子商务领域颇受消费者欢迎且具有影响力的电子商务网站之一。相比同类电子商务网站，京东商城拥有更为丰富的商品种类，并凭借更具竞争力的价格和逐渐完善的物流配送体系等各项优势，赢得了市场占有率。

当当网，是知名的综合性网上购物商城。目前，当当网从早期销售图书的单一购物平台拓展到销售各种百货商品的综合性购物平台。

讨论

你使用过哪种网上购物平台？简单谈一谈你的体会。

（五）移动支付

必读课文

移动支付

移动支付，指用户使用移动终端（通常是智能手机等电子产品）对所消费的商品或服务进行财务支付，而不使用银行卡或者现金支付的一种支付方式。移动支付将互联网、终端设备、金融机构有效地联合起来，形成了一个新型的支付体系。移动支付是互联网时代的产物。移动支付开创了新的支付方式，促使电子货币开始普及。

移动支付打破了传统现金支付对时间和空间的限制。用户可以随时随地进行付款，不再需要面对面交易。同时，移动支付支持个人账户的查询、转账、充值等功能，用户既可以随时了解自己的消费信息，又能够方便地管理个人账户。另外，移动支付安全性很高。用户在付款时，需要输入密码或验证指纹，这一操作较好地保护了用户的隐私。

目前，移动支付已经渗透到中国人生活的方方面面。人们可以通过移动支付进行话费充值、水电费缴纳、网上购物等各类支付活动，极大地便利了人们的生活。中国人常用的具有支付功能的软件有支付宝、微信等。

拓展知识

支付宝

支付宝，中国知名的第三方支付平台。支付宝网络技术有限公司成立于2004年。如今，支付宝已经融合支付、生活、政务、理财等多项服务，成为一个开放性的生活服务平台。它不仅提供便捷的支付、转账、收款等功能，还支持线上信用卡还款、缴纳水电费、查看物流信息等活动，其功能全面覆盖人们的生活。支付宝还与国内外众多银行以及国际金融机构建立战略合作关系，成为金融机构在电子支付领域最为信任的合作伙伴。

在中国，支付宝的手机支付功能处于领先地位。2008年，支付宝发布移动电子商务战略，推出手机支付业务。2009年，支付宝推出中国首个独立移动支付客户端。2010年，支付宝推出中国首个二维码支付技术。用户点击软件中的"扫一扫"，对准二维码进行识别即可完成支付。这一新型支付方式更加便捷省时，进一步推动了电子货币的发展。目前，支付宝是全球最大的移动支付厂商。

讨论

你使用过哪种移动支付软件？简单谈一谈你的体会。

(六) 网络导航

必读课文

手机导航

在日常生活中，随着智能手机的普及，人们大多使用智能手机进行导航。目前，中国使用最多的手机导航软件有高德地图、百度地图和腾讯地图。

高德地图，是高德软件有限公司于2011年5月上线的手机导航软件。高德软件有限公司是中国领先的数字地图内容、导航和位置服务解决方案提供商。公司拥有导航电子地图甲级测绘资质和互联网地图服务甲级测绘资质。

百度地图，是北京百度网讯科技有限公司于2005年上线的手机导航软件。百度地图具备全球化地理信息服务能力。2013年，百度地图导航宣布永久免费。2019年，百度地图上线全球首个地图语音定制功能。

腾讯地图，是深圳市腾讯计算机系统有限公司于2013年上线的手机导航软件。腾讯地图为用户提供包括智能路线规划、精准导航、实时路况、换乘方案、公共出行等位置和出行相关服务。

拓展知识

北斗卫星导航系统

北斗卫星导航系统，是中国自行研制的全球卫星导航系统。该系统完全由中国自主建设、独立运行，为全球用户提供稳定、安全的定位、导航和授时服务。目前，中国已将它运用于交通运输、气象预报、通信授时等多个领域。

北斗卫星导航系统是中国重点建设的工程。1994年，中国"双星导航定位系统"正式立项，并以"北斗星"命名。2000年，中国成功发射了两颗北斗卫星，建成中国第一代卫星导航定位系统（"北斗一代"）并投入使用。2004年，中国启动具有全球导航能力的北斗卫星导航系统的建设（"北斗二号"）。2012年，中国建成"北斗二号"系统，将服务范围扩大至亚太地区。2020年，中国已经基本建成北斗三号系统，并为全球提供相关服务。

北斗卫星系统不仅是中国的导航系统，而且是全球的导航系统。北斗导航系统已经成为全球四大卫星导航系统之一，并为全球人民提供服务。

讨论

简单介绍一下你所使用的手机导航软件。

第十一章

人工智能

一 机器人

必读课文

机器人

机器人，亦称"智能机器人"，是能模仿人的某种活动的一种智能机械，机器人能模拟人类部分逻辑思维活动，具有类似视觉、听觉、嗅觉等的感觉功能，可在人所不能适应的环境下代替人的工作。机器人可以辅助或代替人类完成危险、繁重的任务，解放人力，进一步提高工作效率。

中国历史上最早的机器人是西周时期的"伶人"木偶机器人，有行走、跑步、唱歌、跳舞等功能。中国的机器人专家从应用环境出发，将机器人分为工业机器人和特种机器人两大类。中国于20世纪70年代开始研制工业机器人。进入80年代，在高技术浪潮的冲击下，中国机器人技术的开发和研究得到政府的重视与支持。1987年，中国成立了第一届智能机器人主题专家组。从20世纪90年代起，中国先后研制出各种用途的工业机器人，并实施了一批工业机器人应用工程，形成了一批机器人产业化基地，为机器人产业的发展奠定了基础。进入21世纪，机器人被广泛应用于工程制造、医疗卫生等行业。

拓展知识

水下机器人

水下机器人，又称"无人遥控潜水器"，是一种工作于水下的极限作业机器人。水下环境恶劣危险，人的潜水深度有限，所以水下机器人已成为开发海洋的重要工具。水下机器人的研发是中国机器人事业的发展重点之一。40多年来，中国科学家潜心研究智能机器人在海洋中的应用，并取得一定成就。

中国自20世纪80年代初开始研究开发遥控水下机器人。1984年，中国第一台遥控水下机器人"海人一号"在中国科学院沈阳自动化研究所诞生。1987年，中国科学院沈阳自动化研究所建成我国第一个自主水下机器人试验床HR-02。1994年，中国第一台自主水下机器人"探索者"号研制成功。进入21世纪，在国家"863"计划、中国大洋协会和中国科学院战略先导专项的支持下，中国先后研制了"潜龙"系列和"探索"系列自主水下机器人，用于大洋调查。"潜龙一号"自2013年起多次执行大洋调查任务。2020年，"潜龙四号"首次执行大洋调查任务。

讨论

你看过哪些有关机器人的电影？简单谈一谈你的体会。

（二） 无人机

必读课文

无人机

无人机，指无驾驶人员或驾驶（控制）人员不在机上的飞机和直升机，运用无线遥感设备对飞机进行控制。无人机既可以完成高危险、高难度的任务，也可以进行航拍摄影、地形测绘等日常工作。无人机不仅在军事战争中具有重要的战略地位，而且逐渐渗透到人们的日常生活和工作中。

中国的无人机事业发端于20世纪60年代。在苏联拉-17无人机的基础上，中国于1966年开始独立制造无人机。同年，中国第一架无人机"长空一号"首飞成功，中国独立研发无人机的事业由此起步。此后，中国又根据美国的"火蜂"无人机，制造出长虹-1无人机。它是一架高空多用途无人机，主要用于军事侦察、地质勘测等军事和科学研究。1972年该机型首飞成功，并于1980年正式装备部队。

20世纪末，中国无人机事业进入快速发展阶段。2009年，中国国庆阅兵仪式上出现的无人机方阵，向全世界展现了中国强大的军事实力。2012年以后，民用无人机开辟新的市场，陆续发掘出航拍、物流送货等新功能。

拓展知识

无人机应用

中国无人机事业虽然起步较晚，但它的发展受到国家航空科技部门的高度重视，发展迅速。近年来，中国较为先进的无人机主要有翼龙无人机、大疆无人机、ASN-206等机型。

翼龙无人机，是一种军民两用的多功能无人机，是中国最为先进的无人机。翼龙无人机在军事方面可以执行侦察、监视、攻击地面等任务，用于反恐和边界巡逻。此外，翼龙无人机还可以应用于灾情监视、大气观测、大地测量等方面。

大疆无人机，是民用无人机中的佼佼者。大疆无人机可以用于航拍摄影，进行纪录片、广告或是重大事件的拍摄记录。大疆无人机还可进行环境监测，用于大气污染执法行动。另外，大疆无人机还被用于物流服务中，提高物流效率。

ASN-206 是一种多用途无人驾驶飞机。它最大特点是装有实时视频侦察系统，包括垂直或全景相机、红外探测设备等装置，可执行昼夜空中侦察、战场监视、边境巡逻等任务。

讨论

你知道哪些无人机？简单谈一谈你的看法。

三 物联网

必读课文

物联网

物联网，是在互联网基础上发展而来的新一代网络技术，是一次新的技术革命。物联网的目的是将所有的事物都与网络连接起来，便于识别管理，从而到达"智慧"的状态。

早期物联网在中国又被称为"传感网"。1999 年，中国科学院启动了传感网的研究和开发。2005 年，国际电信联盟正式提出"物联网"的概念。2009 年，物联网被正式列为国家五大新兴战略性产业之一。同年，国家传感网创新示范区正式获得批准。至 2012 年，中国已经完成传感网示范基地建设。在十几年的研究中，中国物联网技术趋于成熟，产业规模进一步扩大。

在中国，物联网的应用范围广泛。在保护环境方面，政府运用物联网技术，实时监控大气质量、湖泊水质、工业污染排放等，切实改善环境质量。在交通领域，使用物联网技术可以实现智能化管理交通状况等，还可以自动监测和报告公路情况，提升交通管理能力。

拓展知识

物联网应用

中国的物联网在生活、交通、医疗、物流等方面应用潜力巨大。

在交通方面，物联网将道路交通信息整合，形成严密的交通网络。目前，中国许多城市已经使用 ITS 智能交通运输系统。例如，北京建立交通管理中心；上海成功实施高架路速度管理；广州建立健全的交通综合信息平台，依靠车上的 GPS 全球定位系统将交通信息上传至交通综合信息平台，使得平台可以分析出道路拥堵情况。广州还将通信、监控、道路收费集合到一个系统中，便于管理。另外，国家智能交通系统工程技术研究中心还积极进行智能交通系统的开发与研究，力图进一步完善智能交通体系。

在居家生活方面，物联网创造了一个智能家居时代。海尔集团开发出"海尔智家"系统，它以 U-home 系统为平台，把所有设备与网络连接起来，实现"物物互联"，实现智能家居、安防等系统的智能化管理和数字共享，使得用户随时随地都可以通过物联网与家中的电器联通互动。

讨论

你接触过哪些物联网技术？简单谈一谈你的体会？

（四）云计算

必读课文

云计算

云计算，又称为"网格计算"，指通过网络"云"将巨大的数据计算处理程序分解成无数个小程序，然后通过多部服务器组成的系统处理和分析这些小程序，得到结果并返回给用户。云计算是信息时代的又一次技术革新，是对计算机资源的协调和整合，使得用户可以在"云"上获取无限的资源，不受时间和空间的限制。在过去的十几年中，中国的云计算技术发展迅速。

2008 年，IBM 在中国成立云计算中心——IBM 大中华区云计算中心。2009 年，阿里软件在江苏建立国内首个"电子商务云计算中心"。同年，中国建立首个企业云计算平台——中化企业云计算平台。2010 年，中国政府在北京、上海、深圳、杭州、无锡 5 个城市率先开展云计算服务创新发展试点示范工作。2011 年，中国在重庆市建成国内最大的云计算试验区。2018 年，"中国云"走出中国、迈向世界。中国参与智利连锁超市、英国共享单车系统等工程的建设，为全球用户提供优质服务。

拓展知识

云计算公司

中国主要的云计算公司和品牌有华为云、阿里云、腾讯云等。

华为云，是华为公司旗下公有云品牌，成立于 2005 年。华为云是基于浏览器的云管理平台，致力于为用户提供稳定、安全、可持续发展的云计算基础服务。华为云坚持自主创新，在研发过程中引入多项华为新技术，使得华为云成本降低、弹性灵活、安全高效。

阿里云，是阿里巴巴集团旗下云计算品牌，创立于2009年，是全球领先的云计算和人工智能技术的科技公司。阿里云致力于通过在线公共服务，为用户提供安全、可靠的计算和数据处理能力。阿里云的服务范围广泛，不仅为中国联通、中国石化、飞利浦集团等大型企业提供优质而稳定的服务，也在春运购票系统、"双十一"购物节等应用场景中服务于普通用户。

腾讯云，是腾讯公司2010年正式对外提供服务的产品，包括云服务器、云安全、云数据库等产品，为开发者和企业提供一站式服务方案。腾讯云致力于打造面向市场的最高质量、最佳生态的公有云服务平台。

讨论

> 你接触过哪些云计算技术？简单谈一谈你的体会。

（五）大数据

必读课文

大数据

大数据，是一种规模巨大的数据集合，有大量、高速、多样、价值密度低和真实性五大特点。大数据可以对大规模资料和信息进行智能处理，帮助用户获得更高质量的资料。大数据是信息技术发展的产物，代表信息时代进入新的阶段。

随着科技的发展与进步，中国迎来大数据时代。2014年，大数据首次被写入中国政府工作报告中，这一年被称为中国大数据元年。从此，大数据开始在中国快速发展。中国的大数据发展主要集中在北京以及东部沿海地区，以北京、上海、广州等发达城市为主。其中，北京的大数据产业发展最为迅速。目前，中国在大数据内存计算等方面有了关键性的技术突破。

大数据在工业、企业、交通、医疗等领域均有应用。在中央和地方政府的支持下，中国互联网公司已经建成大数据服务平台。2021年11月15日，工信部正式发布《"十四五"大数据产业发展规划》，明确了推动大数据产业高质量发展的保障措施。随着中国数字建设的深入发展，大数据的开发与应用将成为中国科技发展的重点。

拓展知识

大数据应用

大数据的广泛应用有助于政府和企业为中国人民提供更加优质和精确的服务。

2018年，中国建成政府主导的数据共享开放平台，打破了政府部门和其他事业单位的数据壁垒。随后，政府进一步推进政务信息资源共享和整合，实现跨系统、跨地区、跨业务的政务信息联动，大大便利了人民的生活。例如，浙江省基于大数据应用推出让企业和群众"最多跑一次"政务改革，实现信息的整合，大大提高了政府部门和事业单位的办事效率。

淘宝数据魔方，是淘宝平台推出的大数据应用方案。在淘宝中完成的每一笔交易都会在大数据中留下交易时间、交易数量、商品价格等信息。同时，这些信息会与买方的年龄、性别、地址等个人信息特征相匹配。在掌握了这些信息后，淘宝平台就可以给消费者提供更适合的商品，帮助消费者以更优惠的价格买到更适合的商品，从而提高交易成功率。商家也可以通过大数据了解自己的经营状况、宏观的行业发展情况等，从而进一步改良商品、调整价格，制定更完善的经营策略。

讨论

> 你接触过哪些大数据应用案例？简单谈一谈你的体会。

(六) 人脸识别

必读课文

人脸识别

人脸识别，是基于人的面部特征进行身份识别的生物特征识别技术。人脸识别主要用于身份识别。人脸识别对输入的人脸图像或视频，会先判断是否存在人脸。若存在人脸，系统则会自动提取人脸的面部特征，并将其与系统内部的人脸进行对比，从而识别用户身份。中国研发人脸识别技术的企业不在少数，较为成功的企业有海康威视、科大讯飞等。

人脸识别技术在中国被广泛应用于政府、安全、银行等领域。在门禁系统中，计算机通过检测用户的面部特征并与计算机中用户的面部进行对比，从而确定户主。在公共交通领域，中国许多机场和高铁站都使用高清人脸证件比对系统，帮助识别用户身份。在公共安全领域，中国还将人脸识别技术应用于查案，利用大量的数据库查找并锁定嫌疑人的身份信息。在金融领域，刷脸支付是中国目前广为流行的支付方式。人们通过刷脸支付可以防止个人信息泄露，提高支付效率。

中国的人脸识别技术已经应用于各个领域，为人们的生活带来极大便利。

拓展知识

刷脸支付

刷脸支付，是基于人工智能、机器视觉、3D 传感、大数据等技术实现的新型支付方式。相比传统支付方式，刷脸支付不需要用户输入密码，不用担心密码泄露的问题，付款速度快，具有安全、高效、便捷的优势。

2013 年，芬兰一家公司推出了全球第一款基于脸部识别系统的支付平台。2014 年，百度、中国科学院重庆研究院、蚂蚁金服、支付宝、微信支付等率先开启了刷脸支付的技术研发和商用探索。2015 年被称为刷脸支付元年，阿里巴巴展示了支付宝的刷脸支付技术。2018 年，支付宝宣布其刷脸支付已经具备商业化能力并计划进行大规模推广。随着智能手机的普及和人脸识别功能的推出，刷脸支付开始在中国大面积使用与推广。目前中国普遍使用的刷脸支付工具是支付宝、微信。2020 年 1 月，为规范人脸识别线下支付应用创新，防范刷脸支付安全风险，中国支付清算协会组织制定了《人脸识别线下支付行业自律公约（试行）》。

刷脸支付的发展及普及，对于提升用户移动支付体验、提高商户经营效率、带动经济社会智能化发展具有重要作用。

讨论

你接触过哪些人脸识别技术？简单谈一谈你的体会。

第十二章

航空航天

一 战斗机

必读课文

战斗机

　　战斗机，指以高空导弹、航空机关炮等为基本武器，具有空战能力的作战飞机，主要有歼击机、强击机等类型。战斗机机动性好、飞行速度快、机载武器火力强，适于进行空战。

　　中国于20世纪50年代中期开始制造战斗机。1956年，中国成功制造第一架国产喷气式歼击机——歼-5，开启了中国战斗机制造的新篇章。在增强本国综合国力的同时，中国也向越南、阿尔巴尼亚、巴基斯坦等国家出口歼-5战斗机，保卫其他国家的航空安全。1959年，歼-6试飞成功，随后开始批量生产。1966年、1979年，歼-7、歼-8战斗机先后定型并投入生产。1984年，歼-8Ⅱ飞机升空试飞，不久便投入生产。1998年，歼-10战斗机首飞成功。它是中国自主研发的新型战斗机，通信设备先进，作战半径大。2011年，中国研发的歼-20战斗机首飞成功。歼-20战斗机是第五代战斗机。

　　中国是世界上拥有五代战斗机的三个国家之一，通过不断自主研发战斗机保卫了中国领空安全。

拓展知识

歼-20战斗机

歼-20战斗机，代号"威龙"，是中国航空工业集团有限公司成都飞机设计研究所研制的一款具备高隐身性、高态势感知、高机动性等能力的隐形第五代制空战斗机。歼-20战斗机是中国最新一代双发重型隐形战斗机，用于接替歼-10、歼-11等第四代战斗机。歼-20战斗机将担负中国空军未来对空、海的主权维护任务。

在总体设计中，歼-20战斗机采用单座、双发、双垂尾、带边条的鸭式气动布局，隐身能力强。其中，歼-20战斗机的全动双垂尾设计提高了歼击机的稳定性能。歼-20战斗机上还装有雷达、大屏幕液晶信息显示系统等先进装备，便于飞行员随时了解战争态势，及时提供空战决策。

2011年1月11日，首架歼-20隐形战斗机进行测试。2016年11月1日，在第十一届中国国际航空航天博览会上，歼-20首次进行空中飞行展示。2017年7月，歼-20战斗机亮相中国人民解放军建军90周年阅兵式。2018年2月9日，歼-20战斗机开始列装中国人民解放军空军作战部队。

中国自主研发的歼-20战斗机代表了中国战斗机研究的最高水平，充分显示了中国空军强大的科技实力和创新能力。

讨论

简单谈一谈你的国家使用的战斗机。

（二）运输机

必读课文

运输机

运输机，指专门用来运输人员或货物的飞机。运输机按用途可分为军用、民用、通用运输机。

中国最早的军用运输机诞生于抗日战争期间。1944年，中国南川第二飞机制造厂成功研发中运1号木质双发中型运输机。1948年，中运2号运输机在重庆试飞。1957年，以苏联安-2运输机为原型，由南昌飞机制造厂制造的运-5轻型多用途单发双翼运输机定型首飞。运-5运输机，是中国第一种自行制造的运输机。运-5运输机属于军民两用运输机，广泛应用于训练、跳伞、体育、运输和农业任务中。1970年，中国航空工业西安飞机工业公司研制生产的运-7军民两用支线运输机首飞成功。1984年，运-7飞机开始正式交付民航使用。1986年，运-7飞机投入民用航空客运服务。运-8运输机，是由中国航空工业陕西飞机制造公司研发的中程多用途运输机，可用于执行空投、空降、海上作业等任务。运-12运输机，是中国航空工业哈尔滨飞机制造公司自行设计生产的轻型双发多用途运输飞机，于1980年初开始设计，1985年后陆续获得中国、英国、美国、法国等国家的适航认证。

拓展知识

运-20运输机

运-20运输机，代号"鲲鹏"，是中国自主研发的新一代军用大型运输机。运-20运输机作为大型多用途运输机，可在复杂气象条件下，执行各种物资和人员的长距离航空运输任务。与中国空军现役伊尔-76运输机比较，运-20运输机的发动机和电子设备有了很大改进，载重量也有提高，短跑道起降性能优异。

　　中华人民共和国成立后相当长的一段时间内，中国只有中小型运输机。随着经济发展和科技实力逐步增强，中国航空工业开始为航空军事运输力量提供新的机型。1993年，中国航空工业西安飞机工业公司开始了大型运输机的前期论证。2007年，中国启动大型运输机项目。2013年，中国第一架自主研发的运-20战略运输机首飞成功，标志着中国大型运输机的诞生。2016年，运-20战略运输机完成试飞，批量交付部队。2020年2月13日，中国空军出动运-20运输机向武汉空运医疗队队员和物资。2022年1月28日，中国空军出动运-20运输机向汤加运送救灾物资。

讨论

> 简单介绍一下你所了解的运输机。

三　舰载机

必读课文

舰载机

　　舰载机，指以航空母舰或其他水面舰艇为起降基地的海军飞机、直升机的统称。该机型作用广泛，可以攻击水下、地面和空中的目标，执行多种任务。舰载机的性能决定了航空母舰的战斗力，舰载机数量越多，航空母舰实力也相对越强。中国舰载机的起步较晚，代表机型是歼-15舰载机。

　　歼-15舰载机，代号"飞鲨"，是中国参考苏-33战斗机原型机，在国产歼-11 战斗机基础上研发的单座双发重型舰载战斗机，属于第四代战斗机改进型。歼-15 舰载机在歼-11 战斗机的基础上增添鸭翼、2 台发动机、起落装置、增升装置等，且拥有可折叠机翼，大大提升了飞机性能。2009 年，歼-15 舰载机首飞成功。2012 年，第一架歼-15 舰载机在中国航空母舰辽宁舰上完成着舰和起飞测试。2013 年，歼-15 舰载机在辽宁舰上起降，完成首次驻舰飞行。2017 年，歼-15 舰载机随辽宁舰抵南海海域训练。2019 年，歼-15 舰载机参加庆祝中华人民共和国成立 70 周年阅兵式。

舰载机是海军作战的重要武器。随着中国海军实力和科技水平的提高，舰载机的种类和数量将进一步增加。

拓展知识

航空母舰

航空母舰，是一种以舰载机为主要作战武器，并作为其海上活动基地的大型水面战斗舰艇。航空母舰的建设是舰载机发展的基础。航空母舰有巨大的甲板和舰岛，能为舰载机提供起飞和降落的场地。

20 世纪 70 年代起，中国人民解放军海军开展对航空母舰的研究。1998 年 2 月，中国购买了苏联海军制造的"瓦良格"号航空母舰。2005 年，"瓦良格"号进入大连造船厂，由中国人民解放军海军进行改造。2012 年 9 月，"瓦良格"号航空母舰正式更名为"辽宁"号，交付中国人民解放军海军，用于科研、实验和训练。2013 年 11 月，中国海军在南海以辽宁舰为核心编组了航空母舰战斗群，标志着辽宁舰开始具备海上编队战斗群能力。2014 年 2 月，中国第一艘国产航空母舰开始建造。2017 年 4 月，该航空母舰正式下水。2019 年 12 月，中国第一艘国产航空母舰山东舰交付中国人民解放军海军。中国航空母舰的诞生和服役使得中国研发舰载机成为可能。2022 年 6 月 17 日，中国第二艘国产航空母舰福建舰正式下水。

讨论

简单介绍一下你所了解的舰载机。

（四）运载火箭

必读课文

中国火箭

火箭，是一种利用火箭发动机推进的飞行器，既可以在大气层内飞行，也可以在大气层外飞行。火箭是中国古代的重大发明之一。

中国唐朝时期，火药便运用于军事领域，由火药制造的武器被称为"火箭"。北宋时期，军官岳义方、冯继升制造出了世界上第一个以火药为动力的火箭。这种最早的原始火箭在工作原理上与现代火箭没有什么不同。12世纪中叶，原始火箭经过改进后，被广泛用于战争。13世纪中叶，蒙古人入侵中亚、西亚和欧洲，把中国的火箭技术传入了欧洲及世界其他地区。

中华人民共和国成立后，中国发射过多次试验性火箭。1956年，中国第一个火箭研究机构成立，标志着中国航天事业拉开序幕。1960年，中国自行设计制造的探空火箭发射成功。1965年，中国开始研制固体探空火箭。1970年，中国"长征一号"火箭运载"东方红一号"卫星发射成功，迈出了中国发展航天技术的第一步，标志着中国正式进入航天时代。1980年，中国向太平洋预定海域成功发射远程运载火箭。1981年，中国成功攻克"一箭三星"技术，用一枚火箭发射三颗卫星，成为世界上第三个掌握一箭多星发射技术的国家。1990年，中国"长征三号"运载火箭成功发射美国制造的"亚洲一号"通信卫星，成为世界上第三个进入国际卫星发射服务市场的国家。

拓展知识

长征系列运载火箭

长征系列运载火箭，是中国自行研制的航天运载工具。20 世纪 60 年代，中国开始研制长征系列运载火箭。1970 年 4 月 24 日，"长征一号"运载火箭首次发射"东方红一号"卫星成功。2022 年 1 月 26 日，中国在酒泉卫星发射中心成功发射长征四号丙运载火箭。

目前，中国长征系列火箭已有四代：第一代运载火箭突破了中国航天技术的瓶颈，完成了中国运载火箭技术从无到有的飞跃；第二代运载火箭在第一代火箭基础上做了技术改进，并采用数字控制系统；第三代运载火箭致力于提高任务可靠性和任务适应能力；第四代运载火箭采用无毒无污染推进剂，旨在保护环境。通过不断的技术改进和创新，长征系列火箭的运载能力大幅提高。

多年来，长征系列运载火箭有力地支撑和保障了中国载人航天、月球探测、北斗卫星导航、高分辨率对地观测系统等一系列重大工程任务的成功实施，为推动相关领域发展、加快科技强国和航天强国建设奠定了坚实基础。

讨论

简单介绍一下你所了解的运载火箭。

（五） 载人航天

必读课文

载人航天

载人航天，是人类驾驶和乘坐载人航天器在太空中从事各种探测、研究、试验、生产和军事应用的往返飞行活动。载人航天活动可以帮助人类更广泛和更深入地认识整个宇宙，并充分利用太空和载人航天器的特殊环境进行各种研究和试验活动，开发太空极其丰富的资源。

中国政府很早就意识到了载人航天事业在未来国际竞争中的重要性。在中国第一颗人造地球卫星上天之后，钱学森于1971年提出"中国要搞载人航天"。当时国家将这个项目命名为"714工程"，并将飞船命名为"曙光一号"。1975年，中国成功发射并回收了第一颗返回式卫星，为中国开展载人航天技术的研究打下了坚实的基础。

1992年1月，中国载人航天工程被正式列入国家计划，该工程又称"921工程"。2003年10月，中国载人飞船"神舟五号"发射成功，杨利伟成为"中国飞天第一人"。这是中国首次完成的载人航天任务。中国成为继俄罗斯和美国后第三个掌握载人航天技术的国家。

拓展知识

神舟飞船

神舟飞船，是中国自行研制，具有完全自主知识产权，达到或优于国际第三代载人飞船技术的一种载人航天器。

1999年11月，中国第一艘无人试验飞船"神舟一号"成功发射与回收。2001年1月，中国成功发射了"神舟二号"无人飞船。2002年3月和12月，中国先后成功发射"神舟三号"无人飞船和"神舟四号"无人飞船。2003年10月和 2005 年 10 月，中国成功发射"神舟五号"载人飞船和"神舟六号"载人飞船。2008 年，中国第三艘载人飞船"神舟七号"成功发射，航天员翟志刚执行了出舱活动。中国成为世界上第三个掌握空间出舱活动技术的国家。2011 年 11 月，"神舟八号"飞船成功发射。2012 年 6 月和 2013 年 6 月，"神舟九号"载人飞船和"神舟十号"载人飞船先后发射成功，并与"天宫一号"目标飞行器在太空中成功对接。2016 年 10 月 17 日，"神舟十一号"载人飞船发射成功，并与"天宫二号"空间实验室在太空中成功对接。2021 年，"神舟十二号"载人飞船和"神舟十三号"载人飞船先后发射成功。

讨论

简单介绍一下你所了解的宇宙飞船。

（六）空间探测

必读课文

空间探测

空间探测，指利用探空火箭和宇航器对空间和天体的物理现象、物理过程，以及化学组成进行的直接探测。空间探测以探空火箭、人造地球卫星、人造行星和宇宙飞船等飞行器为主，并与地面观测台站网、气球相配合构成完整的空间探测体系。

中国的空间探测始于 20 世纪 60 年代。1964 年，中国成功发射了一枚生物火箭。1970 年 4 月，中国发射了第一颗人造地球卫星"东方红一号"。1975 年 11 月，中国发射了一颗返回式人造卫星。1980 年 5 月，中国远程运载火箭发射成功。1984年4月，中国第一颗地球静止轨道试验通信卫星发射成功。1986年2月，中国发射了一颗实用通信广播卫星。1988年9月，中国发射了一颗气象卫星"风云一号"。1999年11月，中国成功发射了第一艘"神舟一号"试验飞船。2003年10月，中国成功发射了第一艘载人飞船"神舟五号"。航天员杨利伟成为第一个乘坐中国自己制造的飞船进入太空的中国人。2004年1月，中国开始实施绕月探测工程。2020年7月，中国首次执行火星探测任务的"天问一号"探测器发射成功。

拓展知识

探月工程

2004年1月，中国绕月探测工程正式立项，被命名为"嫦娥工程"。2006年2月，中国将"载人航天与探月工程"列入国家十六个重大科技专项。中国探月工程在不同阶段有不同任务：第一期的任务是实现环绕月球探测；第二期是实现月球软着陆和自动勘察任务；第三期是实现无人采样返回任务。中国探月工程三期圆满收官后，探月四期已全面启动。

2007年10月，"嫦娥一号"月球探测器在西昌卫星发射中心成功发射，在月球表面执行探测月球的物质组成成分、月壤性质、太空环境等任务。2010年10月，"嫦娥二号"月球探测器成功发射，获得了更清晰的月球表面图像和更精确的月球相关数据。2013年12月，"嫦娥三号"月球探测器成功发射。"嫦娥三号"携带"玉兔号"月球车第一次实现月球软着陆。"嫦娥三号"利用测月雷达完成世界上第一幅月球地质剖面图，并证明月球没有水。2020年11月，"嫦娥五号"月球探测器成功发射，携带月球样品顺利返回地球。

讨论

简单介绍一下你所了解的空间探测活动。

文化传承篇

第十三章

传统文化

一 音乐

必读课文

中国音乐

中国音乐，指中国的民族音乐。中国音乐的历史可以追溯到上古黄帝时代。中国音乐曾经对中国周边地区的音乐产生了深远影响。同时，中国音乐在吸收外来音乐的过程中不断充实发展。

在距今6000年前的新石器时代，中国的先民们就已经可以制作骨哨。根据文献记载，中国远古的音乐具有歌、舞、乐互相结合的特点。在中国古代，诗和歌是不分的，即文学和音乐是紧密相连的。现存最早的汉语诗歌总集《诗经》中的诗都是可以口头传唱的。唐诗、宋词也是可以歌唱的，如苏轼描写中秋佳节的《水调歌头》。

中国古代对音乐是非常重视的，一个有修养的人应该精通"琴棋书画"。这里的"琴"就是流传至今的古琴。除古琴外，中国古代的乐器还有古筝、箫、笛子、琵琶、二胡、扬琴、钟和鼓。中国古代代表性的音乐有《广陵散》《高山流水》《梅花三弄》等。中国近代以来的代表性音乐有《二泉映月》《渔舟唱晚》和《梁祝》等。

拓展知识

古 琴

古琴，又称"七弦琴"，是中国传统拨奏弦鸣乐器，"八音"分类中"丝"的代表乐器。中国古琴有3000年以上的历史。

据中国文献记载，舜定琴为五弦，周文王增一弦，武王伐纣又增一弦为七弦。古琴是中国古代文化地位最崇高的乐器，位列四艺"琴棋书画"之首，有"左琴右书"之说。古琴被中国古代知识分子视为高雅的代表，也是人们吟唱时的伴奏乐器。在古代，古琴一直都是知识分子必备的知识和必修的科目。在中国的诗词歌赋与故事中常见古琴的身影，俞伯牙、钟子期因《高山流水》而成知音的故事就是其中之一。隋唐时期，中国古琴传入东亚各国。近代，伴随华人的足迹，古琴走向世界各地，成为中华文化的象征。

2003年11月7日，联合国教科文组织世界遗产委员会宣布，中国古琴被选为世界非物质文化遗产。2006年，中国将古琴列入第一批国家级非物质文化遗产名录。

讨论

你听过哪些中国古典音乐？简单谈一谈你的体会。

(二) 诗歌

必读课文

中国诗歌

诗歌，是文学的一大样式。中国古代称不合乐的为诗，合乐的为歌，现在一般统称为诗歌。诗歌是用高度凝练的语言，生动形象地表达作者丰富的情感，集中反映社会生活并具有一定节奏和韵律的文学样式。诗歌是中国最早出现的一种文学体裁，起源于上古社会生活，因劳动生产、两性相恋、原始宗教等而产生的一种有韵律、富有感情色彩的语言形式。诗歌生动地反映了中国先民的生活情况和内心祈愿，用简短、生动的形式展现了中华民族语言的力量。《诗经》是中国第一部诗歌总集。汉族诗歌历经汉魏六朝乐府、唐诗、宋词、元曲、明清诗歌和现代诗的发展阶段。

中国的古代诗歌，也称"旧体诗"，是指用文言文和传统格律创作的诗。广义的中国古代诗歌包括各种中国古代的韵文，如赋、词、曲等；狭义的则仅包括古体诗和近体诗。古诗创作是中国文人表达心中思绪的方式之一。中国的现代诗歌，也称"新体诗"，是指五四运动以来的新体诗，其特点是用白话语言写作，表现科学、民主的新时代内容，打破了旧诗词格律的束缚，形式上灵活自由。

拓展知识

唐 诗

唐诗，是唐朝诗歌的总称，是中华民族珍贵的文化遗产之一，是中华文化宝库中的一颗明珠。唐诗对世界上许多国家的文化发展产生了很大影响，对后人研究唐朝的政治、民情、风俗、文化等都有重要的参考意义。唐代是中国古代诗歌史上最繁荣最辉煌的时期。

唐诗的形式是多种多样的。唐朝的古体诗没有固定的句数和字数，主要有五言、七言和杂言。唐朝近体诗有绝句和律诗两种形式。绝句和律诗又各有五言和七言之分。

唐朝的诗人分为很多流派。山水田园诗派的代表人物是王维和孟浩然，代表作品有《九月九日忆山东兄弟》《过故人庄》等。边塞诗派的代表人物是高适、岑参、王昌龄和王之涣，代表作品有《燕歌行》《白雪歌送武判官归京》《出塞》和《凉州词》等。浪漫诗派的代表人物是李白，代表作品有《梦游天姥吟留别》《蜀道难》等。现实诗派的代表人物是杜甫，代表作品有"三吏""三别"等。

讨论

你读过哪些中国古代诗歌？简单谈一谈你的体会。

三 戏曲

必读课文

中国戏曲

中国戏曲，是中国传统戏剧形式，包含文学、音乐、舞蹈、美术、杂技等各种因素，中国戏曲经过汉、唐时期，到宋、金时期才逐渐形成比较完整的戏曲艺术。据1985年统计，中国各民族各地区的戏曲剧种共有340种左右。

中国戏曲的特点是将众多艺术形式以一种标准聚合在一起，在共同具有的性质中体现各自的个性。戏曲音乐是汉族戏曲中的音乐部分，包括声乐部分的唱腔、韵白，器乐部分的伴奏、开场及过场音乐。戏曲音乐以唱腔为主，有独唱、对唱、齐唱和帮腔等演唱形式，是发展剧情、刻画人物性格的主要表现手段。

中国戏曲与希腊悲剧和喜剧、印度梵剧并称为世界三大古老的戏剧文化。中国戏曲经过长期的发展演变，逐步形成了以京剧、越剧、黄梅戏、评剧、豫剧五大戏曲剧种为核心的中华戏曲。

拓展知识

越　剧

越剧，是中国第二大剧种，在国外被称为"中国歌剧"。越剧是中国五大戏曲剧种之一，有"第二国剧"之称。越剧，发源于浙江嵊州，发祥于上海，繁荣于全国，流传于世界。越剧在发展中汲取了昆曲、话剧、绍剧等特色剧种的优点，经历了由以男子越剧为主到以女子越剧为主的历史性演变。

越剧长于抒情，以唱为主，声音优美动听，表演真切动人，唯美典雅，极具江南灵秀之气。越剧多以"才子佳人"题材为主，艺术流派纷呈。越剧主要流行于上海、浙江、江苏、福建、江西、安徽等中国南方地区。越剧的代表性作品有《梁山伯与祝英台》《西厢记》《碧玉簪》《追鱼》《情探》《珍珠塔》《柳毅传书》《五女拜寿》《沙漠王子》等。

1953年，上海电影制片厂摄制的《梁山伯与祝英台》是中华人民共和国成立后的第一部大型彩色戏曲电影。2006年，越剧被列入首批国家级非物质文化遗产名录。

讨论

你都看过或听过中国哪些戏曲？简单谈一谈你的体会。

(四) 绘画

必读课文

国 画

中国画,简称"国画",指具有悠久历史和优良传统的中国民族绘画,在世界美术领域中自成独特体系。国画的绘画工具和材料有毛笔、墨、国画颜料、宣纸、绢等。国画的题材可分为人物、山水、界画、花卉、禽鸟、走兽、虫鱼等。

中国有书画同源之说,即中国古代的文字和绘画都来源于早期的象形字。新石器时期的陶器和青铜器上就绘有各种装饰画。战国时期,中国就出现了画在丝织品上的绘画——帛画。汉朝和魏晋南北朝时期,中国的绘画以宗教绘画为主。隋唐时期,中国的山水画和花鸟画已发展成熟,宗教绘画达到顶峰。五代两宋时期的人物画转为描述世俗生活,山水画、花鸟画跃居画坛主流。元、明、清时期,中国的水墨山水画和写意花鸟画得到突出发展。

随着社会经济的逐渐稳定,中国各历史时期涌现出很多热爱生活、崇尚艺术的伟大画家,其中代表性的画家有顾恺之、阎立本、张择端、唐寅、郑板桥、徐悲鸿和潘天寿等。

拓展知识

山水画

山水画,简称"山水",是以描写山川自然景色为主体的绘画,由地理形势图和人物画的背景演变而成,为中国画的一种。中国山水画分为青绿山水、水墨山水、金碧山水、浅绛山水、小青绿山水和没骨山水。中国山水画的代表画家有展子虔(qián)、王维、范宽和张宏等。

中国的山水画在秦汉时期就已经出现。魏晋南北朝时期,中国的山水画逐渐发展，但仍附属于人物画。隋唐时期，山水画逐步成熟，成为独立的画派。这一时期，中国出现众多山水画流派和画家，如展子虔的设色山水、李思训的金碧山水、王维的水墨山水、王洽的泼墨山水等。两宋时期，中国的山水画已经非常繁荣，出现大量画家，如荆浩、李成、董源、范宽、许道宁、宋迪、米芾（fú）等。元朝时期，山水画趋向写意，以虚带实，侧重笔墨神韵，开创新风。明清以来，山水画有所发展，表现手法上讲究经营位置和表达意境等。

中国各历史时期的代表山水画有隋朝展子虔的《游春图》、唐朝李思训的《江帆楼阁图》、北宋范宽的《溪山行旅图》和元朝黄公望的《富春山居图》。

讨论

你见过中国传统画吗？简单谈一谈你的观后感。

（五）书法

必读课文

中国书法

书法，是一种文字表现的艺术形式，中国传统艺术之一，指用中国式的圆锥形毛笔书写汉字的法则。中国书法是在中国文化里产生和发展起来的。汉字是中国书法中的重要因素。中国的汉字书法被誉为无言的诗歌、无形的舞蹈、无图的绘画、无声的音乐等。

中国的书法艺术开始于汉字的产生阶段。书法艺术的第一批作品不是文字，而是一些象形文字或图画文字。从夏、商、周时期到秦汉时期，中国的各种书法字体相继出现，其中篆书、隶书、草书、行书、楷书五种字体逐渐定型，书法艺术开始了有序发展。书法艺术的繁荣期，是从东汉开始的。东汉时期，中国出现了专门的书法理论著作，最早的书法理论提出者是杨雄。两晋时期，在书法史上最具影响力的书法家当属王羲之。唐朝时期，楷书、行书、草书发展到了新的境地，对后代的影响远远超过了以前任何一个时代。欧阳询、虞世南、褚遂良、颜真卿、柳公权等都是这一时期的书法大家。清朝，中国的书法分为帖学与碑学两大发展时期。

拓展知识

文房四宝

文房四宝，指中国独有的书法绘画工具，即笔、墨、纸、砚四种文具的统称。中国文房四宝的名称起源于南北朝时期。

笔，即毛笔。毛笔的笔杆一般用竹管制，也有用犀牛角、象牙或金银制的。好的毛笔具有尖、齐、圆、健四大优点。自元朝以来，浙江湖州生产的"湖笔"是中国最著名的毛笔品种。墨，是书写、绘画的色料。在人工制墨发明之前，一般利用天然墨或半天然墨作为书写材料。根据原料的不同，墨可分为油烟墨、漆烟墨、松烟墨等。纸，是中国古代四大发明之一。宣纸是手工制造的供毛笔书画用的独特的纸，质地柔韧，洁白平滑，色泽耐久，吸水力强。砚，也称"砚台"，是中国书写、绘画时研磨色料的工具，被中国古人誉为"文房四宝之首"。汉朝时，砚已非常流行。宋朝时，砚已普遍使用。

文房四宝独具一格，既表现了中华民族不同于其他民族的风俗，又为民族文化和世界文化的进步和发展做出了贡献。

讨论

你见过中国书法吗？简单比较一下你写的中文字和中国书法的异同。

（六）手工

● 必读课文

中国手工

中国手工，丰富多彩，其中有代表性的是陶瓷、玉雕、木雕、竹编和剪纸。

陶瓷，是陶器和瓷器的统称，由陶土和瓷土两种原料混合制成。在唐朝，中国陶瓷的制作技术和艺术创造达到了很高的水平。中国陶瓷远销日本、印度、波斯和埃及，在国际文化交流中发挥了重要作用。

玉雕，指玉石经加工雕琢成为精美的工艺品，是中国古老的雕刻品种之一。工艺师在制作过程中，只有根据不同玉料的天然颜色和自然形状精心设计、反复琢磨，才能把玉石雕制成精美的工艺品。

木雕，是雕塑的一种，是从木工中分离出来的一个工种。木雕在中国常常被称为"民间工艺"。木雕种类复杂，流派繁多，其中浙江东阳木雕享誉全国。

竹编，是用山里的毛竹编织成的各种用具和工艺品。竹编不仅具有较强的实用价值，而且具有深厚的历史底蕴。目前，中国主要的竹编产品有斗笠和竹篮等。

● 拓展知识

中国剪纸

中国剪纸，是一种用剪刀或刻刀在纸上剪刻花纹，用于装点生活或配合其他民俗活动的民间艺术。在中国，剪纸交融于各族人民的社会生活，是民俗活动的重要组成部分。剪纸在唐朝最为盛行，南宋时期发展成为一种职业。剪纸凝聚着中华民族几千年来的历史文化，是中国广为流行的民间艺术之一。

窗花，是用于贴在窗户上作装饰的剪纸。窗花在中国北方最为普遍。在以前，北方农家窗户多是木格窗，有竖格、方格或带有几何形的花格，上面糊一层洁白的"皮纸",逢年过节便要更换窗纸并贴上新窗花,以示除旧迎新。窗花的形式有装饰窗格四角的角花,也有折枝团花,还有连续成套的戏文或传说故事窗花。

剪纸蕴含丰富的文化历史信息,表达了广大民众的社会认知、道德观念、实践经验、生活理想和审美情趣,具有认知、教化、表意、抒情、娱乐、交往等多重社会价值。2006年,剪纸艺术遗产被列入第一批国家级非物质文化遗产名录。

讨论

你会做哪些中国传统手工?简单谈一谈你的体会。

第十四章

饮食文化

一、调料

必读课文

中国调料

调料,是人们用来调制食品的辅助用品。正所谓"五味调和百味香",调料在中国的饮食文化中起着重要的作用。好的调料,可以起到去除原料异味,增加食品香味,赋予菜肴色泽,杀菌消毒的作用等。在中国饮食文化中,调料大致可以分为咸味调料、甜味调料、酸味调料、辣味调料、鲜味调料五种。

大多数菜品都离不开咸味。烹饪应用中咸味是主味,是绝大多数复合味的基础味,有"百味之主"之说。在文献记载中,中国最早使用食盐约在5000年前的黄帝时期。咸味调料包括酱油、食盐和酱调料等。甜味调料可以使食品甘美可口,还可以用来去苦和去腥。在中国烹饪中,南方地区使用甜味调料较多。中国在东汉时期就有用甘蔗汁制成的糖。甜味调料有蜂蜜、食糖等。酸味调料在烹饪中也被广泛使用,有固涩的作用,可助肠胃消化,还能去除腥味、解油腻。酸味调料有醋、番茄酱等。辣味调料可以消除食味紧张、增进食欲。辣味调料有花椒、辣椒、姜、葱、蒜等。鲜味调料有鱼露、味精、蚝油等。

拓展知识

酱　油

　　酱油，俗称"豉油"，主要由大豆或黑豆、小麦或麸皮、食盐经过制油和发酵等程序酿制而成。酱油是中国传统液体调味品。酱油色泽呈红褐色，有独特酱香，滋味鲜美，有助于促进食欲。酱油一般分为老抽和生抽两种：生抽用于提鲜；老抽用于提色。酱油的成分比较复杂，除食盐的成分外，还有多种氨基酸、糖类、有机酸、色素及香料等成分，以咸味为主，亦有鲜味、香味等。酱油不仅能增加和改善菜肴的味道，还能增添或改变菜肴的色泽。

　　酱油是由酱演变而来的，中国是世界上最早制造和食用酱的国家。早在3000多年前，中国周朝就有制作酱的记载了。最初，酱油是中国古代帝王御用的调味品，是由鲜肉腌制而成的，与现今的鱼露制造过程相近。因为风味绝佳，酱油渐渐流传到民间。后来人们发现由大豆酿制而成的酱油风味相似且便宜，才广为流传食用。随着中国对外文化交流的开展，酱油逐渐传播到日本、韩国和东南亚地区。

讨论

> 简单介绍一下你的国家美食的调料，说一说它们和中国调料的异同。

二 中国菜系

● 必读课文

中国菜系

中国是一个餐饮文化大国，长期以来受地理环境、气候物产、文化传统以及民族习俗等因素的影响，各个地区形成了不同的菜系，其中鲁菜、川菜、粤菜、闽菜、苏菜、浙菜、湘菜、徽菜被称为"八大菜系"。

鲁菜，指的是山东菜，以清香、鲜嫩、味厚纯正而著称，特别精于制汤，清浊分明。

川菜，指的是四川菜，讲究色、香、味、形，尤在"味"字上下功夫，以味的多、广、厚著称。

粤菜，指的是广东菜，特点是丰富精细的选材和清淡的口味。

闽菜，指的是福建菜，以海鲜为主，素以制作细巧、色调美观、调味清鲜著称。

苏菜，指的是江苏菜，口味趋甜，刀工精细，火候精微，色调清新，造型别致。苏州菜突出主料，强调本味，清淡可口，尤以制汤而著称。

浙菜，指的是浙江菜，其特色是清鲜嫩爽，滋味兼得。

湘菜，指的是湖南菜，多将辣椒当主菜食用。

徽菜，指的是安徽菜，传统是用火腿调味，特点是重色、重油、重火功。

● 拓展知识

浙 菜

浙菜，是浙江地方风味菜系。浙菜食材选用广博，主料注重时令和品种，刀工精细，菜品精致，擅用火候调味，菜品清鲜嫩爽。浙江菜主要由杭州、宁波、绍兴、温州四种地方风味菜组成。

杭州菜制作精细，常用爆、炒、烩、炸等烹饪技法，具有清鲜、爽嫩、精致、醇和等特点。杭州菜的名菜有西湖醋鱼、东坡肉、龙井虾仁、油焖春笋等。宁波菜多以海鲜为主料，炖、烤、蒸是常用的烹饪手法。宁波菜口味鲜咸适度，菜品讲究鲜嫩软滑，注重本味。宁波菜的名菜有雪菜大汤黄鱼、冰糖甲鱼、锅烧鳗、溜黄青蟹，宁波烧鹅等。绍兴菜的主料以鱼虾河鲜和鸡鸭家禽、豆类、笋类为主，菜品香酥绵糯，汤浓味醇。绍兴菜的名菜有糟熘虾仁、干菜焖肉、头肚醋鱼、清蒸鳜鱼等。温州菜也称"瓯菜"，以海鲜为主，口味清鲜，淡而不薄。温州菜的名菜有三丝敲鱼、橘络鱼脑、蒜子鱼皮等。

讨论

> 简单介绍一下你的国家的美食有哪些菜系。

三 中国餐具

必读课文

中国餐具

餐具，指用餐时直接接触食物的非可食性工具，用于辅助食物分发或摄取食物的器皿和用具。中国日常使用的餐具包括金属器具、陶瓷餐具、茶具酒器、玻璃器皿、纸制器具、塑料器具等各种容器类工具和手持用具等。在餐桌上，中国人使用频率最高的餐具是筷子、勺子、碗和碟子。

筷子，是中国人最常用的餐具，直接用于夹菜。中国人用筷子的时间上限还不确定，但至少已有3000年的历史。

勺子，是喝汤盛饭用的工具。勺子是中国使用历史最悠久的餐具，大致有

7000多年的历史。勺子的种类有很多，喝汤时盛汤用的是汤匙，炒菜用的有柄的是炒勺。

相较于西方人常用的盘子，中国人大多喜爱用碗。碗可分为大碗和小碗。饭碗属于小碗，是用来盛饭的餐具。汤碗属于大碗，用来盛公用的汤。汤碗里有一个公用的勺子用来盛汤。

碟子，是一种盛食品或调味品的小而浅的器皿。碟子比盘子小，多为圆形。碟子也有其他的形状，如椭圆形、长方形等。

拓展知识

筷 子

筷子，古称"箸"，夹取食物的用具，通常用竹、木、骨、瓷、金属、塑料等材料制作。筷子是华夏饮食文化的标志之一，也是世界上最常用的餐具之一。筷子发明于中国，后传至朝鲜、日本、越南等国家。公筷亦起源于中国。不管是分餐还是使用公筷，在中国都有着悠久的历史。

民间关于筷子的传说也不少，一说姜子牙受神鸟启示发明丝竹筷，一说妲己为讨纣王欢心而发明用玉簪作筷，还有大禹治水时为节约时间以树枝捞取热食而发明筷子的传说。普通筷子的长度约为22～24厘米，形状多为上粗下细，上方下圆。这种造型的优点是拿起来方便，不容易转动。筷子夹菜入口的一端光滑圆润，不会伤着唇舌。

在中国，筷子的使用有很多讲究：放置筷子时，必须成对；用筷子吃饭时，不要碰到附近的人；与人交谈时，应放下筷子以示礼貌；筷子不要垂直插入碗中；等等。

讨论

你的国家使用哪些餐具？有哪些餐具使用风俗？

（四）时令美食

必读课文

时令美食

一年四季，按时而吃，是中国饮食文化的一大特征。从古至今，中国一直按季节变化来调味、配菜。

春天，特别适合吃一些温补的食物，而韭菜就是非常好的选择。春天是菠菜最嫩的季节，也是吃菠菜最适宜的时节。此时的菠菜被称为"春菠"，根红叶绿，鲜嫩异常，尤为可口。这时的笋也特别鲜美，春天也是特别适合吃笋的季节。

夏天，是尝鲜的季节。李子、樱桃、香梅、蚕豆、新茶都是应时佳品。在炎热的夏季，人们会来一碗冰镇酸爽的酸梅汤或者冰爽甜蜜的绿豆汤解暑。夏季还适宜吃些苦味的食物，如苦瓜、苦菜、苦笋、莴苣。

秋天，是丰收的季节，美食最为丰盛。如大闸蟹在秋季最为肥美。而秋令时节，正是鲜藕应市的时候，排骨藕汤也是秋天的美味。

冬天，北方仍然保留着冬至吃饺子习俗。腊八节的时候，大家会坐在一起喝腊八粥，不少地方还有泡腊八蒜、吃腊八豆等食俗。其他如火锅、生滚粥等美食也是冬天取暖的佳品。

拓展知识

清明时令美食

清明，是中国的二十四节气之一，每年4月5日或4日。在这个时节，应该注意养生。

清明前后，最适宜吃的时令蔬菜之一是荠菜。荠菜有助于增强免疫功能，适合清明时节食用。螺蛳也是这个时间段的美食。清明前后，春暖花开，大地复苏，潜伏在泥土中休眠的螺蛳纷纷爬出泥土。此时螺肉肥美，是食用螺蛳的最佳时令。清明也是适合吃虾的好时间。在这个时间段，河鲜肥美，尤为可口。香椿又名"香椿芽"，被称为"树上蔬菜"，香椿一般在清明时节发芽，谷雨前后采摘，可用于制作香椿炒鸡蛋、香椿炒竹笋、香椿拌豆腐等各类菜肴。它不仅营养丰富，而且具有较高的药用价值，还具有消炎、解毒、杀虫的功效。

此外，清明前后适宜享用的美食还有青团和艾粄等小吃。在清明时节，江南一带有吃青团的习俗。青团是用艾草的汁拌进糯米粉里，再包裹进豆沙馅儿或者莲蓉馅儿，吃起来不甜不腻，带有清淡悠长的清香。艾粄，是广东省客家地区清明时节特有的应节小吃。

讨论

你的国家在不同季节都有哪些特色美食？和中国的有哪些异同？

（五）茶

必读课文

中国茶

茶叶，俗称"茶"，一般包括茶树的叶子和芽。茶叶源于中国。中国是茶树的原产地，是最早发现茶并把它发展成为一种文化的国家。

巴蜀地区是中国茶叶的摇篮。早在战国时期，巴蜀地区就已经形成规模化的茶区，并以茶为贡品。秦统一中国后，饮茶习俗逐渐传播到中国其他地区。西汉时，茶发展成为宫廷的高级饮料，并且出现了专门饮茶的用具。两晋时期，长江中下游地区开始种植茶叶。随着东晋王朝在南方的建立，西南地区的茶叶种植和饮茶习俗逐渐扩展到浙东宁波和温州沿海一带。到了唐朝，长江中下游地区已经成为中国茶叶的生产和技术中心。宋朝时期，中国的茶业重心由东部向南部转移，岭南一带的茶业逐渐发展起来。如福建建安成为中国团茶、饼茶制作的主要技术中心。明清以后，中国茶叶的产区基本稳定，茶叶的发展主要体现在茶叶制作方法的改良上。

拓展知识

中国茶道

茶道，指烹茶、饮茶的程式和技艺。茶道源于中国，盛行于中国南方地区以及日本。中国有着独特的茶道精神，即"和、静、怡、真"。

"和"，是儒家、佛教、道教共通的哲学理念，讲究天和、地和、人和，意味着宇宙万物的有机统一与和谐，并因此产生讲求实现天人合一的和谐之美。

"静"，是中国茶道修身养性、追求自我的必由途径。只有"静心"，才能通过淡淡的茶汤品味人生真谛，才能在茶事活动中明心见性，才能通过小小的茶盏领悟宇宙的奥秘，才能通过茶道修习来锻炼人格、超越自我。

"怡"，乃和悦、愉快之意。在饮茶的过程之中，或吟诗作对，修身养性，寄托情怀，交朋结友；或提神醒脑，辅助参禅悟道；或利用茶叶的药用价值，增强体质，延年益寿。

"真"，意为真理、真性、真诚。"真理"，指在品茶中领悟出"道"，得到精神的升华。"真性"，指在品茶中表露出真正的自我，无拘无束，任由思想海阔天空。"真诚"，指在品茶中坦诚相见，交流感情，沟通思想。

讨论

你的国家有品茶的习惯吗？简单介绍一下。

六　酒

必读课文

中国酒

酒，指用高粱、大麦、米、葡萄或其他水果发酵制成的饮料，是人类生活中的主要饮料之一。中国制酒历史源远流长，酒品种类繁多。从文学艺术创作、文化娱乐到饮食烹饪、养生保健等，酒在中国人的日常生活中都占有重要地位。

中国酿酒最初起源于夏初或夏朝以前的时期，距今已经有 4000 余年的历史了。在中华民族 5000 年的历史长河中，酒和酒类文化一直占据着重要地位。酒是一种特殊的食品，是属于物质的，但同时又融于人们的精神生活之中。中国历史上有很多关于酒的故事，如晋朝诗人陶渊明不能一日无酒，唐朝大诗人李白酒喝得越多诗写得越好，宋朝梁山好汉武松一口气喝了 18 碗酒，赤手空拳打死了一只猛虎等。在中国，酒已经广泛地融入了人们的生活，贴近生活的酒文化也因此得到了空前的丰富和发展。与生日宴、婚庆宴、丧宴等相关的酒俗、酒礼已经成为中国人的一项重要生活内容。

中国酒分为白酒、黄酒、果酒、配制酒和啤酒。中国的名酒也有很多，茅台、五粮液、汾酒、竹叶青、泸州老窖、古井贡酒、绍兴加饭酒、张裕葡萄酒、长城干红葡萄酒等，都是享誉世界的名酒。

拓展知识

中国黄酒

黄酒，亦称"老酒"，是以糯米、黍米、黑米、玉米、小麦等为原料，经过蒸料，拌以麦曲、米曲或酒药，进行糖化和发酵酿制而成的一类低度原汁酒。黄酒，源于中国，与啤酒、葡萄酒并称世界三大古酒。黄酒，是中国的汉族特产，属于低度酿造酒。在3000多年前的商周时期，中国人就开始大量酿制黄酒。

中国黄酒的产地较广，品种很多，比较有名的有房县黄酒、绍兴老酒、龙岩沉缸酒、九江封缸酒、福建老酒、无锡惠泉酒、江阴黑杜酒、绍兴状元红、女儿红等。根据生产工艺的不同，黄酒可分为糯米黄酒、黍米黄酒、大米黄酒和红曲黄酒。糯米黄酒以酒药和麦曲为糖化、发酵剂，主要生产于中国南方地区。黍米黄酒以米曲霉制成的麸曲为糖化、发酵剂，主要生产于中国北方地区。大米黄酒为一种改良的黄酒，以米曲加酵母为糖化、发酵剂，主要生产于中国吉林、山东以及湖北房县等。红曲黄酒以糯米为原料，红曲为糖化、发酵剂，主要生产于中国福建及浙江两地。

讨论

> **你的国家有饮酒的习惯吗？简单介绍一下。**

第十五章

中外差异

一 见面交际

必读课文

见面交际

中国有着独特的交际文化。例如，见面打招呼的时候，中国人通常是寻找一个话题，跟对方闲聊几句，以示友好和礼貌，如"你吃了吗？""你忙什么呢？""你去哪儿呀？"等。值得注意的是上述打招呼的方式只能在较熟悉的人之间进行。如果熟人之间不打招呼，就会引起对方的猜疑："此人对我为何如此冷淡？"这是中国人特有的心态。而西方人很注重个性和隐私，可能认为我"干什么、去哪儿、吃没吃饭"完全属于个人的隐私，与见面打招呼没有关系。

在交际过程中，称呼是传递给对方的第一信息。不同的称呼反映了交际双方的角色身份、社会地位和亲疏程度的差异。所以称呼不能随意出口，应当注意一些细节问题。比如，不能误读称呼者的姓名，不能将未婚妇女称为"夫人"。此外，在当代中国，"小姐"的称呼是带有贬义色彩的，因此不能称呼女性为"小姐"。

当见面谈论天气的时候，西方人只限于对天气作客观的评价，而中国人一谈到天气常常会嘘寒问暖，以示关怀，仿佛是一家人似的亲切。

拓展知识

见面礼仪

见面礼仪，指日常社交礼仪中最常用与最基础的礼仪。握手是现代人常用的一种礼节，一般在相互见面、离别、祝贺、慰问等情况下使用。

拱手礼，又叫作"揖礼"，是中国传统的礼节之一，已有2000多年的历史，常在人们相见时采用。拱手礼，即两手互握合于胸前。行礼时，不分尊卑，拱手齐眉，上下加重摇动几下，重礼可作揖后鞠躬。

鞠躬，即弯身行礼，是表示对他人敬重的一种礼节。"三鞠躬"称为最敬礼。在中国，鞠躬常用于下级对上级、学生对老师、晚辈对长辈，亦常用于服务人员向宾客致意，演员向观众掌声致谢。

值得注意的是，中国不同民族的见面礼仪也有所不同。例如黑龙江满族传统的礼仪表现在衣、食、起、居、言、行、举、止各个方面，按辈分、性别不同，满族的见面礼分做跪叩礼、抱腰礼、擦肩礼、拉拉礼、抚鬓礼等。

讨论

> 你的国家有哪些见面礼仪？与中国有哪些差异？

二 生活方式

必读课文

生活方式

生活方式，指个人及其家庭日常生活的活动方式，包括衣、食、住、行以及闲暇时间的利用等。中国与西方生活方式的不同，主要表现在语言、饮食、教育、建筑等方面。

语言方面，汉字是象形文字，方块字。汉语含蓄、典雅、华美；西方语言直白、坦率，有些奔放。

饮食方面，在用餐方式上，中西方存在巨大差异。中国人喜欢热闹，倾向于大家围在一起聚餐；西方人喜欢在安静、优雅的环境里就餐，每个人都有自己的餐具，是提前分配好的。中国人主食以谷物为主，其次是蔬菜，植物类占主导地位；西方人主食则以肉食居多。

教育方面，西方教育的主导思想是：每个人都是特殊人才，给予所有学生机会去发挥自己的特长；中国教育则强调集体、团体意识、很少关注个体的差异。

建筑方面，中西建筑风格的不同，从本质上看是因为文化的不同。中国文化重视人，而西方文化重视物。中国建筑重视道德与艺术，而西方建筑重视科学与宗教。

拓展知识

饮食生活

在"食"上，中国人的主食以谷类及其制品如面食为主，副食则以蔬菜为主，辅以肉类。而西方人的主食则以肉类、奶类为主。在"饮"上，中国人习惯饮茶；西方人则喜欢喝咖啡等饮料。

在饮食方式上，在中国，无论是哪种宴席，大家都是团团围坐，共享一席。中国的宴席要用圆桌，这就从形式上营造了一种团结、礼貌、共趣的气氛。西方奉行分餐制，各点各的菜，想吃什么点什么，这也表现了西方人对个性的尊重。中国大多数宴会上将长幼有序、尊重长者作为排座的标准，而西方排座位的礼俗则是女士优先、尊重妇女。中国人还喜欢劝酒、夹菜，举杯共饮，气氛和睦生趣。而西方人则没那么热情，且客人与主人之间也没那么客气，他们更注重个人的独立性。

讨论

简单谈一谈你的国家的生活方式，并比较与中国生活方式的异同。

三 审美思维

必读课文

审美思维

审美思维是人在审美中对客观对象概括、间接、能动的反映。中国人在审美思维上体现出人文主义精神，而西方审美思维更多体现的是科学主义精神。

中国人和西方人在审美思维方式上最大的差异在于强调的是整体性还是个体性。中国人强调整体性和综合性，主张在把握审美对象时，不要孤立地、静止地看待某一方面，而要系统地、全局性地去把握对象。整体思维的特点集中表现为天人合一、天人和谐。用现代哲学语言讲，就是人与自然的统一、主体与客体的统一、主观与客观的统一等。西方人在思维上则注重局部和个体，强调分析和实证，偏重对世界某一部分或部门的专门而精确的研究和考察。分析性、多元性、发散性是其基本特征。"黄金分割""多样统一""天人相分"等形式观念就是这种思维的具体表现。西方思维逻辑性的特点使得人们在审美活动中，喜欢把艺术类比于自然科学，强调理性分析审美范畴。

拓展知识

建筑风格

在建筑上，中国人讲究含蓄蕴藉，最好是曲径通幽。这一处假山，那一处竹林花草，所到之处皆有不同之景。人为地做出湖泊、小山、小桥、流水等，追求天人合一。中国造园讲究的是含而不露。和西方人不同，中国人认识事物多借助于直接的体验，认为直觉并非感官的直接反应，而是一种心智活动，一种内在经验的升华，不可能用推理的方法求得。园林的造景借鉴诗词、绘画，力求含蓄、深沉、虚幻，并借以求得大中见小，小中见大，虚中有实，实中有虚，或藏或露，或浅或深，从而把许多全然对立的因素交织融汇。苏州园林是中国建筑的典型代表。

讨论

简单谈一谈你的国家的传统建筑。与中国的传统建筑有哪些异同？

（四）时间观念

必读课文

时间观念

时间观念是人类观察感知到的自然时间或物理时间。中西方时间观念的差异主要体现在以下几点：

一是多元制时间观和单一制时间观。中华民族是比较典型的多元制时间观的民族，强调的是对时间的适应。人们做事更讲究时机和火候，灵活性强，但计划性较少。相反，西方人则是典型的单一制时间观，看重的是对时间的安排。

二是循环时间观和线性时间观。在中国人的观念中，时间是周而复始、循环不止的，也就是说时间的变化与自然的状态相协调，如昼夜交替、季节的往复、植物的周期生长等。受基督教的影响，西方人喜欢把眼光投向未来，所以人们常持线性的时间观，认为时间是一种线性的单向持续运动。

三是时间的持续性与即刻性。在中国文化中，人们关注时间的持续性，做事讲究四平八稳。做一件事情所花费的时间越长越能显示其重要性。而西方人更看重时间的即刻性，做事重视效率，强调在尽可能短的时间内完成事情。

拓展知识

时间取向

时间是环境语言中的一个重要方面，不同的文化孕育了不同的时间观念和时间行为。中西方在过去和未来时间取向上的不同就体现了很多的文化差异。

中国人在时间取向上就是采取过去取向。中国人喜欢回顾历史，在社会伦理方面表现出对父母和长者的尊重。中国人十分在意老祖宗的规矩是什么，有哪些成功的经验和失败的教训，通常将过去作为衡量现在的标准及今天事情成败的重要参考。所以，中国有成语"前车之鉴""前事不忘，后事之师""吃一堑，长一智"等。对于未来，中国人没有像对过去那样感兴趣，因为它是不可知的、无法捉摸的。

与中国人的时间取向不同，西方人是以未来为时间取向的。他们强调未来，期待未来会比现在更精彩。汉语称呼中的"老""大"等常表示敬意的词，在西方却无此含义。因为在西方人心目中，"老"就意味着青春已逝，是不好的代名词，如果确实要表示敬意，就必须用"respected"或"senior"。

讨论

简单谈一谈你的国家的时间观念与中国有哪些异同。

（五）思维模式

必读课文

思维模式

中国人偏好形象思维，西方人偏好抽象思维。形象思维包含一个想象的过程。这种思维方式是感性的、直觉的。抽象思维，指根据概念进行判断、推理的思维活动。

中国人偏好综合思维，西方人偏好分析思维。中国人偏向于综合思维和整体优先，中国人在观察分析事物的时候，不是就事论事，把事物进行拆分、解析，而是把事物当成一个整体看待，充分注重该事物与其他事物的联系。西方人偏向于分析的思维模式。对于西方人而言，要弄清楚一件事物，必须要先把事物进行分割和拆开，才能弄清内部的结构。

中国人偏好求同思维，西方人偏好求异思维。中西文化都注意到了事物的矛盾对立。中国文化强调的是"统一"，注重求同的思维方式，强调万物一体、和谐共生。在伦理上，为顾全大局和整体，必要时中国人会不惜牺牲个人或局部利益以维护整体利益。而在西方文化中，求异的思维方式则比较普遍，注重追求个体生存的意义。

拓展知识

综合思维

综合思维强调整体。例如，中医把人体看作一个整体，运用阴阳五行学说明五脏之间的依存和制约关系。分析思维强调部分或个体。因而西医建立在人体解剖学的基础上，根据人体九大系统的生理结构来解释病理现象。

在艺术门类的分类上，也反映出中国重整体的特点。例如，中国的国粹京剧就是一种综合性的表演，讲求唱、念、做、打。这种表演方式在西方可以分解为歌剧、舞剧、话剧。再如，中国的国画中不只有画，还常常配有诗词、书法、篆刻等内容。而西方绘画中一般只有画，最多在画上署上画家的名字。因而，中国艺术门类的分类往往不那么明确，中国人比较习惯综合类的审美情趣。

在语言层面上，也有这样的表现。例如，在时间的表达法上，中文的顺序是年—月—日—时—分—秒。西方人，尤其是英国人的表达则是分—时—日—月—年。中国人表达空间的顺序习惯从大到小，从整体到部分，而西方人则恰恰相反。

讨论

简单谈一谈你的国家的思维模式与中国有哪些异同。

(六) 聚会方式

必读课文

聚会方式

聚会，指多人在特定时间和特定地点聚集在一起进行交流的活动。中国和西方的聚会方式有着较大差异。

首先，是聚会时间。中国人的聚会一般在白天，如果是晚上聚会，也会很早就开始集合。主人甚至要更早就开始忙碌，因为聚会的首要活动往往是聚餐。聚会结束的时间基本上也比较早，不会到第二天才结束。而西方的聚会开始得很晚，而且往往到第二天才会结束。

其次，是聚会地点。中国人的聚会大多是在家中。例如，请客吃饭便是由邀请者在家中准备一桌好菜，等待被邀请者来访。而西方人的聚会多选择在餐厅或酒吧。

最后，是参加聚会的人物。中国人的聚会一般主要由相互认识的人参加，携带与主人不熟悉的人参加聚会被认为是不礼貌的行为。西方人的聚会则会有很多不熟悉的面孔出现。

值得注意的是，在中国人的聚会中，美食是很重要的，聚餐是聚会的重头戏。人们往往在餐桌上谈笑风生。而在西方人的聚会中食物并不占主要地位。

拓展知识

中国人聚餐

中国有一句俗语叫"民以食为天"。可见，吃饭问题在中国人的日常生活中是一件很重要的事情。

中国人的聚餐不仅仅是为了吃，其背后还有很多意义。如流传至今的"鸿门宴""青梅煮酒论英雄""杯酒释兵权"等,就体现了中国人聚餐的重要性。在中国,饭局名目繁多,无论是过节、结婚、丧葬、庆生、谈判、搬家,都会有聚餐。其实,聚餐不仅仅是吃饭,蕴含着许许多多的社会内涵。

除此之外,中国人的饭局也很讲究礼节。从座位的安排到上菜的顺序,从谁先动第一筷到什么时候可离席,都有明确的规则。这些规则把"礼仪之邦"的概念诠释得淋漓尽致。如在中国人的饭局上,靠里面正中间的位置要给最尊贵的人坐,上菜时要依照先凉后热、先简后繁的顺序。

在中国,人际交流大多在餐桌上进行。在餐桌上,中国人能做到一边饮酒,一边吃饭,一边交流。

讨论

简单谈一谈你的国家的聚会方式与中国有哪些异同。

>>>>
Introduction

China is located in the east of Asia and on the west coast of the Pacific Ocean. China has a vast territory, with a total land area of about 9.6 million square kilometers and a total sea area of about 4.7 million square kilometers. The topography of China is high in the west and low in the east, with a stepped distribution. The different temperature and precipitation in China form a wide variety of climates. There are 34 provincial administrative units in China, including 23 provinces, 5 autonomous regions, 4 municipalities directly under the central government and 2 special administrative regions. China has a large population base and many ethnic groups. China is rich in resources, but average per capita is low.

China, is one of the countries with the longest history in the world. The Youchao, Suiren, Fuxi, Shennong and Xuanyuan (Yellow Emperor) of the prehistoric period are revered as the originators of Chinese humanity. The Xia, Shang and Zhou dynasties were the periods of slavery society in China. The period from the Qin Dynasty to the Qing Dynasty was the period of feudal society in China. After the Revolution of 1911, China established a republican system of government. In 1949, the People's Republic of China was founded.

After the founding of the People's Republic of China, China has made world-renowned achievements through planned large-scale construction, laying a solid foundation for the development of the national economy, gradually moving from a traditional agricultural country to a modern industrial powerhouse. Since the reform and opening up, China's economy has enjoyed unprecedentedly rapid growth. In the 21st century, China's economy continues to grow steadily and rapidly. At present, China has become the second largest economy in the world and one of the world's most promising economic powers.

After the founding of the People's Republic of China, China's science and technology has been greatly improved, with major scientific and technological achievements in the fields of computers, aerospace, bioengineering, new energy, new materials and laser technology. In the 1980s and 1990s, the Chinese government launched the 863 Program and the Strategy of Invigorating China through Science and Education, both of which have greatly contributed to the development and progress of science and technology in China. China has a large number of public research institutions that produce considerable results every year and its international competitiveness in science and technology has increased rapidly.

Chinese civilization is the root of contemporary Chinese culture and has its origins in prehistoric times. During the Han and Tang dynasties, Chinese culture, including

Confucianism, Buddhism and Taoism, as well as writing, painting, architecture, and sculpture, flourished. Chinese culture had an important influence on Japan and the Korean Peninsula and spread to Southeast Asian countries such as Vietnam and Singapore, forming the East Asian cultural circle with Chinese culture as the pivot. Since the Ming and Qing dynasties, with the increasingly frequent cultural exchanges between the East and the West, Chinese culture has gone global and occupied an important position within the world cultural system.

China, as an ancient civilization with a long history stands rock-firm in the East of the world.

Geographical Variations

Chapter 1

Physical Geography

1 Oceans

Required Reading Text

Seas of China

China's seas comprise the Bohai, Yellow, East and South China Seas at the edge of China's mainland, spanning the temperate, subtropical and tropical zones. The eastern and southern mainland coastline is 18000 kilometers. The waters of the Inland and Border Seas cover an area of about 4.7 million square kilometers.

The Bohai Sea is the northernmost sea in China, surrounded by land on three sides and located among Liaoning, Hebei, Shandong and Tianjin. The Bohai Sea is rich in prawns, crabs and yellow croakers. The Yellow Sea is located between China's mainland and the Korean Peninsula, from the mouth of the Yalu River in the north, in the south, from the Qidong Cape in the north coast of the mouth of the Yangtze River to boundary of the southwest corner of Republic of Korea's Jeju Island and the East China Sea. The Yellow Sea has long been affected by the injection of large amounts of yellowish-brown sediment of the Yellow River and other rivers and contains large amounts of sand. The near-shore water is yellow and the Yellow Sea is also named after it. The East China Sea is one of the three largest marginal seas in China and the widest marginal sea on the Chinese continental shelf. The East China Sea is rich in yellow croakers, hairtails, cuttlefish, etc. and is also rich in undersea oil and gas resources. The South China Sea named after its location in the south of China. The South China Sea is rich in natural resources, with a wide variety of flora and fauna and abundant mineral resources.

Extended Text

The South China Sea

The South China Sea, located in the south of China, is one of the three major marginal seas of China and is the largest and deepest sea area in China's coastal waters. The South China Sea extends from the southeast to the Philippine Islands and from the southwest to Vietnam and the Malay Peninsula, with the southernmost part of the South China Sea, Zengmu Ansha, near Kalimantan Island. The South China Sea is connected to the Pacific Ocean and the Indian Ocean through the Bashi Channel, the Sulu Sea and the Strait of Malacca.

There are over 200 islands and reefs in the South China Sea, commonly known as the South China Sea Islands. The South China Sea Islands include Dongsha Islands, Xisha Islands, Zhongsha Islands and Nansha Islands. The South China Sea Islands have been used and developed by the Chinese in ancient times and are an integral part of China's territory. After the establishment of Hainan Province in 1988, the South China Sea Islands became part of Hainan Province. In 2012, China established Sansha City in Hainan Province to govern the Xisha Islands, Zhongsha Islands, Nansha Islands and the waters.

The South China Sea and the South China Sea Islands are all in the south of the Tropic of Cancer, closing to the equator, in the equatorial belt, with a tropical maritime monsoon climate, with high temperatures and high humidity all year round and summer in all seasons. The South China Sea is one of the main areas of global typhoon activity, and typhoons can be generated every month. The South China Sea is an essential link between China and Southeast Asia, South Asia, West Asia and Africa and it is also one of the most important sea routes from Western Europe to the Far East.

Discussion

> Are there any sea route from China to your country? Which sea areas do they pass through?

② Plateaus

Required Reading Text

Plateaus of China

A plateau refers to an elevation of 500 meters or more with a relatively gentle top surface. The four major plateaus in China are the Qinghai-Xizang Plateau, the Yunnan-Guizhou Plateau, the Inner Mongolia Plateau and the Loess Plateau.

The Qinghai-Xizang Plateau, known as the "roof of the world" is the largest plateau in China and the highest in the world. Located in the west and southwest of China, the Qinghai-Xizang Plateau covers an area of about 2.5 million square kilometers, with an average altitude of over 4000 meters. The Qinghai-Xizang Plateau is the source of major rivers in East Asia, Southeast Asia and South Asia.

The Yunnan-Guizhou Plateau, located in southwestern China, is bordered by the Qinghai-Xizang Plateau to the west. The Yunnan-Guizhou Plateau is one of the most complete and typical regions in the world in terms of karst landform development and has a rich and diverse natural environment. The Yunnan-Guizhou Plateau is the watershed of three major water systems: the Yangtze River, the Xijiang River and the Yuanjiang River.

The Inner Mongolia Plateau, the second largest plateau in China, is part of the Mongolian Plateau. The Inner Mongolia Plateau is mainly dominated by low, gentle hills and wide, shallow basins. The eastern part of the plateau is covered with grasslands, serving as an important livestock base in China; while the western part has a dry climate, consisting of steppe, desert steppe and desserts.

The Loess Plateau, is located on north of the Qinling and Weihe Plain, south of the Great Wall, west of the Taihang Mountains and east of the Taohe River and the Ushing Mountains. The Loess Plateau has loose soil, broken terrain and serious soil erosion. After years of comprehensive management, the soil erosion on the Loess Plateau has been controlled to some extent. Loess Plateau is rich in coal, oil, bauxite, etc.

Extended Text

Pamir Plateau

The Pamir Plateau, located in the southwestern part of Xinjiang Uyghur

Autonomous Region, southeastern Tajikistan and northeastern Afghanistan, China. The Pamir Plateau is a large knot of mountains formed by the rendezvous of the Tianshan Mountains, Kunlun Mountains, Karakorum Mountains and Hindu Kush Mountains. The Pamir Plateau is 4000 to 7700 meters above the sea level and has several peaks. In China, the Gonger Peak is 7649 meters and the Muztagh Peak is 7509 meters.

The Pamir Plateau has an alpine climate with pronounced vertical variations in the natural landscape. The Pamir Plateau is extensively glaciated and is one of the largest mountain glaciers in the world. The mountain glaciers make some deserts and rivers get water. Fidchenko Glacier in the northwest corner of the Pamir Plateau is 71.2 kilometers long, one of the longest highland mountain glaciers in the world. The eastern part of the Pamir Plateau is the main breeding ground for goats and argali. The central part of the Pamir Plateau is gently undulating and has wide valleys. Grapes and other fruits can be cultivated in the valleys of the Pamir Plateau where irrigation is available.

The Pamir Plateau is part of what is known in China as the Onion Range. The famous historical Silk Road could reach Central Asia and the Mediterranean countries after crossing the Pamir Plateau.

Discussion

> Find on a map, what plateaus did the Silk Road from Xi'an of China to Rome of Italy pass through in ancient times?

③ Plains

Required Reading Text

Plains of China

A plain refers to a wide, low and flat area with an altitude of less than 200 meters. It is divided into alluvial plains, erosion plains and lacustrine plains according to the genesis. There are three major plains in China, namely the Northeast Plain, the North China Plain and the Middle and Lower Yangtze River Plain, which are distributed on the third terrain step in eastern China.

The Northeast Plain is the largest plain in China, located between the Great and Little Xing'an Mountains, the Changbai Mountains and the Yanshan Mountains, and is mainly formed by the alluvial deposits of the Liaohe, Songhua and Nengjiang Rivers. The Northeast Plain has short, warm and rainy summers and long, cold winters with little snow. The soil of the Northeast Plain is deep, fertile and rich in organic matter, making it an important grain base in China.

The North China Plain is the second largest plain in China, located at the lower reaches of the Yellow River, covering an area of about 310000 square kilometers. The North China Plain is a typical alluvial plain. The terrain of the North China Plain is flat and endless. There are many rivers and lakes and transportation is convenient. The North China Plain is China's political, economic, cultural and transportation center.

The Middle and Lower Yangtze River Plain refers to the middle and lower reaches of the coastal plain which is in the east of the Three Gorges of the Yangtze River in China, formed by the alluvial deposits of the Yangtze River and its tributaries. The Middle and Lower Yangtze River Plain is flat, with many lakes and thousands of miles of fertile land. The Middle and Lower Yangtze River Plain is famous as the land of fish and rice in China, and are also an exceptionally rich region in terms of water resources.

Extended Text

Guanzhong Plain

The Guanzhong Plain, in central Shaanxi Province, between the Qinling Mountains and the Northern Shaanxi Plateau, is a river valley basin surrounded by mountains on three sides and open to the east, also known as the Weihe Plain or the Guanzhong Basin. The Guanzhong Plain extends from Baoji in the west, to Tongguan in the east, to the Qinling Mountains in the south, and to the Northern Shaanxi Plateau in the north. The Guanzhong Plain is more than 300 kilometers long from east to west, wide in the east and narrow in the west, with an elevation of about 400 meters. The Guanzhong Plain has flat terrains, fertile soils, mild climates, abundant water and convenient irrigation. With superior natural and economic conditions, the Guanzhong Plain has been one of the most affluent areas in China's history in terms of agriculture. At present, the Guanzhong Plain is still one of the developped areas of industry, agriculture and culture in China, and is also an important wheat and cotton producing area in China.

With convenient transportation and surrounded by mountains and rivers, starting from the Western Zhou Dynasty, 10 dynasties, including Qin, Western Han, Sui and Tang dynasties, have built their capitals in the Guanzhong Plain for more than 1000 years. As the political, economic and cultural center of the ancient dynasties, Guanzhong Plain was called "Guanzhong" because it was located within the four "gates", with Tongguan in the east, Dasanguan in the West, Wuguan in the south and Xiaoguan in the north.

The Guanzhong Plain is rich in history and culture, and was the homeland of the Qin Dynasty during the Spring and Autumn Period and the Warring States Period. At the end of the Warring States Period, the state of Qin unified the country from the east and established China's first feudal dynasty, the Qin Dynasty, which is why the Guanzhong Plain is also known as the Qinchuan or the 800-mile Qinchuan.

Discussion

What are the other alluvial plains in China? Do you have similar alluvial plains in your country?

4 Basins

Required Reading Text

Basins of China

A basin is an area of the earth's surface that is high around and low in the middle. The main basins in China are the Tarim Basin, Junggar Basin, Qaidam Basin and Sichuan Basin. They are mostly located on the second step of the terrain, and their characteristics are different due to their different locations.

The Tarim Basin, located in the south of Xinjiang, China, is the largest inland basin in China. The Tarim Basin is located among the Tianshan Mountains, Kunlun Mountains and Altun Mountains, and extends from the Pamir Plateau in the west to the depression of Lop Nor in the east, covering an area of about 530000 square kilometers. The edge of the Tarim Basin is the gobi, and the central part south of the Tarim River is the desert and salt lakes. Between the basin's edge and the desert are alluvial fans and alluvial plains, with oases spread out. The climate of the basin is arid with little rain and has a large temperature difference between day and night. The basin is rich in oil and gas resources.

The Junggar Basin, located in the northern part of Xinjiang, is an unequal triangle among the Tianshan Mountains, Altay Mountains and the western mountains. The basin is a semi-enclosed inland basin with a high topography in the east and a low topography in the west. The edge of the basin is an oasis at the foot of the mountains, and most of the cultivated crops are annual, producing cotton and wheat. The central part of the basin is a vast grassland and desert, partly covered by shrubs and herbs. The southern part of the basin is an important demonstration base for agriculture, industry, energy, culture, science and education in Xinjiang.

The Qaidam Basin, located in the northern part of Qinghai Province, among Mingshan Mountains, Altun Mountains, Qilian Mountains and Kunlun Mountains, has an average altitude of 2600 to 3000 meters. The Qaidam Basin is a giant inland basin with the highest topography in China. The topography of the basin slopes from northwest to southeast, with the gobi, hills, plains and lakes in order from the edge to the center. The climate of the basin is arid, and precipitation is scarce. The basin is rich in mineral resources.

Extended Text

Sichuan Basin

The Sichuan Basin, located in the eastern part of Sichuan Province and the upper reaches of the Yangtze River in China, is bounded by the Yunnan-Guizhou Plateau in the south, the Qinghai-Xizang Plateau in the west, and the Daba Mountains in the north. According to geographical differences, the Sichuan Basin can be divided into three parts from west to east: the Chengdu Plain, the Mid-Sichuan and the parallel ridges and valleys in eastern Sichuan. The soil of the Sichuan Basin is purple, making it one of the most fertile natural soils in China, hence it is also called Purple Basin.

With its mild climate and abundant rainfall, especially since the construction of the Dujiangyan Water Conservancy Project during the Warring States Period, the Chengdu Plain became a highly developed agricultural and handicraft region in Chinese history, and became the main food supply base and taxation source for the central dynasty, known as the land of heaven. The Sichuan Basin was densely populated, with prosperous economy and flourishing culture. The major cities in the basin are Chengdu, Chongqing, Mianyang, etc.

The Sichuan Basin is one of the most diverse and complete regions in China in terms of animal species, including the giant panda and the Sichuan golden monkey, which belong to the national first-class protected animals. The Sichuan Basin has mineral resources such as coal, salt, natural gas and petroleum. In addition to the road network, there are railroad trunk lines such as Chengdu-Chongqing, Chengdu-Kunming and Baoji-Chengdu and a water transport network mainly on the Sichuan River.

Discussion

> What other basins are there in China or your country? Are they also rich in oil?

5 Deserts

Required Reading Text

Deserts of China

A desert, an area where the surface is fully covered by sand with a short of water, dry climate, rare plants. The arid region of northwest China is the most concentrated area of deserts in China. The main deserts in China are the Taklimakan Desert, the Gurbantunggut Desert and the Badain Jaran Desert.

The Taklimakan Desert, located in the middle of the Tarim Basin in Xinjiang, is the largest desert in China and one of the world's famous great deserts. Influenced by the wind, the desert dunes move from time to time. The dunes move to the southeast in the west under the influence of northwest wind, and to the southwest in the east under the influence of northeast wind. There are fewer plants in the desert, mainly the populus and red willow. Taklimakan has a glorious history and culture, and the ancient Silk Road passes through the southern end of the desert.

The Gurbantunggut Desert, located in the middle of Junggar Basin in Xinjiang, is the second largest desert in China. The vast majority of the desert interior is fixed and semi-fixed sand dunes. Under the influence of northwest wind and west wind, the desert forms a large sand monopoly belt with northwest-southeast direction. The desert has plenty of water sources and richer plant species, such as the white haloxylon ammondendron and artemisia, which are excellent winter pastures. There are large salt mines in the northwest of the desert.

The Badain Jaran Desert, is located in the western part of Alxa Right Banner and the eastern part of Ejin Banner in Inner Mongolia Autonomous Region. The desert has an arid climate, little precipitation and strong light. The towering sand mountains, the mysterious sounding sands and the tranquil lakes constitute the unique and fascinating landscape of the Badain Jaran Desert, which attracts many domestic and foreign tourists.

Extended Text

Ulanbuh Desert

The Ulanbuh Desert is located in the west-central part of Inner Mongolia Autonomous Region, with north to Wolf Mountain, northeast to the Hetao Plain, east to the Yellow River, south to the northern side of Helan Mountains, and west to the Jilantai Salt Pond.

The terrain of the Ulanbuh Desert slopes from southeast to northwest, with drifting sands in the south, ridge dunes in the middle and fixed and semi-fixed dunes in the north. The northern part of the Ulanbuh Desert is the ancient alluvial plain of the Yellow River, and there is a large area of flat soil between the dunes, which can be developed and used after land leveling. There are potential advantages for developing agriculture in these flat soil areas and many farms have been opened up. The Ulanbuh Desert is flat and slopes gently to the west from the bank of the Yellow River, so that the Yellow River water can be diverted for irrigation by gravity. The semi-fixed and fixed dune areas in the west and southwest of the desert are distributed with a lot of natural pastures, in which the reaumuria soongorica, haloxylon ammodendron, nitraria tangutorum and other psammophytes, xerophytes and halophytes extremely adaptable to the local environment.

The main reasons for the formation of Ulanbuh Desert are drought and wind. Coupled with people's indiscriminate felling of trees and destruction of grassland, the surrounding natural environment was once very poor. With the large-scale treatment of the country and the attention of the western region to maintain the pastoral economy, the ecological environment of Ulanbuh Desert gradually turned better.

Discussion

Have you ever been to a desert? What are the landscapes in the desert?

⑥ Mountains

Required Reading Text

Mountains of China

A mountain range is a mountain body that extends linearly in a certain direction, often consisting of multiple mountains. The mountain ranges in China can be divided into five types according to direction: east-west, northeast-southwest, northwest-southeast, north-south and curved mountains, and the representative ones are the Himalayas, the Kunlun Mountains, and the Hengduan Mountains.

The Himalayas, an arc-shaped mountain range, are located in the southern part of the Qinghai-Xizang Plateau and are the highest mountain range in the world. The climate is very different between the north and south sides of the Himalayas, with a warm and humid climate on the southern slopes and a dry climate on the northern slopes. The topography, hydrology, biology, soil and agricultural production differ greatly between the north and south slopes. The main peak of the mountain range is the world's highest peak, Qomolangma, located in the middle of the Himalayas.

The Kunlun Mountains, an east-west mountain range, are also known as the spine of Asia. The Kunlun Mountains are located in central Asia, starting from the eastern Pamir Plateau in the west, traversing the two autonomous regions of Xinjiang and Xizang, and extending eastward to the territory of Qinghai Province. The Kunlun Mountains are high in the west and low in the east, and can be divided into three sections according to the terrain: west, middle and east, each of which has several peaks above 6000 meters in elevation.

The Hengduan Mountains are the longest, widest and most typical north-south trending mountain range in China. The Hengduan Mountains are located in the southeastern part of the Qinghai-Xizang Plateau and is often referred to as the north-south mountain range in the western part of Sichuan Province and Yunnan Province and the eastern part of the Xizang Autonomous Region. It is named "Hengduan Mountains" because the mountain range crosses the east-west traffic. The Hengduan Mountains have a distinct vertical climate variation and are rich in forest resources and hydroenergy resources.

Extended Text

The Five Great Mountains

The Five Great Mountains are the collective name for the five most famous mountains in traditional Chinese culture, namely the Mount Tai in the east, the Mount Hua in the west, the Mount Song in the middle, the Mount Heng in the south and the Mount Heng in the north.

The Mount Tai, located in the middle of Shandong Province, is a world natural and cultural heritage. In the myth of "Pan Gu creating the world", after Pan Gu died, his head became the Mount Tai; his belly became the Mount Song; his left arm became the Mount Heng; his right arm became the Mount Heng, and his two feet became the Mount Hua. Therefore, the Mount Tai is called the first mountain in the world and is the top of the five mountains.

The Mount Hua is located in the eastern part of Shaanxi Province and the north of the Qinling Mountains. It is a famous Taoist mountain, and was the birthplace of the Huashan school of Quanzhen Taoism during the Yuan Dynasty. The Mount Hua is so dangerous that there is a saying that "the Mount Hua has had only one road since ancient times". The Xiyue Temple on the mountain, built in the period of Emperor Wu of the Han Dynasty, has only one shrine and temple dedicated to Xiyue for many generations.

The Mount Song, located in the north of Dengfeng City in Henan Province, consists of Thaishi Mountain and Shaoshi Mountain. It is the birthplace of Zen Buddhism and a sacred Taoist site in China, and is also the home of Shaolin Temple, the source of Chinese Kungfu. The Mount Song is a national scenic spot of the World Geological Group.

The Mount Heng (衡山), located in the central part of Hunan Province, is the most famous Taoist holy land and Buddhist shrine in China. There are 72 famous peaks in Mount Heng, among which Zhurong, Tianzhu, Furong, Zigai and Shilin peaks are the tallest. The Mount Heng has a large green area, with ancient trees and exotic flowers everywhere, and is known as the only one of the five mountains.

The Mount Heng (恒山), located in the north of Shanxi Province and the northwest of Hebei Province, is one of the sacred places of Taoism. Legend has it that Zhang Guolao, one of the Eight Immortals, became an immortal after living in seclusion on Mount Heng.

Discussion

What are the other famous mountains in China besides the Five Great Mountains on the map?

Chapter 2

Human Geography

① Population

Required Reading Text

Population of China

Population is the sum of people living in a specific social system and in a specific area. Historically, China's population has always occupied a large proportion of the world's population. In the modern period, China's population grew slowly due to wars, etc. After 1949, China's population grew rapidly due to the development of production and longer life expectancy.

According to the 7th national census in 2020, China's population exceeded 1.4 billion. The data show that China's population has continued to grow at a low rate for a decade. The size of China's households continues to shrink, with an average population of less than three people per household, due to factors such as China's population mobility and young people living independently after marriage. The regional distribution of China's population is about 40% in the eastern region, about 26% in the central region, about 27% in the western region, and about 7% in the northeastern region. Compared with 2010, the proportion of population in the eastern and western regions has increased, while the central and northeastern regions have decreased. The population has further concentrated in economically developed regions and urban clusters. In the gender composition, the gender ratio of men to women is basically the same as that in 2010. In terms of age composition, the aging of the population has further deepened. Among the urban and rural population, the urban population exceeded 900 million, and the proportion of urban population further increased.

Extended Text

Population Policy

The population policy refers to the policies formulated and adopted by a country to regulate or influence the quantity, quality, composition and distribution of the population in order to achieve certain population goals. Population policies of different countries are adjusted according to the actual situation of their population development.

The population policy in ancient China was much related to the marriage policy. After long wars in some dynasties, the population was greatly reduced. To solve this problem, the government promoted population growth through early marriages. For example, the State of Yue in the Spring and Autumn Period set the age of 20 for men and 17 for women as the latest age for marriage. If a man or woman did not marry beyond this age, the parents were punished.

In the 1980s, China adopted family planning as a basic state policy, i.e., planned childbirth in accordance with its population policy. The main elements of the policy were to promote late marriage, late childbearing, fewer and better births, and only one child per couple. The purpose of the policy is to control population growth in a planned manner and promote long-term balanced population development.

In the early 21st century, the family planning policy was adjusted in the economically developed regions of China. In 2016, China implemented a policy of two children per couple, and in 2021, China further optimized its fertility policy by implementing a policy of three children per couple.

Discussion

What are your country's population policies? What are the similarities and differences with China's population policies?

② Ethnicity

Required Reading Text

Ethnic Groups of China

An ethnic group is a community of people historically formed at different stages of social development. A country can have different ethnic groups, and an ethnic group can live in different countries. China is a unified multi-ethnic country with 56 ethnic groups, including Han, Zhuang, Hui, Manchu, and Uyghur. The Han ethnic group is the main ethnic group in China, and the other 55 ethnic groups are collectively called ethnic minorities.

The Han ethnic group is the result of a long-term fusion of the ancient Chinese and other ethnic groups. The Han people have made brilliant achievements in both social sciences and natural sciences. The Han people are an ethnic group with a long history and the largest population in the world. The Han people are found throughout the country, mainly in the Yellow River, the Yangtze River and the Pearl River basins and the Songliao Plain. In addition to China, the Han people are also found in Southeast Asia, North America and Western Europe.

The Zhuang ethnic group, one of the most populous ethnic minorities in China, has an ethical language of Zhuang language. The Zhuang people developed from a group of ancient Chinese Baiyue. The Zhuang people are mainly distributed in southern China. Guangxi Zhuang Autonomous Region is the main distribution area of the Zhuang people. In addition to China, the Zhuang people are also found in the northern part of Vietnam, which is adjacent to China.

The Hui ethnic group is one of the more populous ethnic minorities in China. The Hui people were mainly Central Asians, Persians and Arabs who migrated to China in the 13th century, and gradually formed by absorbing Han, Mongolian and Uyghur components during their long-term development. The Hui people are mainly distributed in northwest China. Ningxia Hui Autonomous Region is the main distribution area of the Hui people.

Extended Text

Manchu

Manchu is one of the populous ethnic groups in China and its language is

Manchu and Chinese. Manchu people are mainly distributed in northern China. Liaoning, Hebei, Heilongjiang and Jilin provinces are the main distribution areas of the Manchu.

Northeast region is the homeland and birthplace of the Manchu. The origin of the Manchu, can be traced back to more than 2000 years ago to the Sushen and later to the Jurchens (an ancient nationality in China). In the Liao Dynasty, the Jin Dynasty was established by the Jurchens. Subsequently, the Jin Dynasty and the Northern Song Dynasty united to destroy the Liao. After the rise of Mongolia, the Jin Dynasty was destroyed by the Yuan Dynasty. In the middle and late Ming Dynasty, the Jin Dynasty was re-established by the Jurchens, which was called the Later Jin Dynasty and later changed to the Qing Dynasty. In 1644, the Qing army entered Shanhai Pass and gradually unified the country. In 1911, the Revolution of 1911 broke out and the Qing Dynasty fell.

The Manchu people are mainly engaged in agriculture, as well as fishing, animal husbandry, farming and so on. The Manchu children's songs and folk songs have many traces of hunting lives. Manchu men wear Chinese and women wear cheongsam, becoming a representative of traditional Manchu dress. Manchu food is very special. The most representative of the Manchu and Chinese jacket food culture integration is the "Manchu-Han Banquet". In ancient times, marrying older women was popular in the Manchu marriage, and there was a saying that if the woman was 3 years older than the man, the man would be as happy as holding golden bricks. Since the Qing Dynasty, Manchu education and culture have developed greatly, represented by Cao Xueqin and Lao She.

Discussion

> Which ethnic group do you belong to? What are the characteristics of your ethnic group?

③ Provincial-Level Administrative Regions

Required Reading Text

Provincial-Level Administrative Regions of China

There are 34 provincial-level administrative regions in China, including 23 provinces, 5 autonomous regions, 4 municipalities directly under the central government and 2 special administrative regions, with the following abbreviations.

North China: Beijing, "Jing"; Tianjin, "Jin"; Hebei Province, "Ji"; Shanxi Province, "Jin"; Inner Mongolia Autonomous Region, "Neimenggu".

Northeast China: Liaoning Province, "Liao"; Jilin Province, "Ji"; Heilongjiang Province, "Hei".

East China: Shanghai, "Hu"; Jiangsu Province, "Su"; Zhejiang Province, "Zhe"; Anhui Province, "Wan"; Fujian Province, "Min"; Jiangxi Province, "Gan"; Shandong Province, "Lu"; Taiwan Province, "Tai".

Central China: Henan Province, "Yu"; Hubei Province, "E"; Hunan Province, "Xiang".

South China: Guangdong Province, "Yue"; Guangxi Zhuang Autonomous Region, "Gui"; Hainan Province, "Qiong"; Hong Kong Special Administrative Region, "Hong Kong"; Macao Special Administrative Region, "Macao".

Southwest China: Chongqing, "Yu"; Sichuan Province, "Chuan" and "Shu"; Guizhou Province, "Gui" and "Qian"; Yunnan Province, "Yun" and "Dian"; Xizang Autonomous Region, "Zang".

Northwest: Shaanxi Province, "Shan" and "Qin"; Gansu Province, "Gan" and "Long"; Qinghai Province, "Qing"; Ningxia Hui Autonomous Region, "Ning"; Xinjiang Uygur Autonomous Region, "Xin".

Extended Text

Zhejiang Province

The provincial capital of Zhejiang is Hangzhou. Zhejiang has 11 prefecture-level cities under its jurisdiction, of which Hangzhou and Ningbo are sub-provincial cities. Zhoushan is the only island city in Zhejiang Province.

Zhejiang is located in the southeast coast of China, east of the East China Sea, south of Fujian, connected to Anhui and Jiangxi to the west and bordered by Shanghai and Jiangsu to the north. The largest river in Zhejiang is the Qiantang River, also known as "Zhejiang". With four distinct seasons, moderate temperatures, more light, and abundant rainfall, Zhejiang is one of the regions in China with abundant precipitation.

Zhejiang Province is one of the provinces with the least variation in economic development within China. Hangzhou and Ningbo have long ranked among the top 20 economies in China. Zhejiang Province is known as the land of fish and rice and has the highest marine fishery catch in China. The main coastal port in Zhejiang is Ningbo-Zhoushan Port. Hangzhou Xiaoshan International Airport is one of the top ten airports in China.

The important natural scenery of Zhejiang includes the West Lake, Qiandao Lake, Dongqian Lake, Qiantang River Tide, Siming Mountain, Tiantai Mountain and Yandang Mountain. The humanistic scenery includes the Song Dynasty Town, Xitang Ancient Town, Lu Xun's Former Residence, Hengdian World Studios and Xiangshan World Studios. Zhejiang is represented by the thinker Wang Shouren, the literary scholar Lu Xun and the scientist Tu Youyou.

Discussion

> Which Chinese provinces have you visited or known about? Talk about your impression of these provinces.

(4) Cities

Required Reading Text

Cities of China

Cities are settlements with a certain population density and building density, a high concentration of secondary and tertiary industries, and a predominantly non-agricultural population. The major cities in China are Beijing, Hong Kong, Shanghai, Taipei, Guangzhou, Shenzhen, Hangzhou, Nanjing, Chengdu, and Wuhan.

Beijing, known as Yanjing and Beiping in ancient times, is the capital of China, the political center, cultural center, international communication and science and technology innovation center of China, a modern international metropolis, the national transportation center, and the general hub of railroad, highway and air transportation.

Hong Kong, known as the Hong Kong Special Administrative Region of the People's Republic of China, is a highly prosperous free port and cosmopolitan city, and is the center of the Guangdong-Hong Kong-Macao Greater Bay Area. Hong Kong is an important international financial, trade, shipping, tourism and information center, and is internationally recognized as the freest and most open economy.

Shanghai is the third largest city in the world and one of the national central cities. Shanghai is one of China's international economic, financial, trade, technology and shipping centers, and is the core city of the Yangtze River Economic Belt and the Yangtze River Delta City Cluster. Shanghai port's container throughput ranks first in the world.

Taipei, the capital of Taiwan Province of the People's Republic of China, is also the political, economic, cultural and transportation center of Taiwan Province. Taipei is the largest city in Taiwan Province, with well-developed tertiary industries such as finance, trade, wholesale and tourism. Industry in Taipei is dominated by the manufacture of electric motors and appliances.

Extended Text

Guangzhou

Guangzhou is known as Yangcheng (ram city) and Huangcheng (flower city). Guangzhou is the capital of Guangdong Province, a sub-provincial city and a megacity. Guangzhou is one of the national central cities, the central city of Guangdong-Hong Kong-Macao Greater Bay Area and the Pearl River Delta city cluster, and the economic, cultural and transportation center of South China. Guangzhou is one of the first coastal open cities in China, the southern gate of China to the world, and a hub city of the Belt and Road.

From the Qin and Han dynasties to the Ming and Qing dynasties, Guangzhou has been an important port city for China's foreign trade and the starting point of China's Maritime Silk Road. During the Tang and Song dynasties, Guangzhou became a world-famous oriental port and established China's first institution "the Municipal Shipping Department" to manage foreign trade affairs. During the Ming and Qing dynasties, Guangzhou was the only port city for foreign trade in China for a long period. After the Opium War in 1840, Guangzhou was one of the five ports of commerce forced to open in China.

Guangzhou has superior natural conditions and rich material resources, and is one of the richest regions in China in terms of fruit trees, with many varieties of lychees, bananas, pineapples and so on. Guangzhou is rich in tourism resources, and its famous natural and humanistic landscapes include Yuexiu Mountain, Guangzhou Tower, the Baiyun Mountain, Sun Yat-sen Memorial Hall and Huangpu Miltary Academy.

Discussion

Which city in China have you studied or worked in? What are the characteristics of this city?

(5) Ports

Required Reading Text

Ports of China

Ports are water and land transportation hubs located along rivers, lakes, seas and reservoirs where ships can safely enter, exit and berth. The major ports in China are Shanghai Port, Tianjin Port and Guangzhou Port.

Shanghai Port, a port in Shanghai, China, a major hub port on the coast of China, was formed in the Sui Dynasty. During the late Qing Dynasty, Shanghai Port was one of the first five earliest commercial ports in China, and was a major port for China's foreign trade. The port area mainly consists of the Yangtze River mouth port area, the Hangzhou Bay port area, the Huangpu River port area and the Yangshan port area, which is the largest port in China and the largest container port in the world.

Tianjin Port, the port in Tianjin, China, is the largest comprehensive port in northern China, and is an artificial deep-water port with the highest navigational grade in the world. It was shaped in the Tang Dynasty, and in 1860, Tianjin Port became a port for foreign trade. Tianjin Port is located at the downstream of the Haihe River and its entrance to the sea, at the western end of Bohai Bay, at the intersection of Beijing-Tianjin-Hebei city cluster and Bohai Bay economic circle.

Guangzhou Port is the port of Guangzhou City, Guangdong Province, China. Guangzhou port was formed in the Qin and Han dynasties. During the Qing Dynasty, Guangzhou Port was a port of commerce and foreign trade for China. It is an important hub of China's comprehensive transportation system and an important port for foreign trade in South China.

Extended Text

Ningbo-Zhoushan Port

Ningbo-Zhoushan Port, a port in Ningbo and Zhoushan City, Zhejiang Province, China, is a result of the merger and reorganization of Ningbo Port and Zhoushan Port, which has been the world's largest port in terms of cargo throughput since 2009.

The history of Ningbo Port can be traced back to prehistoric times. After the establishment of Mingzhou in the Tang Dynasty, the port of Mingzhou rapidly developed into a major port for China's ocean-going and offshore trade. In the early Ming Dynasty, Mingzhou was changed to Ningbo. In the early and middle of the Ming Dynasty, Ningbo Port became the only port for China's trade with Japan. In the late Ming Dynasty, Ningbo Port was banned from foreign trade and became a transshipment port for Chinese goods from north to south. In 1842, Ningbo Port was opened to the public again.

Zhoushan Port has a long history and was once a haven and transit port for China's north-south shipping and international shipping during the Tang and Song Dynasties. During the Republic of China, nine wooden wharves were built in Dinghai and Shenjiamen. In 1987, Zhoushan Port was officially opened to the public. There are eight port areas in the port: Dinghai, Shenjiamen, Laotangshan, Gaoting, Qushan, Sijiao, Lühuashan and Yangshan.

At present, there are 19 port areas in Ningbo-Zhoushan Port, among which the main port areas are Beilun, Yangshan, Liuheng, Qushan, Chuanshan, Jintang, Daxie, Cengang, Meishan.

Discussion

> What other ports along the Chinese coast are you familiar with? Give examples to illustrate their characteristics.

6 Railroads

Required Reading Text

Railroads of China

The railroad is a land-based mode of transportation. The first railroad in China was built in Shanghai. China's total railroad is the second longest in the world. The main types of railroads in China are national trunk railroads, inter-regional trunk railroads and urban rail transit.

National trunk railroads are the railroads with key economic, political, cultural and defense benefits in the national region. In 2004, China announced the Medium and Long-Term Railway Network Plan. By 2005, there were 11 national trunk railroads in China, including six north-south railroad lines, namely, Beijing-Harbin Railway to Beijing-Shanghai Railway, Beijing-Kowloon Railway, Beijing-Guangzhou Railway, Jiaozuo-Liuzhou Railway, Baoji-Chengdu Railway to Chengdu-Kunming Railway and Chengdu-Chongqing Railway to Chongqing-Guiyang Railway; five east-west railroad lines, namely, Beijing-Baotou to Baotu-Lanzhou Railway, Longhai to Lanzhou-Xinjiang Railway, Shanghai-Kunming Railway, Xiangyang-Chongqing Railway and Nanning-Kunming Railway.

Inter-regional trunk railroads are the railroad systems connecting different city groups, city belts or provincial administrative regions within a certain distance. Some of the more representative regional trunk rail lines in China are Guangzhou-Shantou Railway and Jinhua-Ningbo Railway.

Urban rail transit, which serves urban passenger transportation, is usually powered by electricity. It is often referred to as green transportation because of its high speed, safety, punctuality, low cost and energy saving. The first cities in China to open urban rail transit lines are Hong Kong, Beijing, Tianjin, Taipei, Shanghai, and Guangzhou, etc.

Extended Text

High-Speed Railways of China

The China high speed railway is a high-speed railroad built and used in China. The mileage of high-speed railroad in China is over 40000 kilometers, which is the first in the world. China high-speed railway trains are divided into high-speed EMU travel trains, intercity EMU travel trains and EMU travel trains with the beginning letters "G" "C" and "D" respectively. In 2016, China announced the new Medium and Long-term Railway Network Plan, in which the main high-speed railway corridor consists of eight vertical high-speed railroads and eight horizontal high-speed railways.

Eight longitudinal railways include: Dalian-Beihai high-speed railway, Beijing-Shanghai high-speed railway, Beijing-Hong Kong high-speed railway, Harbin-Hong Kong high-speed railway, Hohhot-Nanning high-speed railway, Beijing-Kunming high-speed railway, Baotou-Haikou high-speed railway, and Lanzhou-Guangzhou high-speed railway.

Eight horizontal railways include: Suifenhe to Manzhouli high-speed railway, Beijing to Lanzhou high-speed railway, Qingdao to Yinchuan high-speed railway, Lianyungang to Urumqi high-speed railway, Shanghai to Chengdu high-speed railway, Shanghai to Kunming high-speed railway, Xiamen to Chongqing high speed railway, Guangzhou to Kunming high-speed railway.

Discussion

> What types of railways are available in your city in China? Which of these railways have you taken?

Chapter 3

People and Environment

① Forests

● Required Reading Text

Forests of China

A forest usually refers to a large area of trees; in the forestry sector, a forest means a large number of trees on the vast land, including the animal and plants living on this area. Forests are rich in species, complex structures and diverse functions, and are known as the lungs of the earth. Forests are an important part of natural resources. Human development cannot be achieved without the use of forest resources.

China's forest resources are small in quantity and uneven in regional distribution. China's forest resources can be divided into three regions: northeast, southwest and south of China. The forests in the northeast are the main natural forest areas in China. After logging and artificial transformation, the proportion of planted forests in the northeastern forests has gradually increased. The forests in the southwest region are the second most important natural forest area in China, mainly located in the southeast of the Qinghai-Xizang Plateau. Southern mountainous areas are large, with good climatic conditions and potential for forestry production, and many of China's endemic tree species are produced in southern regions.

China has a long history of utilizing forest resources. In agricultural societies, people cut down trees for energy and wood was the raw material for building houses and making various products. Currently, China has responded to the desertification in northern China by planting trees and has achieved some success.

Extended Text

The "Three-North" Shelter Forest Program

The "Three-North" Shelter Forest Program refers to China's large-scale artificial forestry ecological projects in northwest China, northern China and western northeast China. The "Three-North" Shelter Forest Program starts from Heilongjiang in the east and reaches Xinjiang in the west, covering 13 provinces (autonomous regions and municipalities), including Xinjiang, Qinghai, Gansu, Ningxia, Inner Mongolia, Shaanxi, Shanxi, Hebei, Liaoning, Jilin, Heilongjiang, Beijing and Tianjin.

The "Three-North" regions are dotted with deserts, sandy areas and the vast gobi. Precipitation is scarce and droughts and other natural disasters are very serious. Therefore, the construction of the "Three-North" Shelter Forest is necessary for China to improve the ecological environment, reduce natural disasters and maintain living space. The program started in 1978 and is planned to end in 2050, in three phases and eight stages. It has the functions of preventing wind, fixing sand, conserving soil and water, regulating climate and improving the environment. At present, the "Three-North" Shelter Forest Program has built a number of shelter forest systems, initially curbing the trend of ecological deterioration in the "Three-North" regions and promoting regional rural industrial restructuring and economic development.

The "Three-North" Shelter Forest Program is large in scale, fast and highly effective, and is known as the China's Great Wall in green. In 2003, the "Three-North" Shelter Forest Program was awarded the Guinness Certificate for the largest afforestation project in the world.

Discussion

Are there any forest parks around your city? Can you describe it?

② Animal Husbandry

Required Reading Text

Animal Husbandry of China

Animal husbandry refers to raising animals and the herding of livestock. Animal husbandry is an important part of Chinese agriculture, and is one of the two pillars of agricultural production along with farming. Animal husbandry provides people with animal foods such as meat, milk, eggs and fat, as well as raw materials such as wool, skins, feathers and bones for light industry. In ancient times, cattle, horses and donkeys are important livestock for China's agriculture and transportation industry.

Chinese animal husbandry has a long history. During the primitive society, the ancient Chinese already artificially raised "six animals" such as horses, cattle, sheep, chickens, dogs, and pigs. In the Yellow River basin, people already started to raise birds and animals in captivity and domesticate cattle and horses. During the Xia, Shang and Zhou dynasties, veterinarians and horse breeding officials have emerged in China. The *Historical Records* recorded the breeding and herding activities of people during the Xia, Shang and Zhou dynasties. During the Spring and Autumn Period, cattle became the main animal power for farming. Idioms such as "Tian Ji's horse racing strategy" "Bo Le judging horses" and "thousands upon thousands of horses and soldiders" show that horses have become part of Chinese life.

In contemporary times, Chinese rural families raise animals such as pigs, cows, sheep, horses, chickens, ducks, geese, and rabbits. The domesticated economic animals in China include deer, foxes and minks. Chinese livestock are divided into two types: captive-bred and wild farmed. The main forms of production of livestock farming in China are dairy production, pig production, cattle and sheep production and egg and broiler production.

Extended Text

The Four Pastoral Regions

A pastoral area is an economic type of area with large amount of grassland resources and where grassland animal husbandry is the main production method. China's pastoral areas are mainly located in the west and northwest, of which the four major pastoral areas in China are Inner Mongolia Pastoral Area, Xinjiang Pastoral

Area, Xizang Pastoral Area and Qinghai Pastoral Area.

Inner Mongolia Pastoral Area, the largest natural pasture grazing area in China, extends from the Greater Khingan Mountains in the east to the Ejina Gobi in the west. The pasture area of Inner Mongolia Pastoral Area is the first in China, and the livestock breeds are mainly Sanhe cattle, Sanhe horses, red steppe cattle, Inner Mongolia fine-wool sheep, Ujimqin sheep, Inner Mongolia white cachmere goats, and bactrian camels. The main livestock products in pastoral area, such as wool, cashmere, woollen yarn, woollen material, and woollen blankets, occupy an important position in the country.

Xinjiang Pastoral Area is a mountainous pastoral area. The pastoral areas of Xinjiang are mainly located in north of the Tianshan Mountains in northern Xinjiang and the western parts of mountainous areas in western Xinjiang. The diverse types of pastures and the wide variety of forage species in pasture areas of Xinjiang provide favorable conditions for the development of many kinds of livestock. The main livestock breeds in the pastoral areas of Xinjiang include fine-wool sheep, lambskin sheep, Ili horses, Tacheng cattle, etc.

Xizang Pastoral Area is a unique alpine grassland livestock area. In recent years, Xizang Pastoral Areas have started to artificially plant pasture and expand pasture. The main livestock breeds in Xizang Pastoral Area are yaks, Xizang sheep, Xizang goats and yellow cows, etc., and the number of Xizang sheep and yaks is the largest.

Qinghai Pastoral Area, mainly located in the Qingnan Plateau, Qilian Mountains and Qaidam Basin, has a long history of animal husbandry.

Discussion

What kind of meat delicacies have you eaten in China? What are the similarities and differences with the meat cuisine in your country?

③ Fisheries

Required Reading Text

Fisheries of China

The fishery, also known as aquaculture, is a production business in which aquatic economic plants and animals inhabiting and breeding in the sea and inland waters are exploited for rational harvesting, artificial multiplication and breeding, as well as storage and processing of aquatic products. The fishery is an important part of Chinese agriculture, providing people with a wide variety of food, as well as important raw materials for the pharmaceutical and chemical industries. Fisheries are generally divided into marine fisheries and freshwater fisheries.

Chinese fishery production has a very long history. Fish is one of the main foods of primitive men. In the ancient Chinese work *The Classic of Mountains and Seas*, it is recorded that ancient Chinese could catch fish in the water with one hand. During the Xia, Shang and Zhou dynasties, shells became one of the important forms of currency. The state recognized the importance of fishing and prohibited fishing at certain times. During the Spring and Autumn Period and Warring States Period, a Chinese man named Fan Li summarized the techniques of fish farming and promoted them along the southeastern coast. During the same period, government officials who managed the fishing industry have also emerged in China.

After the Qin and Han dynasties, China's marine and freshwater fisheries developed simultaneously. As ships became larger and sailed farther, Chinese coastal fishermen gradually went offshore for fishing. Some fishermen also engaged in the transportation of people and goods while fishing. The government's management of the fishing industry also extended to the control of fishermen, fishing vessels and fishing areas. By now, fishing has become one of the important ways of earning a living for China's coastal residents.

Extended Text

Zhoushan Fishing Ground

Fishing grounds refer to the waters where fish and other aquatic economic animals are highly concentrated, suitable for fishing operations, and can obtain a certain yield. Chinese coastal fishermen have discovered many offshore fishing grounds during their long-term fishing activities, the largest of which is the Zhoushan Fishing Ground.

Zhoushan Fishing Ground is located in the northeast of Zhejiang Province in the East China Sea. Zhoushan Fishing Ground is the traditional fishing area of fishermen in Zhejiang, Jiangsu, Fujian and Shanghai. With a fishing history dating back to the Xia, Shang and Zhou dynasties, Zhoushan Fishing Ground has long been known for their rich fishing resources. During the Ming and Qing dynasties, Zhoushan Fishing Ground became one of the most important fishing grounds in China, with various fishing seasons throughout the year. The main fishery products of Zhoushan fishery are large yellow croakers, little yellow croakers, hairtails and cuttlefishes. Zhoushan Fishing Ground can be divided into eight fishing grounds, including Daji, Shengshan, Langgang, Huangze, Daiqu, Zhongjieshan, Yangan and Jintang Fishing Grounds.

In recent times, with the increase in the number of fishing boats and the construction of coastal industries, the marine fishery in Zhoushan Fishing Ground has been overfished and the sea has been polluted. The output of products in Zhoushan Fishing Ground has dropped sharply. After the 1980s, the fishing season in Zhoushan Fishing Ground could no longer be formed naturally. Therefore, the government imposed a closed season on various fishing grounds along the Chinese coast. During the closed season, coastal fishing boats were not allowed to fish in the sea.

Discussion

What Chinese fishery products have you seen or eaten? What are the similarities and differences with the fishery products in your country?

④ Minerals

Required Reading Text

Minerals of China

Minerals refer to all natural minerals or rock resources buried in the ground that can be used by human beings. China is one of the countries with the longest history of developing and utilizing mineral resources in the world.

During the primitive human period, the production and use of stone tools was the main marker to distinguish the Paleolithic and Neolithic periods. During the Xia, Shang and Zhou dynasties, China moved from the Stone Age to the Bronze Age, with the representative bronzes being the Houmuwu Square Cauldron. During the Spring and Autumn Period and the Warring States Period, China moved from the Bronze Age to the Iron Age. During the Qin and Han dynasties, the use of iron in China has been very common. In addition, gold became the main circulating object. During the Northern Song Dynasty, the production of gold, silver, copper, iron, lead, tin, mercury and other minerals reached historically unprecedented levels, and mineral taxes even became an important national revenue. The use of minerals in ancient China not only promoted the development of China's productive forces, but also promoted the development of politics, economy, culture and social progress.

At present, China has a wide variety of mineral resources with large reserves. Some of the mineral reserves rank among the best in the world, but the per capita possession is lower than the world average. China's mineral resources have more poor mines and fewer rich mines, more co-existing mines and fewer independent mines. China's mineral resources are unevenly distributed, showing a wide distribution but particularly concentrated reserves, such as more coal and rare earth in Northeast and North China, and more nonferrous metals and phosphorus in the south.

Extended Text

Minerals Distribution

China's main mineral resources are gold, silver, copper, iron and tungsten.

The gold ore is distributed in Jiaodong, Xiaoqinling (including westernregion of Henan Province), Heilongjiang, North China, Jidong, the Shaanxi-Gansu-Sichuan border area and Qilian Mountains area, Middle and Lower Yangtze River, and Guizhou, Guangxi and Yunnan border area.

Silver ore, which is very widely distributed in China, is mainly found in the northern Jiangxi, the Southern Shaanxi and the northwest Hubei, the south Henan, the north China-Jixi, Nanling, and the Jiangsu and Zhejiang. China is one of the first countries in the world to discover and utilize silver ore.

Copper ore, with relatively abundant resources, is mainly distributed in East and Southwest China, with specific provinces such as Jiangxi, Yunnan, Hubei, Shanghai, Jiangsu, Gansu, Anhui, Shanxi and Liaoning.

Iron ore is very widely distributed with abundant resource reserves, but the proportion of iron-rich ore is very small, mainly in Beijing, Shanxi, Inner Mongolia, Shandong, Hebei, Hubei, Yunnan, and Anhui.

Tungsten ore is an advantageous mineral resource in China. China is rich in tungsten ore and ranks first in the world in terms of reserves, production and export volume. China's tungsten ore is mainly distributed in Hunan, Jiangxi, Guangxi, Guangdong, and Yunnan.

Discussion

Please classify and explain the countries which are the main sources of mineral resources imported by China.

(5) Energy

Required Reading Text

Energy of China

Energy, a natural resource that produces various types of energy such as mechanical, thermal, light, electromagnetic, and chemical energy. China's major energy sources are coal, oil, natural gas, hydro-electric energy, and wind energy.

Coal. China is rich in coal resources and its reserves are among the highest in the world. The geographical distribution of China's coal resources is unbalanced, with more in the north and less in the south, more in the west and less in the east. China's northern coal resources are concentrated in Shanxi, Shaanxi, Inner Mongolia, Henan and Xinjiang; southern coal resources are concentrated in Sichuan, Yunnan and Guizhou.

Oil. The total amout of oil in China is relatively abundant, but its geographical distribution is uneven, with more in the east and west and less in the middle. China's land oil resources are concentrated in the basins of Songliao, Tarim, Junggar, North China, Sichuan and Ordos. China's offshore oil resources are mainly distributed in Bohai Bay.

Natural gas. China's natural gas is mainly coal-formed gas, mainly located in large basins such as Bohai Bay, Junggar, Tarim, Sichuan, Ordos, Qaidam and Songliao.

Hydro-electric energy. Hydro-electric energy is a renewable energy source. China is one of the countries in the world with relatively abundant Hydro-electric energy resources. China's hydro-electric energy resources are unevenly distributed, mainly concentrated in the southwest, northwest and south-central regions.

Wind-electric energy. Wind energy is a renewable energy source. China's wind energy is relatively abundant, with more concentrated areas in the southeast coast and its islands, northern Xinjiang, Inner Mongolia and northern Gansu.

Extended Text

The "Three Barrels of Oil"

The "three barrels of oil" are the abbreviations of three Chinese oil companies: China National Petroleum Corporation, China Petroleum & Chemical Corporation and China National Offshore Oil Corporation.

China National Petroleum Corporation, CNPC for short, is a central enterprise with its headquarter in Beijing and 15 oil fields under its management, including Daqing, Liaohe, Changqing, Xinjiang, Dagang, North China and Southwest oil fields. Founded in 1998, CNPC is a comprehensive international energy company and one of the top 500 companies in the world.

China Petroleum & Chemical Corporation, abbreviated as Sinopec, founded in 1983, is the largest supplier of refined oil products and petrochemicals in China, the world's largest oil refining company and one of the top 500 companies in the world.

China National Offshore Oil Corporation, abbreviated as CNOOC, is headquartered in Beijing and has five listed companies at home and abroad. Founded in 1982, CNOOC is the largest offshore oil and gas producer in China and one of the top 500 companies in the world.

Discussion

> Which countries does China mainly import its oil from? Which routes are used to transport oil to China?

6 Protected Areas

Required Reading Text

Nature Reserves

The nature reserve refers to a natural ecosystem and natural landscape area that the state has determined by law for long-term protection and basically left it change naturally.

There was a simple idea of nature protection in ancient China. *The Book of Yi Zhou* records, "in spring, mountains and forests were not boarded with axes to make the grass and trees grow; in summer, rivers and ponds were not netted to make the fish and turtles grow." It shows that officials at that time had measures to seal off the mountains and prohibit fishing in order to profect resources. The people also often spontaneously designated some areas where woodcutting was not allowed, and formulated a number of township rules and regulations to manage, some of which had the prototype of nature reserves.

Since the founding of the People's Republic of China, China has developed in the establishment of nature reserves. In 1956, the first natural reserve in China, Dinghu Mountain National Nature Reserve, was established in Guangdong Province. Since the 1970s, The cause of nature conservation in China has been developing rapidly. At present, there are 34 nature reserves in China that have joined the World Network of Biosphere Reserves, including Changbai Mountain, Dinghu Mountain and Wolong.

Changbai Mountain National Nature Reserve, located at the junction of Antu County, Fusong County and Changbai Korean Autonomous County, Jilin Province, mainly protects the volcanic landscape and forest ecosystem. The reserve was established in 1960 with a total area of 190000 hectares, of which 130000 hectares are absolute reserves and 60000 hectares are general reserves. With severe and long winters and warm and humid summers, this area is the only mountainous area with alpine tundra on the eastern continent of Asia.

Extended Text

Marine Nature Reserves

The marine nature reserve is an area where a certain area of coasts, estuaries, islands, wetlands or sea areas, including the object of protection, is divided by law for the purpose of marine natural environment and resource protection for special protection and management. The establishment of marine nature reserve is one of the most effective means to protect marine biodiversity and prevent the deterioration of the marine ecosystem. At the end of 1988, the State Oceanic Administration formulated and promulgated the *Outline for the Establishment of Marine Nature Reserves*.

In September 1990, five marine nature reserves were listed as the first batch of national marine nature reserves: Changli Golden Coast Nature Reserve in Hebei, which mainly protects the natural coastal landscape and the ecological environment of the sea area; Shankou Mangrove Nature Reserve in Guangxi, which mainly protects the mangrove ecosystem; Dazhou Island Marine Nature Reserve in Hainan, which mainly protects the golden swallows and its coastal ecological environment; Sarrya Coral Reef Nature Reserve in Hainan, which mainly protects coral reefs and their ecosystems; Coastal Nature Reserve of Nanji Island in Zhejiang, which mainly protects shells, algaes and their ecological environment.

In 1993, five marine nature reserves, including the Tianjin Ancient Coast and Wetland National Nature Reserve, joined the World Network of Biosphere Reserves. In 1995, the State Oceanic Administration promulgated the *Measures for the Management of Marine Nature Reserves*, which began to plan and manage marine nature reserves in accordance with the law.

Discussion

> Which nature reserves do you know about in China? Give a brief introduction.

Historical Evolution

Chapter 4

Ancient China (I)

1. Xia Dynasty

Required Reading Text

Xia Dynasty

The Xia Dynasty, the first slavery dynasty in Chinese history, was the first hereditary dynasty recorded in Chinese history. The Xia Dynasty was founded by Yu. The Xia Dynasty had 17 emperors and lasted for more than 400 years before it was finally destroyed by Tang.

The Xia Dynasty began when Shun ceded the position of tribal leader to Yu. After his death, Yu passed the throne to his son Qi, indicating that the hereditary system officially replaced the abdication system. This history is regarded as the beginning of family-controlled country in Chinese history. The territory of the Xia Dynasty stretched from the western part of Henan Province and the southern part of Shanxi Province in the west to the border of Henan Province and Shandong Province in the east, to the northern part of Hubei Province in the south, and to the southern part of Hebei Province in the north. After the establishment of the Xia Dynasty, the various tribes of it had patriarchal relations with the central royal family in terms of blood, by enfeoff in politics, and by supply and tax in economy. The reign of the Xia Dynasty was unstable and experienced changes such as the loss of the country by Tai Kang and the rise of the country by Shao Kang. The tyranny at the end of the Xia Dynasty led directly to the uprising of Tang who was the leader of the Shang tribe. Finally, the Xia Dynasty fell in the Battle of Mingtiao.

Extended Text

Emperor Yu's Flood Control

Emperor Yu's flood control, an ancient Chinese myth and legend, is one of famous legends of the great flood of ancient times.

During the Yao and Xun periods, the Central Plains of China was flooded, submerging crops and hills and flooding people's houses, displacing people and forcing them to leave their homes. In this situation, Yao was determined to eliminate the floods and began to search for someone who could control them. At first, Yu's father was elected to rule the floods, but he did not have any success for several years. When Shun became the leader of the tribal alliance, he sought the talents of his ministers to see who could control the floods. The ministers recommended Yu to control the floods. At that time, Yu had just been married for only four days. In order to control the floods, Yu had to leave his wife at home and passed by the house three times in several years without returning home. During the period of flood control, Yu led Bo Yi, Hou Ji and a group of assistants to travel around to investigate the geographical environment and design plans to control the water. Yu learned from his father's lesson of blocking water. He used the method of channeling, opening many rivers together with the mass, and finally diverting the floods to the sea successfully.

After 13 years of hard work, Yu finally succeeded in controlling the water. People re-established their homes and were no longer threatened by floods. Agricultural production also gradually resumed, and the people lived in peace.

Discussion

> Is there a legend of flood control in your country? What are the differences and similarities with Chinese legends of flood control?

② Shang Dynasty

Required Reading Text

Shang Dynasty

The Shang Dynasty, the second dynasty in Chinese history, lasted from about 1600 BC to 1046 BC. The Shang Dynasty had 31 emperors and lasted for more than 500 years.

The ancestors of the Shang Dynasty were from a tribe that emerged from the middle and lower reaches of the Yellow River. Legend has it that its ancestor Qi was a man with Yu at the same time. At the end of the Xia Dynasty, the Shang monarch, Tang, destroyed Xia in the Battle of Mingtiao and established the Shang Dynasty in Bo with Shang as the state name. At the beginning of the Shang Dynasty, the capital was frequently moved. After Pan Geng moved the capital to Yin, the capital of the Shang Dynasty was gradually stabilized. That is why the Shang Dynasty was also called Yin or Yinshang in later times. Due to the incompetence of Di Xin, the last ruler of the Shang Dynasty, the Zhou Dynasty rose up to invade the Shang Dynasty and defeated the Shang army in the Battle of Muye. Eventually, the Shang Dynasty was replaced by the Zhou Dynasty.

The Shang Dynasty was at the height of Chinese slavery. State power was initially established during the Shang Dynasty, and the social order of slavery was firmly established. Bronze smelting technology reached its peak during the Shang Dynasty, and a wide variety of bronze vessels was used for divination and ritual purposes. The representative of Shang bronze wares is the Houmuwu Square Cauldron, which is an outstanding work in the history of bronze casting. In addition, the inscriptions on bones or tortoise shells, which were the earliest mature script in China, had already appeared during the Shang Dynasty and were used to record divination records and divination rhetoric during the Shang Dynasty.

Extended Text

Pan Geng's Migration to Yin

The migration of Pan Geng to Yin was a historical event that took place in the middle and late Shang Dynasty, when Pan Geng decided to move the capital to Yin to save the country from a political crisis.

At the beginning of the Shang Dynasty, the capital was set at Bo. During the next 300 years, the capital of the Shang Dynasty was moved five times. At the beginning of the reign of Emperor Pan Geng, the north of the Yellow River was threatened by floods and frequent political crises within the royal family. Therefore, Pan Geng decided to move the capital to Yin. Due to the frequent relocation of the capital by the previous Shang monarchs, people were suffering and they did not want to move again. At the same time, the nobles were also reluctant to move the capital because of their desire for comfort. Pan Geng's decision to move the capital was opposed by almost all the people in the country. However, Pan Geng still insisted on moving the capital. He urged the nobles to move the capital with him, while severely suppressing the opposing people. Pan Geng defeated the opposition, taking his people across the Yellow River and moving the capital to Yin.

After Pan Geng's move to Yin, the capital of the Shang Dynasty was finally fixed in Yin, and the people no longer suffered from frequent capital moves. As a result, the political situation of the Shang Dynasty was stable, and the political, economic and cultural development flourished. For more than 250 years during the late Shang Dynasty, Yin became the center of the nation's political, economic, and cultural development.

Discussion

> Which Chinese bronze artifacts have you seen? Talk about the bronzes you know about.

③ Zhou Dynasty

Required Reading Text

Zhou Dynasty

The Zhou Dynasty was the third slavery dynasty in Chinese history after the Shang Dynasty. The Zhou Dynasty inherited the state system of the Xia and Shang dynasties, and was the turning point in the development of ancient Chinese slavery society to its peak and the beginning of its decline.

The Zhou was an ancient tribe that lived on the Loess Plateau which located in today's central Shaanxi and eastern Gansu provinces. During the Shang Dynasty, Zhou was one of its vassal states. When King Wen of Zhou was the head of the Zhou State, the Zhou State was strong and powerful. In 1046 BC, King Wu of Zhou, the son of Wen, led his troops to fight against the Shang army at Muye. The Battle of Muye overthrew the Shang Dynasty and the Zhou army won a great victory establishing the Zhou Dynasty. The Zhou Dynasty was divided into two periods: Western Zhou and Eastern Zhou. In 771 BC, the Western Zhou Dynasty fell. In 770 BC, Emperor Ping of Zhou moved eastward and re-established the Zhou Dynasty, which was called the Eastern Zhou. The Eastern Zhou was divided into two periods: the Spring and Autumn Period and the Warring States Period, with the event of "Partition of Jin by Three Families" as the node. In 249 BC, Qin destroyed the Eastern Zhou.

After Wu established the Zhou Dynasty, politically, he implemented an enfoffment system of feudal royal families and meritorious officials. Economically, the Zhou Dynasty implemented the nine-square system, which promoted the development of small farming economy and improved productivity. Culturally, the Zhou Dynasty practiced the rites and music system to regulate the internal relations of the nobility and maintain the feudal rule.

Extended Text

Contention of a Hundred Schools of Thought

The Contention of a Hundred Schools of Thought refers to the situation and culture of academic debates during the Spring and Autumn Period and Warring States Period. The Warring States Period was a time of great social change, and various social conflicts were intricate and complex. The intense political struggle and economic and cultural prosperity had a profound impact on all social classes at that time. People expressed their attitudes and put forward their ideas, wishes and demands on many issues in the great social changes at that time. The various schools of thought during the Warring States Period wrote books and discussed politics, which contributed to the social change and cultural development.

The four most influential schools of thought are Confucianism, Legalism, Taoism, and Mohism. The founder of Confucianism was Confucius. He traveled around the world and put forward ideas such as "governance based on virtue" "to subdue yourself and return to propriety" "education for all without distinction". In his later years, Confucius wrote books and devoted himself to teaching. Mencius and Xun Zi inherited and developed Confucianism from Confucius. Among a hundred schools of thought, Confucianism has had the most profound influence on China.

The representative figure of Legalism was Han Feizi. Han Feizi was the master of Legalism in pre-Qin Dynasty. He advocated strict punishment and harsh laws. The founder of Taoism was Lao Zi. Zhuang Zi inherited and developed Lao Zi's ideas and was the representative figure of Taoism during the Warring States Period. The founder of Mohism was Mo Zi, who proposed the theories of "universal love" "denouning unjust wars" and "concurrent love and mutual benefit".

The various academic ideas formed during this period became the main source of Chinese thought and culture in the future.

Discussion

Give an example of a Chinese idiom story of the Zhou Dynasty and briefly explain its historical background.

④ Qin Dynasty

Required Reading Text

Qin Dynasty

The Qin Dynasty was the first unified feudal dynasty in Chinese history. In 359 BC, Duke Xiao of Qin relied on Shang Yang to change the law, which led to the economic development of Qin and made it the richest vassal state in the late Warring States Period. King Yingzheng of Qin destroyed the six states of Han, Wei, Chu, Yan, Zhao and Qi one after another and completed the unification of China. In 221 BC, Ying Zheng became the emperor and was called Qin Shi Huang (the first emperor).

The Qin Dynasty abolished the enfoffment system and established the prefecture-country system to govern the whole country. The Qin Dynasty unified the writing script, the width of vehicles and the units of measurement. Externally, the Qin Dynasty conquered the Xiongnu in the north and the Baiyue in the south, and built the Great Wall to resist foreign invasion from the north. Internally, the Qin Dynasty built the Chi Road to improve transportation throughout the country. The Chi Road was the earliest national road in Chinese history, centering on Xianyang, the capital of the

Qin Dynasty, and leading to all parts of the country. In 210 BC, Qin Shi Huang fell ill and died, and his son Hu Hai took the throne. In 209 BC, Chen Sheng and Wu Guang started a peasant uprising. In 207 BC, the Qin Dynasty fell.

The Qin Dynasty ended the 500-year division of the lords since the Spring and Autumn Period and the Warring States Period, and became the first centralized state in Chinese history. The Qin Dynasty's centralized system laid the foundation for the rule of a great unified dynasty in China and had a profound impact on Chinese history.

Extended Text

The Battle of Qin's Destruction of the Six Powers

The battle of Qin's destruction of the six powers, also known as the war of Qin Unification, refers to the war in which the state of Qin destroyed six other vassal states and completed the unification of China at the end of the Warring States Period. In 238 BC, King Ying Zheng of Qin, with the assistance of Li Si and Yu Liao, adopted a foreign policy of befriending distant states while attacking those nearby to eliminate each of them. The specific measures were to enlist Yan and Qi, stabilize Wei and Chu, and destroy Han and Zhao.

Since the reforms of Shang Yang, Qin's economy developed rapidly and its army was strong. After the reign of King Ying Zheng, Qin became stronger and stronger, while the other six states had declined. In 230 BC, Qin destroyed Han. In 228 BC, Qin captured Handan and took the king of Zhao, Qian, as captives. Duke Jia of Zhao fled to the city of Dai, and he called himself the King of Dai. In 226 BC, Qin invaded the capital of Yan, Ji, and King of Yan, Xi, moved his capital to Liaodong. In 225 BC, Qin captured Daliang and Wei fell. In 223 BC, Qin destroyed the state of Chu. In 222 BC, Qin destroyed Yan, captured King Jia, and Zhao fell. In 221 BC, Qin destroyed the state of Qi. Thus, Qin destroyed the six powers and unified China.

During the battle of Qin's destruction of the six powers, Yan sent Jing Ke to assassinate the King of Qin, which is known as Jing Ke's assassination attempt on the King of Qin. In 1998, Chinese director Chen Kaige made the film *The Emperor and the Assassin*, which is the story of the assassination of the King of Qin. In 2002, Chinese director Zhang Yimou's film *Hero* was also based on this story.

Discussion

> What Chinese movies and novels do you know that are set in the Qin Dynasty?

⑤ Han Dynasty

Required Reading Text

Han Dynasty

The Han Dynasty was another great unification dynasty in China after the Qin Dynasty. The Han Dynasty was divided into two periods, the Western Han and the Eastern Han, with 29 emperors, lasting for more than 400 years. The Han Dynasty was the most advanced civilization and powerful empire in the world at that time.

In the peasant uprising at the end of the Qin Dynasty, Liu Bang overthrew the Qin Dynasty and was crowned King of Han. Liu Bang defeated Xiang Yu in the Chu-Han War. In 202 BC, Liu Bang became the emperor and established the Han Dynasty with the capital at Chang'an, which was called the Western Han Dynasty. The early years of the Western Han Dynasty basically followed the political system of the Qin Dynasty. Liu Bang, Emperor Gaozu of Han, organized the demobilization of the army, recruited exiles, stabilized people's lives, and restored and developed production. After that, Emperor Wen of Han and Emperor Jing of Han implemented the state policy of rest and recuperation, creating the prosperity in the reign of Wen and Jing. After the reign of Emperor Wu of Han, the fourth emperor of the Western Han Dynasty, he strengthened centralized power by sending Zhang Qian to the West to open up the Silk Road and defeat the Xiongnu in the north, which initiated the great unity. During the reign of Emperor Xuan, the Western Han Dynasty reached the peak of its power, and the Western region was incorporated into China's territory. It was called steadiness in the reign of Zhao and Xuan in history. In 8 AD, the Western Han Dynasty fell.

In 25 AD, Liu Xiu rebuilt the Han Dynasty and set the capital at Luoyang, which was called the Eastern Han Dynasty. After the reign of Liu Xiu, he resettled the exiles, lightened the tax and rested, so that the political and economic development was possible. After the reign of Emperor He, he sent Ban Chao to manage the western region and the Silk Road was extended to Europe. In 166 AD, the Roman Empire sent ambassadors to China. In 190 AD, there were frequent uprising in various parts of the Han Dynasty, and the world was in chaos. In 220 AD, the Han Dynasty fell.

Extended Text

Wang Mang's Reform

Wang Mang's reform was a series of new measures taken by the new emperor Wang Mang to ease the growing social conflicts in the late Western Han Dynasty. Wang Mang, the founding emperor of the new dynasty, was a political reformer. Wang Mang was born in 45 BC. In 8 BC, Wang Mang became the grand secretary, the highest military governor of the Western Han Dynasty. In 8 AD, Wang Mang proclaimed himself emperor and changed the name of his country to "Xin".

After the establishment of the new dynasty, Wang Mang began to carry out comprehensive social reforms, including land reform, commercial reform and currency reform. In 9 AD, in response to the most prominent land issue of the Western Han Dynasty, Wang Mang issued a decree abolishing the private ownership of land and implementing a state-owned system of land, which could not be bought or sold by private individuals. In 10 AD, Wang Mang appointed officials to manage market prices in Chang'an and the five major cities of the country. Wine, salt and iron were sold exclusively by the state, and no private business was allowed. The state was to monopolize the currency and private individuals were not allowed to mint money.

Wang Mang's land state policy was strongly opposed by landowners and big merchants, some of whom even raised armies against it. Wang Mang's commercial policies strengthened the centralization of power and were a continuation of the economic policies under Emperor Wu, but later became a tool for noble officials to make profits. The monetary reform essentially exploited the wealth of the common people and became one of the reasons for the rapid demise of the Xin Dynasty.

Discussion

> What events and stories do you know about the Han Dynasty in China?

⑥ Jin Dynasty

● Required Reading Text

Jin Dynasty

The Jin Dynasty, a unified dynasty after the Three Kingdoms Period. After the fall of the Eastern Han Dynasty, China entered the Three Kingdoms Period of Wei, Shu and Wu. After that, the Jin Dynasty unified China. The Jin Dynasty was divided into two periods, the Western Jin and the Eastern Jin, of which the Western Jin was a great unification dynasty and the Eastern Jin was one of the six dynasties in southern China. The Jin Dynasty had 15 emperors, lasting for 155 years.

In 265, Sima Yan seized the power of Wei and established the Jin Dynasty, with the capital in Luoyang, known as the Western Jin. Sima Yan was the first emperor of the Jin Dynasty, known as Emperor Wu of Jin in history. In 280, Western Jin destroyed the state of Wu and completed the unification of China. When Emperor Wu of Jin was working to unify the country, he enacted many important political and economic measures and received some results, which are known as the rule of Tai Kang. In 316, the Western Jin Dynasty was extinguished. In the following year, Sima Rui, a member of the Western Jin royal family, continued the Jin Dynasty in southern China, which was called the Eastern Jin Dynasty. In 420, Liu Yu established the Song Dynasty, which was known as the Southern Song Dynasty. At this point, the Eastern Jin Dynasty fell and Chinese history entered the period of the Northern and Southern dynasties.

During the period of the two Jin dynasties, Chinese culture had new developments in literature, art, history and science and technology, represented by Tao Yuanming's *Land of Peach Blossoms*, Wang Xizhi's *The Orchid Pavilion Preface* and Liu Hui's *Sea Island Arithmetic*. At the end of the Western Jin Dynasty, the social unrest in northern China led to the migration of a large number of people southward, and the economic barycenter of China gradually shifted from the north to the south.

● Extended Text

The Battle of Feishui

The Battle of Feishui, which took place in 383, is a famous example in Chinese history of the victory of fewer over many.

After the fall of the Western Jin Dynasty, various minority regimes in northern China were established one after another. In 357, Fu Jian, the great general of the former Qin state, took control of the country. He rehired Wang Meng to strengthen the state. By 376, the former Qin state had destroyed the former Yan, former Liang and Dai and unified northern China.

In 373, Fu Jian captured the Liang and Yi states of the Eastern Jin Dynasty. Thereafter, after a year of hard fighting, the former Qin State captured Xiangyang and Pengcheng, the military strongholds of the Eastern Jin. In order to unify the whole country, Fu Jian launched an attack on the Eastern Jin despite the opposition of the people. In 383, General Fu Jian personally led an army to attack the Eastern Jin. The Eastern Jin sent General Xie Shi and General Xie Xuan to the north to fight. Both sides encountered at the Feishui. Facing the former Qin army which did not all arrive, Xie Shi decided to change his defense and attack immediately. The former Qin army moved backwards, trying to wait for the Eastern Jin army to cross the river before launching an attack. As a result, during the movement, confusion occurred in the rear of the former Qin army. Then, the Eastern Jin army seized the opportunity and launched an attack. Eventually, the former Qin army was defeated.

After the defeat, the former Qin army, which had absolute superiority, gradually declined and went into disintegration. The victory of Eastern Jin prevented a major disruption and destruction in the south and allowed economic and cultural development to continue. The Eastern Jin's generals Xie Xuan, Xie An and Xie Shi were also recorded in the history books for this battle.

Discussion

What are other battles with fewer trops defeating larger ones in China? Does your country have similar battles?

Chapter 5

Ancient China (Ⅱ)

1 Sui Dynasty

Required Reading Text

Sui Dynasty

The Sui Dynasty, another unified dynasty after the Jin Dynasty, had two emperors and lasted 37 years. The first emperor of the Sui Dynasty was Yang Jian, known as Emperor Wen of Sui. During his tenure as emperor, Yang Jian made a series of reforms in political and economic systems and implemented the system of Three Departments and Six Ministries in the central government to consolidate centralized power. Yang Jian reduced taxes several times to promote national agricultural production and stabilize economic development. After Yang Jian's death in 604, his son Yang Guang became the emperor. Yang Guang was known as Emperor Yang of Sui. During his tenure as emperor, Yang Guang built national granaries around Luoyang city. He ordered the digging of the Grand Canal to connect the economic region in the south, the political region in the Central Plains and the military region in the north. He ordered the construction of the Chi Roads and the Great Wall, which promoted the social and economic development as a whole. In 618, the Sui Dynasty fell.

After the Sui Dynasty destroyed Chen and unified the country, its territory extended from the Liao River in the east, to the desert in the north, to Dunhuang in the west, and to Jiaozhi in the south. During the Sui Dynasty, China made a series of achievements in science and technology. Li Chun designed and presided over the construction of the Zhaozhou Bridge, which had the most advanced level of bridge engineering in the world at that time and predated Europe by more than 700 years. Liu Zhuo was the first to propose the formula of "equidistant quadratic interpolation" when he formulated the Imperial Calendar. Lu Fayan's *Cut the Rhyme* laid the foundation for phonetics.

Extended Text

The System of Three Departments and Six Ministries

The system of Three Departments and Six Ministries was a centralized official system in ancient feudal China. It was established in the Sui Dynasty and continued until the end of the Qing Dynasty.

The Three Departments refer to the Department of Imperial Secretariats, Department, and Department of Imperial Affairs. The Department of Imperial Secretariats, an agency for issuing governmental orders, was first set up in the State of Wei during the Three Kingdoms Period. In the Song Dynasty, the Department of Imperial Secretariats was merged with the Department of Chancellor. At the beginning of the Ming Dynasty, the Department of Imperial Secretariats was abolished. The Department of Chancellors, which was in charge of administrative affairs together with the Department of Imperial Secretariats and was responsible for reviewing and signing decrees, was first set up in the Eastern Han Dynasty. Originally an advisory body to the emperor, The Department of Chancellors gradually became the center of the central government organs. The Department of Imperial Affairs, the highest administrative body of the state, developed from the secretarial organ of the emperor in the Han Dynasty. The organization of the Department of Imperial Affairs was finalized in the Sui Dynasty, with six ministries under its jurisdiction, which were responsible for executing imperial edicts.

The six ministries were the Ministry of Personnel, the Ministry of Household Registration, the Ministry of Rites, the Ministry of Wars, the Ministry of Justice, and the Ministry of Works. The Ministry of Personnel was in charge of the appointment, dismissal, examination, promotion and transfer of officials throughout the country. The Ministry of Household Registration was in charge of the national household registration, land and taxation. The Ministry of Rites was in charge of ceremonial systems, such as rituals and music, schools, clothes and crowns, and registers of investitures. The Ministry of Wars was in charge of officers, soldiers, military equipment, and military orders throughout the country. The Ministry of Justice was in charge of all kinds of laws in the country and reviewed cases in various places. The Ministry of Works was in charge of all engineering works, craftsmen and water works.

Discussion

> Do you know any water conservancy projects in Chinese history? Describe them briefly.

② Tang Dynasty

Required Reading Text

Tang Dynasty

The Tang Dynasty was another great unification dynasty after the Sui Dynasty. The Tang Dynasty had 21 emperors and lasted 289 years. The Tang Dynasty was one of the most powerful countries in the world at that time, and had interactions with Asian and European countries. After the Tang Dynasty, the Chinese were often called Tang people overseas and now the Chinese settlements overseas was called Chinatown.

At the end of the Sui Dynasty, the world was in chaos. In 618, Li Yuan became the emperor, established the Tang Dynasty and set the capital in Chang'an. In 626, Li Shimin became the second emperor of the Tang Dynasty and was called Emperor Taizong of Tang. In 628, the Tang Dynasty unified the whole country. Li Shimin practiced economy and improved a series of political systems such as the system of Three Departments and Six Ministries and the imperial examination system, which led to a more stable society. In addition, he actively resisted foreign invasion, promoted ethnic integration and stabilized the frontier. This historical period is known as the "Prosperity of Zhenguan".

In 712, Li Longji succeeded to the throne and was known as Emperor Xuanzong of Tang. During the reign of Emperor Xuanzong, the Tang Dynasty became stronger than ever and was known as the flourishing Kaiyuan reign period. In 755, An Lushan, the general of Tang Dynasty, started a rebellion and the Tang Dynasty turned from prosperity to decline. In 907, the Tang Dynasty fell.

Extended Text

Wu Zetian

Wu Zetian, born in 624, was a native of Shanxi. Wu Zetian was the only female emperor in Chinese history. Wu Zetian became the emperor at the age of 67 and died at the age of 82.

In 635, Wu Zetian's father died of illness and she moved to Chang'an with her mother. In 637, at the age of 14, Wu Zetian was chosen to enter the imperial palace. In 655, Wu Zetian became the empress. In 660, Emperor Li Zhi was unable to deal with state affairs due to illness; Wu Zetian participated in the management of state affairs, and gradually formed the two sages pattern in which Li Zhi and Wu Zetian were in charge of the imperial government together. After Li Zhi's death, Wu Zetian became the empress dowager to manage the country. In 690, Wu Zetian became the emperor, established Wu Zhou, and set the capital in Luoyang.

During her tenure as the emperor, Wu Zetian fought against conservative forces with vested interests, creating favorable conditions for social progress and economic development. In addition, Wu Zetian attached importance to the selection of talents and further improved the imperial examination system. Wu Zetian strengthened the management of officials, rectified the rule of officials, and severely punished corruption. Wu Zetian attached importance to the development of agriculture, reduced the taxation of farmers, and promoted advanced agricultural production experience and production techniques.

In 705, Chancellor Zhang Jianzhi and others staged a coup to restore the Tang Dynasty. In the same year, Wu Zetian died of illness.

Discussion

What movies and TV shows have you seen about the Tang Dynasty in China? Briefly talk about your experience.

③ Song Dynasty

Required Reading Text

Song Dynasty

The Song Dynasty was divided into two phases: the Northern Song and the Southern Song, with 18 emperors, surviving for a total of 319 years. The Song Dynasty was a time in Chinese history when the commodity economy, culture and education, and technological innovation were highly prosperous.

In 960, Zhao Kuangyin established the Song Dynasty, which was known as the Northern Song. Zhao Kuangyin was the first emperor of the Northern Song Dynasty and was known as Emperor Taizu of Song. Zhao Kuangyin strengthened centralized power and deprived military generals of military power. Zhao Guangyi, the younger brother of Zhao Kuangyin, unified the country during his tenure as the emperor. In 1004, the Northern Song Dynasty signed an oath of alliance with the Liao Dynasty to avoid war. After that, the society tended to be stable and the economy gradually prospered. During the reign of Emperor Shenzong of the Song Dynasty, Wang Anshi, a famous reformer, carried out reforms of national policies, known as Wang Anshi's Reform. In 1120, the Northern Song Dynasty allied with the Jin Dynasty and jointly attacked the Liao Dynasty. In 1125, the Jin Dynasty destroyed the Liao Dynasty. In 1127, the Jin Dynasty invaded south and the Northern Song Dynasty was destroyed.

In 1127, Zhao Gou re-established the Song Dynasty in Nanjing, which was called the Southern Song Dynasty. In 1141, the Southern Song Dynasty made peace with the Jin Dynasty and ended the war. In 1234, the Southern Song Dynasty united with Mongolia to destroy the Jin Dynasty. In 1276, the Yuan Dynasty captured the capital of the Southern Song Dynasty, Lin'an, and the Southern Song Dynasty fell.

Extended Text

Wang Anshi's Reform

Wang Anshi's Reform was a political reform movement led by Wang Anshi during the Northern Song Dynasty. The aim of Wang Anshi's Reform was to develop production, enrich the country, strengthen the army, and save the Northern Song Dynasty from political crisis. It covered all aspects of politics, economy, military, society, and culture. Wang Anshi's Reform was another large-scale political reform movement in ancient Chinese history after Shang Yang's Reform.

Wang Anshi, born in 1021, was a Chinese politician, writer, thinker and reformer during the Northern Song Dynasty. In 1047, at the age of 27, Wang Anshi served as the magistrate of Yin County. During his four-year tenure, Wang Anshi built water conservancy and expanded schools. In 1059, Wang Anshi systematically put forward the idea of politicall reform. Wang Anshi summarized his years of experience as a local official and pointed out that the country was facing many economic, social and defense problems. In 1068, the Emperor Shenzong of Song appointed Wang Anshi to preside over the reform. The following year, Wang Anshi began a large-scale reform movement throughout the country, promulgating a series of decrees. These decrees were mainly concerned with finance and military affairs.

Wang Anshi's reforms offended the interests of the conservatives and were opposed. In 1085, when Emperor Shenzong of Song died and Emperor Zhezong of Song took the throne, Wang Anshi's Reform was ceased. The government's revenue increased dramatically and the country's power increased through the reforms.

Discussion

> Name one historical figure in China during the Song Dynasty and briefly talk about his deeds.

(4) Yuan Dynasty

Required Reading Text

Yuan Dynasty

The Yuan Dynasty was the first unified dynasty in Chinese history founded by an ethnic minority, lasting from 1271 to 1368.

In 1206, Temujin unified Mongolia and established the Great Mongolian Empire. It successively destroyed the Western Liao, Western Xia and Jin Dynasty one after another. In 1260, Kublai Khan succeeded to the throne and became the founder of the Yuan Dynasty. In 1271, Kublai Khan established the Yuan Dynasty. In 1276, the Yuan Dynasty destroyed the Southern Song Dynasty and unified China. After that, the Yuan Dynasty continued its foreign expansion. In the middle and late Yuan Dynasty, political corruption was serious and ethnic conflicts intensified. In 1368, Zhu Yuanzhang established the Ming Dynasty. The Yuan Dynasty retreated to the north and was called the Northern Yuan. In 1402, the Northern Yuan was destroyed.

During the Yuan Dynasty, China's territory was larger than that of any other dynasties. The territory of the Yuan Dynasty stretched from the Sea of Japan in the east, to the Tianshan Mountains in the west, from Lake Baikal in the north to the South China Sea in the south. The Yuan Dynasty implemented a system of local provinces, which influenced the administrative system of modern China. To maintain the autocratic dominance of the Mongol aristocracy, the Yuan Dynasty practiced a hierarchy that divided the Chinese into four classes, with the Mongols being the first class. The Yuan Dynasty had a prosperous commodity economy and overseas trade, with frequent diplomatic exchanges with various countries. The Yuan Dynasty was the first dynasty in Chinese history to use paper money as the currency in circulation.

Extended Text

The Great Mongolian Empire

The Great Mongolian Empire refers to the Mongolian regime established by the Mongolian Temujin in the 13th century. Temujin is an outstanding military and political figure in world history. Temujin was born in 1162. In 1189, Temujin was elected as the chief of the Mongols. In 1206, Temujin established the Great Mongolian Empire and was respectfully called Genghis Khan. Temujin died in 1227 at the age of 66.

After the establishment of the Great Mongolian Empire, the country was repeatedly expanded and successively occupied a vast area including East Asia, Central Asia, West Asia and Eastern Europe. In 1218, the Great Mongol Empire destroyed Western Liao and fought westward to the Volga River valley. 1227, the Great Mongolian Empire destroyed Western Xia and in 1234, the Great Mongol Empire destroyed the Jin Dynasty. In 1237, the Great Mongolian Empire occupied Moscow. In 1241, the Great Mongolian Empire invaded Poland, Hungary, Slovakia and the Czech Republic in two ways and arrived near Vienna, Austria. In 1253, the Great Mongolian Empire destroyed the Dali Kingdom. In 1258, the Great Mongolian Empire occupied Baghdad, the capital of Arab Empire. After 1259, the Great Mongolian Empire was gradually split into Yuan Dynasty and four other states.

The establishment of the Great Mongolian Empire accelerated the spread of culture and technology between the East and the West and promoted the cultural exchange of multiple ethnic groups.

Discussion

> Which foreigners do you know came to China in ancient times? What were their deeds?

⑤ Ming Dynasty

Required Reading Text

Ming Dynasty

The Ming Dynasty was the unified dynasty after the Yuan Dynasty. The Ming Dynasty had 16 emperors and lasted 276 years in total. The capital of the Ming Dynasty was set in Nanjing at the beginning and later moved to Beijing.

In 1364, Zhu Yuanzhang established the Western Wu Dynasty. In 1368, Zhu Yuanzhang became the emperor and established the Ming Dynasty with its capital in Nanjing. Afterwards, after several wars, the Ming Dynasty unified China. In 1421, Zhuli, Emperor Chengzu of Ming, moved the capital to Beijing. At the beginning of the Ming Dynasty, the politics was clear, the country was strong, and the society and economy were restored and developed. In 1449, after the Incident of Tumu Fortress, the Ming Dynasty changed from prosperity to decline. During the Wanli period, with the implementation of Zhang Juzheng's reforms, the Ming Dynasty became strong again. During the late Ming Dynasty, political corruption, natural disasters and foreign invasions led to the decline of the country's strength. In 1644, Li Zicheng invaded Beijing and the Ming Dynasty came to an end. After that, several regimes were established in southern China, which were called the Southern Ming. In 1662, the Southern Ming was overthrown.

During the Ming Dynasty, the centralized power system was strengthened and the multi-ethnic state was further unified and consolidated. During the Ming Dynasty, handicraft and commodity economy flourished, and a large amount of commercial capital was transformed into industrial capital, with the emergence of commercial towns and the sprouting of capitalism. Culture and art in the Ming Dynasty showed a trend of secularization, and novels such as *Journey to the West*, *Water Margin* and *Romance of the Three Kingdoms* were created in this period.

Extended Text

Novels of the Ming Dynasty

The novel of the Ming Dynasty, a subject of Chinese literary creation, was developed on the basis of the art of speaking in the Song and Yuan dynasties. During the Ming Dynasty, the novel saw unprecedented prosperity, fully demonstrating its social role and literary value. In the history of Chinese literature, the novel of the Ming Dynasty achieved a status comparable to that of the poetry of the Tang Dynasty, the lyrics of the Song Dynasty and the opera of the Yuan Dynasty. The famous novels of the Ming Dynasty include *Journey to the West*, *Water Margin* and *Romance of the Three Kingdoms*.

Journey to the West was written by Wu Chengen. The novel mainly depicts the story that the Monkey King, who makes a big disturbance in the Heavenly Palace, meets the Tang Monk, the Pig, the Monk Sha and the White Dragon Horse, and travels westward together to get the scriptures through hardship along the way, and finally arrives at the Western Heaven to meet the Buddha. The novel is based on the historical event of the Tang monk taking the scriptures.

Water Margin was written by Shi Nai'an. The novel mainly depicts the story that in the late Northern Song Dynasty, led by Song Jiang, 108 ture men gathered in Liangshan Marsh of Shandong Province. The novel is based on the historical event Song Jiang uprising as the background.

Romance of the Three Kingdoms was written by Luo Guanzhong. The novel is roughly divided into five parts: the Yellow Turbans uprising, the Dong Zhuo's rebellion, the feudal lords of the Three Kingdoms vying for the throne, the Three Kingdoms, and the return of the Three Kingdoms to the Jin Dynasty, depicting nearly 100 years of history from the end of the Eastern Han Dynasty to the beginning of the Western Jin Dynasty.

Discussion

> When did China interacted with your country? Explain briefly.

⑥ Qing Dynasty

● Required Reading Text

Qing Dynasty

The Qing Dynasty, the last feudal dynasty in Chinese history, was the second great unification dynasty established by an ethnic group. The Qing dynasty was ruled by the Jurchen, also known as the "Manchu". In 1616, Jurchen established the Later Jin. In 1636, Huangtaiji became the emperor and established the Qing Dynasty. In 1644, Ming general Wu Sangui surrendered to the Qing Dynasty, and the Qing army set the capital in Beijing. Thus, the Qing Dynasty became the central dynasty ruling China. Subsequently, the Qing Dynasty destroyed various regimes, put down rebellions, recovered Taiwan and unified China.

During the early Qing Dynasty, Chinese traditional society achieved unprecedented development and the country's comprehensive national power was strong. The Qing Dynasty rewarded land reclamation and reduced taxes, so the area of reclaimed land increased throughout the country. The handicraft industry of the Qing Dynasty was mainly textile and porcelain, with Jingdezhen in Jiangxi Province as the porcelain center. The Qing Dynasty developed commerce and had prosperous cities, forming a regional commercial center. With the development of commerce, ten merchant gangs were formed nationwide, among which Shanxi and Anhui merchants dominated the country's financial industry.

In 1840, the Qing Dynasty was invaded by western countries and signed a large number of unequal treaties. At the same time, in the face of internal and external problems, the Qing government also actively carried out the exploration and reform of modernization such as the Westernization Movement and the Hundred Days Reform. In 1912, the last emperor of the Qing Dynasty, Aisin Gioro Puyi, announced his abdication and the Qing Dynasty ended.

● Extended Text

Complete Library in the Four Branches of Literature

Complete Library in the Four Branches of Literature, or *Siku Quan Shu*, was a large series of books compiled during the Qianlong period of the Qing Dynasty. Complete Library in the Four Branches of Literature was the largest cultural project in ancient China, providing a systematic and comprehensive summary of classical Chinese culture. The book presents the structure of knowledge of classical Chinese culture.

Complete Library in the Four Branches of Literature was presided over by Emperor Qianlong, and more than 360 officials and scholars participated in its compilation, which took 13 years to complete. The collection is divided into four parts: Confucian classics, history, philosophy and literature, hence named "Siku", which contains 3503 kinds of books, 79337 volumes and is bound into more than 36000 volumes. In order to store the Complete Library in the Four Branches of Literature, Emperor Qianlong built a book collection pavilion modeled after the building of the Ningbo Book Collection "Tianyi Pavilion". There are seven sets of the Complete Library in the Four Branches of Literature, four of which are stored in northern China and the other three in Yangzhou, Zhenjiang and Hangzhou in the south.

During the 200 years since the completion of the Complete Library in the Four Branches of Literature, many sets have been destroyed by war. Complete Library in the Four Branches of Literature, now in the Taipei Palace Museum, is one of the better-preserved ones. Complete Library in the Four Branches of Literature, which preserves a large number of Chinese documents from all generations, has had a tremendous impact on the cultural development of that time and later, and is a treasure trove of traditional Chinese culture.

Discussion

> Does your country have a literature collection similar to the Chinese Complete Library in the Four Branches of Literature? Give a brief description.

Chapter 6

Modern Times

① Opium War

● Required Reading Text

Opium War

The Opium War refers to a war of aggression waged by Britain against China from 1840 to 1842. The Opium War was the beginning of modern Chinese history.

At the beginning of the 19th century, Britain became the most powerful country in the world in terms of capitalism and established the sun-never-set empire. During the same period, the Qing Dynasty was still an independent feudal state, and the natural economy of self-sufficiency dominated the Chinese society. In the Sino-British trade, China was dominant. To change this situation, Britain smuggled large quantities of opium into China. The Chinese government's dispatch of Lin Zexu to ban opium in Guangzhou became the cause of the Sino-British War.

In August 1839, after the news of Lin Zexu's ban on smoking reached London, the British government began to plan a war against China. In April 1840, the British Parliament passed a resolution to launch a war against China. In June, the British fleet arrived off the mouth of the Pearl River and blockaded the Haikou to cut off China's foreign trade. Subsequently, British troops captured Zhoushan Island in Zhejiang Province as a forward base. In January 1841, the British occupied Hong Kong, and in October, occupied Ningbo of Zhejiang Province. In June 1842, the British captured Wusong and planned to capture Nanjing. In August, the Qing government negotiated peace with Britain and signed the Treaty of Nanking, the first unequal treaty in modern Chinese history.

Extended Text

Destruction of Opium at Humen

Destruction of Opium at Humen refers to the destruction of opium by Lin Zexu in Humen of Guangdong Province in 1839. Destruction of Opium at Humen was the fuse for the Opium War.

In order to change the unfavorable position of trade with China, Britain smuggled large quantities of opium into China, which led to a flood of opium in China. The large quantities of opium into China not only led to the outflow of wealth from China, but also affected the physical and mental health of the population. Therefore, in 1838, Emperor Daoguang of the Qing appointed Lin Zexu to be in charge of the national anti-smoking campaign.

In March 1839, Lin Zexu arrived in Guangdong. He collaborated with Deng Tingzhen and other officials to launch a vigorous anti-smoking campaign. He issued injunctions, arrested opium dealers, and seized large quantities of opium and smoking materials. He issued an order requiring tobacco merchants to hand over all their opium within three days and stating that they were not allowed to sell opium in the future. British and American opium merchants vigorously resisted Lin Zexu's orders In late March, Lin Zexu ordered the siege of the merchant houses, stopped the Sino-British trade, and cut off the traffic between Guangzhou and Macao. In June, Lin Zexu publicly destroyed the seized opium in Humen.

The Destruction of Opium at Humen curbed the spread of opium in China to a certain extent, but did not completely solve the opium problem in China. The anti-smoking campaign increased the Chinese people's awareness of the dangers of opium. Lin Zexu, who was in charge of the Destruction of Opium at Humen, became a national hero in China.

Discussion

Briefly describe an invasion in your country's history and discuss its similarities and differences with the Chinese Opium War.

② Westernization Movement

Required Reading Text

Westernization Movement

The Westernization Movement was also known as Tongguang New Deal, Self-Strengthening New Deal and Self-Strengthening Movement. The Westernization Movement was a military, political, economic, cultural, educational, and diplomatic activity of the late Qing government from the 1860s to the 1890s, which was closely related to capitalism.

After the Opium War, a group of reform-minded middle and upper class bureaucrats in China launched the Westernization Movement with the main purpose of learning foreign industrial manufacturing technologies, strengthening themselves and seeking wealth, and saving the Qing Dynasty from crisis. The Qing government introduced advanced production technologies from the West, established new military industries, trained a new army and built a modern navy such as the Beiyang Navy. Jiangnan Machinery Manufacturing Bureau, Jinling Manufacturing Bureau and Fuzhou Bureau of Shipping were the main military industrial enterprises established in China during this period. The Qing government set up various new civilian industries such as ships, railroads, telegraphs, postal services, mining and textiles, which promoted the development of national industries in modern China. China Merchant's Steamship Navigation Company was the largest civilian enterprise established in Shanghai. In addition, the Qing government built and trained a new type of army in Tianjin. At the same time, the Qing government built a new navy by outsourcing and self-construction. In 1862, the School of Combined Learing was the first cultural and educational institution to cultivate westernization talents and introduce western knowledge.

In 1894, the collapse of the new-style army and navy built by China in the Sino-Japanese War of 1894–1895 marked the bankruptcy of the Westernization Movement. The Westernization Movement objectively stimulated the development of Chinese capitalism and resisted the economic import of foreign capitalism to a certain extent, but did not put China on the road to wealth and power.

Extended Text

Jiangnan Machinery Manufacturing Bureau

Jiangnan Machinery Manufacturing Bureau was a state-run military factory during the late Qing Dynasty. In 1865, Li Hongzhang purchased the American-owned Qiji Iron Factory in Hongkou, Shanghai, and merged it with two existing artillery bureaus. He allocated the machines purchased by Rong Hong from America under the order of Zeng Guofan, and established the bureau. In 1867, the bureau was relocated to Gaochang Temple and expanded into the largest military factory of the Qing government, primarily manufacturing guns and cannons and repairing ships.

In 1867, the Jiangnan Machinery Manufacturing Bureau had a graving dock. In 1868, a translation institute was established, presided over by Xu Shou and Hua Hengfang. In the same year, the bureau built its first steamship, Tianji. The following year, the bureau built the second steamship, Caojiang. In 1883, an arsenal was established. After 1885, shipbuilding was suspended for a long time, focusing solely on repairing ships from various provinces. In 1905, the shipbuilding department was separately established as the Jiangnan Shipyard. Since then, the Jiangnan Machinery Manufacturing Bureau was divided into two parts: Jiangnan Manufacturing Bureau and Jiangnan Shipyard, with the former becoming a specialized arsenal for manufacturing military hardware.

After the Revolution of 1911, the Jiangnan Shipyard was renamed the Jiangnan Shipbuilding Institute, under the jurisdiction of the Navy Ministry of the Beiyang Government. Jiangnan Machinery Manufacturing Bureau was renamed the Shanghai Manufacturing Bureau and was subordinate to Army Ministry. In 1914, Shanghai Manufacturing Bureau was renamed the Shanghai Arsenal. After 1927, Jiangnan Shipbuilding Institute was managed by the navy of the National Government. After the Battle of Songhu in 1932, Shanghai Arsenal was closed, and its site was merged into the Jiangnan Shipbuilding Institute. In May 1949, Jiangnan Shipbuilding Institute was renamed the Jiangnan Shipyard.

Discussion

> What are the economic development measures in your country in modern times? Compare the similarities and differences with the Chinese Westernization Movement.

③ The Reform Movement of 1898

Required Reading Text

The Reform Movement of 1898

The Reform Movement of 1898, also known as the "Wuxu Reform", was a political reform movement during the late Qing Dynasty. Following China's devastating defeat in the Sino-Japanese War of 1894–1895, the national crisis reached an unprecedented level of severity. Kang Youwei and others initiated the movement by rallying over 1300 provincial examination candidates in Beijing to petition Emperor Guangxu, opposing the signing of the Treaty of Shimonoseki and advocating for reform and national rejuvenation. They organized the Society for Strengthening the Nation and launched the Hundred Days Reform.

Kang Youwei, Liang Qichao, Tan Sitong, Yan Fu, and others organized societies, established schools and newspapers across various regions, and promoted reform and renovation, exerting influence nationwide. The political power of the bourgeois reformists led by Kang Youwei received support from a grand councilor, Weng Tonghe, and the governor of Hunan Province, Chen Baozhen. In the winter of 1897, when Germany forcibly occupied Jiaozhou Bay and imperialist powers were conspiring to partition China, Kang Youwei once again rushed to Beijing to petition for reform. In April 1898, Kang Youwei and others established the Society for National Protection in Beijing, with the aim of safeguarding the country, its people, and its culture. Emperor Guangxu accepted the reform proposal and adopted the suggestions of reformers. On June 11, Emperor Guangxu issued the "imperial edict of the self-strengthening of the country", announcing the reform to strengthen the nation. Over the following 103 days, a series of reform decrees were continuously issued, implementing new policies in areas such as politics, economy, military, and culture and education.

However, the conservative faction led by Empress Dowager Cixi controlled the actual political and military power and firmly opposed the reform movement. On September 21, Empress Dowager Cixi staged a coup, imprisoning Emperor Guangxu and executing six reformist leaders, including Tan Sitong, marking the failure of the Reform Movement of 1898.

Extended Text

The Sino-Japanese War of 1894–1895

The Sino-Japanese War of 1894–1895 refers to the war between China and Japan that occurred from 1894 to 1895. This war led to a sharp decline in China's international status, shattered the pursuit of national rejuvenation in modern China, bringing unprecedented and severe national crises to the Chinese nation.

In 1868, Japan embarked on the path of capitalism through the Meiji Restoration, resulting in its growing national strength. Meanwhile, China was in the late Qing Dynasty, and the Qing government initiated the Westernization Movement of 1898 to learn advanced scientific and technological knowledge from the West. In 1872, Japan invaded Ryukyu, a vassal state of China. In 1874, Japan invaded Taiwan, China. In 1879, Japan annexed the Ryukyu Kingdom and renamed it Okinawa Prefecture. By 1887, Japan had formulated a plan to invade China, known as the policy of conquering the Qing Dynasty.

In 1890, Japan experienced an economic crisis. In early 1894, there was an internal conflict in Democratic People's Republic of Korea (DPRK), and Japan took the opportunity to send troops to Democratic People's Republic of Korea. In late July, the Japanese army attacked the Chinese naval and ground forces by surprise. On August 1, China and Japan officially declared war. In the Pyongyang Campaign, the Qing army suffered defeat, and subsequently, the Japanese army controlled the entire territory of Democratic People's Republic of Korea. After the fall of Pyongyang, the Chinese and Japanese navies engaged in the Yellow Sea Naval Battle near the mouth of the Yalu River, and the Japanese army seized control of the Yellow Sea. In October, the Japanese army invaded the Liaodong Peninsula and Shandong Peninsula in China through both land and sea routes. In April 1895, the Qing government signed the Treaty of Shimonoseki with Japan.

Discussion

> What political reform measures did your country take in modern times? Compare and contrast them with the Reform Movement of 1898 in China.

④ The Revolution of 1911

Required Reading Text

The Revolution of 1911

The Revolution of 1911 refers to the bourgeois-democratic revolution that broke out in China in 1911.

In 1905, Sun Yat-sen and others established the Chinese Revolutionary Alliance in Tokyo of Japan, with the platform of "expelling the Tartars, restoring China, establishing the Republic of China, and equalizing land rights". Afterwards, Chinese revolutionaries launched several armed uprisings, shattering the rule of the Qing Dynasty and expanding the influence of the revolution. In June 1911, in opposition to the Qing government's decree on the state ownership of railroads, the Road Protection Movement broke out in Sichuan, Hunan, Hubei and Guangdong provinces. On October 10th, the revolutionaries in Wuchang, Hubei Province, launched the Wuchang Uprising and established the Hubei Military Government. Within two months after the victory of Wuchang Uprising, 14 provinces including Shaanxi, Hunan, Jiangxi and Anhui declared independence one after another. In January 1912, Sun Yat-sen was inaugurated as the provisional president of the Republic of China, and in February, the Qing emperor announced his abdication.

The Revolution of 1911 was a revolution led by the bourgeoisie to oppose the feudal monarchy and establish a bourgeois republic, creating a modern national democratic revolution in a complete sense. The Revolution of 1911 opened the floodgates of historical progress in modern China, initiated unprecedented social changes in China, and explored the way for the development and progress of the Chinese nation, which is of great historical significance.

Extended Text

The May Fourth Movement

The May Fourth Movement refers to the anti-imperialist and anti-feudal patriotic movement launched by the Chinese people on May 4, 1919.

After the end of the First World War, the allied powers of Britain, France, and the United States convened the Paris Peace Conference in January 1919. The Chinese government proposed to the conference that the imperialist powers should abandon their privileges in China, cancel the "Twenty-One Demands", and reclaim the rights of the original German possessions in Shandong, which had been seized by Japan. However, these proposals were rejected by the imperialist countries participating in the conference, and the Beiyang government prepared to sign the treaty. The news of China's diplomatic failure sparked nationwide outrage. On the afternoon of May 4, more than 3000 students in Beijing gathered in front of Tiananmen Square. After the rally, the students held a protest march, which was blocked by the police from the embassies. The government dispatched military police to suppress the protest, arresting over 30 students. Starting from June 3, the government implemented special martial law, which sparked even greater anger among the people. On June 5, workers in Shanghai went on strike; merchants closed their shops; and students suspended classes. More than 150 cities across the country were successively involved, and the center of the movement shifted from Beijing to Shanghai. On June 10, the Beiyang government was forced to release the arrested students. On June 28, the Chinese delegation refused to sign the Treaty of Versailles.

The May Fourth Movement was a thorough, uncompromising anti-imperialist and anti-feudal patriotic movement. It marked the emergence of the Chinese working class onto the political stage, preparing the way for the establishment of the Communist Party of China in terms of ideology and cadres, and signaling the beginning of the new democratic revolution.

Discussion

> What were the effects of World War 1 on China and your country?

⑤ Chinese People's War of Resistance Against Japanese Aggression (1931–1945)

Required Reading Text

Chinese People's War of Resistance Against Japanese Aggression (1931–1945)

Chinese People's War of Resistance Against Japanese Aggression (1931–1945) refers to the just war fought by the Chinese people against Japanese aggression in the 1930s and 1940s. The war lasted 14 years, from September 1931 to September 1945.

On September 18, 1931, the Japanese army launched the September 18th Incident and invaded three provinces in northeastern China one after another, and China's local resistance war began. In January 1932, Japan attacked Shanghai, which led to the first full-scale confrontation between the Chinese and Japanese armies. On July 7, 1937, the Japanese army launched an attack on Lugou Bridge, southwest of Beiping (today's Beijing), starting a full-scale war of aggression against China, and the Chinese army rose up to resist, starting a nationwide War Against Japanese Aggression. In August, the Battle of Songhu in Shanghai broke out. In December, Nanjing fell. In October 1938, after the Japanese invaded Guangzhou and Wuhan, they were forced to stop their strategic offensive and the war entered the stage of strategic stalemate. On December 7, 1941, Japan launched the Pacific War. On August 15, 1945, Japan surrendered unconditionally. On September 2, Japan signed the Instrument of Surrender. China's War of Resistance Against Japanese Aggression ended victoriously.

War Against Japanese Aggression was an important part of the World War II and made great sacrifices and indelible historical contributions to the victory of the World Anti-Fascist War. War Against Japanese Aggression was the first national liberation war in which China achieved complete victory against foreign invasion in modern times, and became a historical turning point of the Chinese nation from decline to revitalization.

Extended Text

The Establishment of the People's Republic of China

On October 1, 1949, the Central People's Government of the People's Republic of China was established, and October 1st became the National Day of the People's Republic of China.

After the victory of the Chinese People's War of Resistance Against Japanese Aggression (1931–1945), China entered the period of the War of Liberation. Facing the all-out civil war launched by the Nationalist Party, the Chinese People's Liberation Army led by the Communist Party of China (CPC) won the three major battles of Liaoshen, Huaihai and Pingjin and the Battle of Dujiang successively, and marched to the central south, northwest and southwest. Eventually, the people's forces led by the CPC overthrew the regime of Nationalist Party and established the People's Republic of China.

On September 21, 1949, the First Plenary Session of the Chinese People's Political Consultative Conference, composed of representatives from all walks of life in China, was held in Beiping (today's Beijing). The meeting adopted the Common Program of the Chinese People's Political Consultative Conference which was a provisional constitution. At 2:00 pm on October 1, the Central People's Government Committee held its first meeting and announced its inauguration. At 3:00 pm, 300000 soldiers and citizens of the capital held a grand opening ceremony in Tiananmen Square, where the first five-star red flag was raised and Mao Zedong proclaimed the establishment of the Central People's Government of the People's Republic of China.

The founding of the People's Republic of China marked the great victory of China's new democratic revolution and the passing of the semi-colonial and semi-feudal era when the Chinese people were enslaved and oppressed, and China had become a new democratic country.

Discussion

What were the effects of World War II on China and your country?

⑥ War to Resist US Aggression and Aid Korea (1950–1953)

Required Reading Text

War to Resist US Aggression and Aid Korea (1950–1953)

War to Resist US Aggression and Aid Korea (1950–1953), was a war fought by the Chinese People's Volunteer Army in the early stages of the founding of the People's Republic of China, in support of the people in DPRK against the American aggression to defend China's security.

On June 25, 1950, the Korean War broke out. On the 27, the president of the United States Truman publicly announced military intervention in DPRK and ordered the Seventh Fleet to invade the Taiwan Strait. In early October, the Central Committee of the Communist Party of China made the strategic decision to "resist US aggression, aid Korea, defend the homeland" in response to the request of the DPRK government and the will of the Chinese people, forming the Chinese People's Volunteer Army. On October 19, the Chinese People's Volunteer Army set off for the DPRK battlefield, marking the beginning of the War to Resist US Aggression and Aid Korea (1950–1953).

The war lasted for two years and nine months, consisting of two phases. In the first phase, the Chinese People's Volunteer Army and the DPRK People's Army conducted strategic counteroffensives primarily through mobile warfare. In the second phase, they shifted to positional warfare. On July 27, 1953, both sides signed the Korean Armistice Agreement, bringing an end to the War to Resist US Aggression and Aid Korea (1950–1953).

The great victory in the War to Resist US Aggression and Aid Korea (1950–1953). had significant and far-reaching implications for both China and the world. This battle solidified the important role of the People's Republic of China in Asian and international affairs.

Extended Text

The First Five-Year Plan

The First Five-Year Plan is the abbreviation of the first five-year plan of the

People's Republic of China. The formulation and implementation of the First Five-Year Plan is a crucial step of great significance for China to achieve industrialization.

The People's Republic of China began to formulate the First Five-Year Plan in 1951. The plan was implemented and modified simultaneously. In March 1954, the formulation of the First Five-Year Plan entered its final stage. In July 1955, the First National People's Congress officially adopted the First Five-Year Plan at its second session and promulgated it nationwide for implementation.

In 1953, China began to implement the First Five-Year Plan, and people across the country enthusiastically participated in the construction of the plan with high political consciousness and enthusiasm for production. The metallurgical industry is the foundation of the entire industry, and the focus of its development is on the large-scale expansion and renovation of Anshan Iron and Steel Company. The coal industry is the focus of energy construction, and the petroleum industry, chemical industry, and weapons industry have also made considerable progress. During this period, the country also concentrated its efforts on the construction of two emerging industrial sectors: aviation and electronics. In the later stage of the First Five-Year Plan, China began to establish two emerging cutting-edge industries: nuclear industry and aerospace industry. By 1957, all tasks of the First Five-Year Plan were overfulfilled ahead of schedule, laying a solid foundation for China to comprehensively start socialist construction.

Discussion

When did your country establish diplomatic relations with China? Please briefly discuss this process.

Economic Development

Chapter 7

Economic Transformation

① Agricultural Transformation

Required Reading Text

Agricultural Transformation

Agriculture is a sector of social production that uses the life functions of plants, animals and microorganisms, which are artificially cultivated to obtain agricultural products. Agriculture is the basis of the national economy, providing people with food, by-products and industrial raw materials. Agriculture in a broad sense includes five forms of industries: plantation, forestry, animal husbandry, fishery, and side occupation. Since the establishment of the People's Republic of China, along with the modernization process of the country, the modernization of agriculture has also made significant progress. Currently, as economic development changes from high-speed growth to high-quality development, China's agricultural development has also transformed.

From the establishment of the People's Republic of China to the 1970s, Chinese agriculture was in the stage of exploring agricultural modernization under the rural collective ownership system. China has implemented a system of collective ownership of rural land, unified purchase and marketing of agricultural products, and agricultural household registration in rural areas. From the late 1970s to the 1990s, Chinese agriculture was in a stage of agricultural modernization led by rural reforms and structural changes. The establishment and institutionalization of the household contract responsibility system with remuneration linked to output made farmers the masters of agricultural development. Since the 1990s, Chinese agriculture has been in a stage of agricultural modernization where farmers left the land and moved from the countryside to the cities and towns. Mechanization inputs have increased significantly and agricultural labor productivity has increased rapidly. China's agricultural modernization is transforming toward a model in which improving labor productivity is the main focus.

Extended Text

The Household Contract Responsibility System with Remuneration Linked to Output

The household contract responsibility system with remuneration linked to output is a form of agricultural production responsibility system in which farmers contract production materials (including land) and production tasks to collective economic organizations on a household basis. The household contract responsibility system with remuneration linked to output is a basic economic system in China's rural areas at this stage.

After the founding of the People's Republic of China, China's agricultural economy has been run on a collective basis. In the autumn of 1978, when some areas in Anhui and Sichuan provinces suffered from disasters, peasants spontaneously resumed the production responsibility system that had emerged in the early 1960s, such as contracting production to groups and households, etc. In May 1980, Deng Xiaoping publicly affirmed the practice of Xiaogang Village's all-round responsibility system in an important talk. On January 1, 1982, the first document on rural work in the history of the Communist Party of China was officially issued. In September 1982, the 12th Party Congress gave full recognition to the rural production responsibility system, which is mainly in the form of contracting production to households, and emphasized that it must be adhered to in the long run and gradually improved. Since then, most Chinese farmers have implemented various forms of the contract responsibility system, the most common of which is the all-round contract.

The Chinese government has continued to consolidate and improve the household contract responsibility system with remuneration linked to output, encouraging farmers to develop a variety of businesses and gradually putting the vast rural areas on the road to prosperity.

Discussion

> Briefly describe your country's agricultural policies. Talk about their similarities and differences with China's agricultural policies.

② Financial System

Required Reading Text

Financial System

The financial system is the sum of the forms and management systems that banks and other financial institutions use to organize and regulate the circulation of money and the movement of funds through various credit activities. The financial system includes the banking system, the currency issuance system, the lending capital management system and the interest rate management system. According to the policy of the Third Plenary Session of the 11th Central Committee of the Communist Party of China on implementing economic system reform and opening up to the outside world, China has carried out a series of major reforms of the financial system since 1979.

After the establishment of the People's Bank of China in 1948, China adopted a grand unified financial system with planned management. After 1949, China confiscated bureaucratic capital banks and transformed private banks and money changers in accordance with the requirements of establishing a socialist ownership system, and at the same time, based on the vigorous development of rural credit cooperatives, established a highly centralized planned economy model. Since 1979, the general direction of China's financial system reform has been to gradually establish a financial system adapted to the operating mechanism of the socialist market economy.

At present, China has established a financial organization system with the People's Bank of China as the core, specialized banks as the main body, and a variety of financial institutions co-existing. The People's Bank of China exclusively exercises central banking functions.

Extended Text

Four Major Banks

Four major banks refer to the four large state-owned banks under the direct control of the state. The four major banks include: Industrial and Commercial Bank of China, Agricultural Bank of China, Bank of China and China Construction Bank.

Industrial and Commercial Bank of China, founded in 1984 and headquartered in Beijing, is a large centrally managed state-owned bank. With a high-quality customer base, Industrial and Commercial Bank of China is the largest commercial bank in China and one of the top 500 companies in the world.

Agricultural Bank of China, founded in 1951 and headquartered in Beijing, is a large centrally managed state-owned bank. Agricultural Bank of China is an important part of China's financial system and is one of the top 500 companies in the world.

Bank of China, founded in 1912 and headquartered in Beijing, is a large centrally managed state-owned bank. The Hong Kong and Macao branches of Bank of China act as local note-issuing banks, and their business scope covers investment banking, insurance, fund and aircraft leasing. Bank of China provides financial services for individual and corporate customers worldwide.

China Construction Bank, founded in 1954 and headquartered in Beijing, is a large centrally managed state-owned bank. China Construction Bank has a broad customer base and maintains banking ties with a number of large conglomerates and leading companies in strategic sectors of the Chinese economy.

Discussion

> Which banks do you know about in China? What kind of business have you done in the bank?

③ Eastern Development

Required Reading Text

Eastern Development

Eastern development refers to a policy of the People's Republic of China to encourage the eastern part of China to take the lead in development in order to give full play to the geographical advantages of the eastern coast. The eastern, northeastern, central and western regions are the four major economic zones of China. The eastern region of China includes Liaoning, Hebei, Shandong, Jiangsu, Zhejiang, Fujian, Taiwan, Guangdong, Hainan provinces, Beijing, Tianjin, Shanghai, Hong Kong and Macao Special Adaministrative Regions.

In the 1980s, China successively established five special economic zones, namely Shenzhen, Zhuhai, Shantou, Xiamen and Hainan, 14 economic and technological development zones, such as Dalian and Qinhuangdao, and then opened up the Yangtze River Delta, Pearl River Delta and Minnan Xiamen-Zhangzhou-Quanzhou Delta as coastal economic open zones. In the 21st century, the State Council has approved Shanghai's Pudong New Area and Tianjin's Binhai New Area as national comprehensive supporting reform pilot zones to test some major reform and opening-up measures first.

The eastern part of the country has taken the lead in development and experimentation, so the eastern part of the country is ahead in development, transformation, reform and transformation, and can play a role in deepening reform and paving the way for early and pilot implementation.

Extended Text

The Yangtze River Delta Region

The Yangtze River Delta in the physical-geographical sense is part of the middle and lower reaches of the Yangtze River Plain, from the Tongyang Canal in the north, to Hangzhou Bay in the south, to Zhenjiang in the west, and to the sea in the east. The Yangtze River Delta in the economic-geographical sense includes 15 cities including Shanghai, Nanjing, Wuxi, Changzhou, Suzhou, Nantong, Yangzhou, Zhenjiang and Taizhou in Jiangsu Province, and Hangzhou, Ningbo, Jiaxing, Huzhou, Shaoxing and Zhoushan in Zhejiang Province. The Yangtze River Delta region is one of the most economically developed and open regions in China.

The Yangtze River Delta region has a long cultural history, and a sizable urban agglomeration was initially formed in the middle and late feudal society of China. During the Ming and Qing dynasties, larger commercial and handicraft cities emerged in the Yangtze River Delta. In modern times, Shanghai became the trade center, financial center and industrial center of the whole Yangtze River Delta and even China. After the reform and opening up, the urban functions of the Yangtze River Delta region were re-divided and reorganized, and Shanghai re-emerged as a cosmopolitan city with its superior geographical location. Entering the 21st century, China clearly defined the strategic positioning of the development of the Yangtze River Delta region as an important international gateway to the Asia-Pacific region, a globally important center for modern service and advanced manufacturing industries, and a world-class urban agglomeration with strong international competitiveness.

Discussion

> What are the big cities or urban agglomeration in your country? Describe them briefly.

(4) Revitalization of the Northeast China

Required Reading Text

Revitalization of the Northeast China

Revitalization of the northeast China is a policy of the People's Republic of China to promote the transformation and revitalization of the northeastern old industrial areas. In August 2004, Premier Wen Jiabao proposed the strategy of revitalization of the northeast China. In September 2018, Xi Jinping, the president of the People's Republic of China, clearly proposed a comprehensive and all-round revitalization of northeast China in the new era.

The Northeast is the cradle of industry in the People's Republic of China. At the early stage of China's socialist industrialization, the Northeast made a historic and significant contribution to the establishment of an independent and perfect national economic system and to the promotion of China's industrialization and urbanization. The Northeast is an important base for China's heavy industry and an important production base for agricultural and sideline products. Since the 1990s, due to various reasons such as institutions and mechanisms, the Northeast began to face numerous obstacles in the process of full integration into the market economy, which need to be solved urgently.

The revitalization of the northeast China includes consolidating and developing modern agriculture, improving the modern industrial system, promoting the development of industrial agglomeration, promoting the sustainable development of resource-based cities, improving infrastructure conditions, strengthening resource conservation and energy saving, taking various measures to increase employment, continuing to deepen the reform of state-owned enterprises, and comprehensively enhancing the level of opening up to the outside world, and so on.

Extended Text

Northeast China

The northeast region of China includes Liaoning, Jilin and Heilongjiang provinces and the eastern part of Inner Mongolia Autonomous Region, referred to as Northeast China.

Liaoning Province, with its capital Shenyang, is bordered by the Yellow Sea and the Bohai Sea to the south, Hebei Province to the southwest, Inner Mongolia Autonomous Region to the northwest, Jilin Province to the northeast, and DPRK to the southeast by the Yalu River. The topography of Liaoning Province is roughly north to south, sloping from east and west to the center. Since the founding of the People's Republic of China, Liaoning has been the cradle of Chinese industry and is known as the "eldest son of the People's Republic of China".

Jilin Province, with its capital Changchun, is connected to Liaoning Province, Inner Mongolia Autonomous Region and Heilongjiang Province, and shares borders with Russia and DPRK, and is located in the geographic center of Northeast Asia. The topography of Jilin Province slopes from southeast to northwest, showing the characteristics of high southeast and low northwest. Jilin Province is a witness to the complete course of political and military conflicts in Northeast Asia in modern times, and is an important industrial base and commodity food production base in China.

Heilongjiang Province, with its capital Harbin, is the northernmost as well as the easternmost land administrative region of China, with Russia across the river to the north and east, Inner Mongolia Autonomous Region to the west, and Jilin Province to the south. Located in the hinterland of Northeast Asia region, Heilongjiang Province is an important gateway to Russia and continental Europe by land from Asia and the Pacific, and an important window of China's opening along the border.

Discussion

> Describe briefly the cities in Northeast China that you know.

⑤ The Rise of Central China

Required Reading Text

The Rise of Central China

The rise of central China is a policy of the People's Republic of China to promote the joint rise of the six central provinces. In March 2004, Premier Wen Jiabao made the first clear proposal in his government work report. In 2006, China defined the central region as an important national grain production base, energy and raw material base, modern equipment manufacturing and high-tech industry base, and comprehensive transportation hub.

The central region of China includes six provinces: Shanxi, Anhui, Jiangxi, Henan, Hubei and Hunan provinces. With the implementation of the rise of central China policy, the central region, connecting east and west, and south and north, has been further developed with the advantages of developed transportation network, dense production factors, abundant human resources and complete industrial categories. At present, the central region is strategically positioned as an important advanced manufacturing center in China, a key area for new urbanization in China, a core area for modern agricultural development in China and an area for building ecological civilization in China.

The central region occupies an important position in the overall economic and social development of China and has made significant contributions to the national economic and social development. The central region is a key region for China's new round of industrialization, urbanization, informatization and agricultural modernization, a region with the most potential to expand domestic demand and raise the level of openness, and an important region to support China's economy to maintain medium-to-high speed growth.

Extended Text

Central China

The central region of China include six provinces: Shanxi, Anhui, Jiangxi, Henan, Hubei and Hunan provinces.

Shanxi Province, with its capital Taiyuan, is bordered by Hebei Province to the east, Shaanxi Province to the west, Henan Province to the south, and Inner Mongolia Autonomous Region to the north. Shanxi Province is a typical mountainous plateau covered by loess, with a high northeast and low southwest topography. Shanxi Province is located inland in the mid-latitude zone and has a temperate continental monsoon climate.

Anhui Province, with its capital Hefei, is connected to Jiangsu Province to the east, Henan and Hubei provinces to the west, Zhejiang Province to the southeast, Jiangxi Province to the south, and Shandong Province to the north. Anhui Province is an important part of the Yangtze River Delta, with historical and natural ties in terms of economy and culture to other regions of the Yangtze River Delta.

Jiangxi Province, with its capital Nanchang, is bordered by Zhejiang and Fujian provinces to the east, Guangdong Province to the south, Hunan Province to the west, and Hubei and Anhui provinces to the north.

Henan Province, with its capital Zhengzhou, is bordered by Anhui and Shandong provinces to the east, Hebei and Shanxi provinces to the north, Shaanxi Province to the west, and Hubei Province to the south. Henan Province is located at the junction of the coastal open areas and the central and western regions, serving as an important comprehensive transportation hub and information flow center for people and logistics in China.

Hubei Province, with its capital Wuhan, is bordered by Anhui Province to the east, Chongqing to the west, Shaanxi Province to the northwest, Jiangxi and Hunan provinces to the south, and Henan Province to the north.

Hunan Province, with its capital Changsha, is bordered by Jiangxi Province to the east, Chongqing and Guizhou Province to the west, Guangdong Province and Guangxi to the south, and Hubei Province to the north.

Discussion

> What cities do you know about in central China? Describe briefly your impression.

⑥ Western Development

Required Reading Text

Western Development

Western development refers to China's policy to improve the economic and social development of the western region. The implementation of the western development strategy is a major decision made by China for the new century. In September 1999, China proposed the western development strategy. In October 2000, China made the implementation of western development and the promotion of coordinated regional development a strategic task. The western development is a major strategic adjustment to the layout of China's economic development.

The scope of western development includes Sichuan, Shaanxi, Gansu, Qinghai, Yunnan, Guizhou provinces, Chongqing, Guangxi zhuang Autonomous Region, Inner Mongolia Autonomous Region, Ningxia Hui Autonomous Region, Xinjiang Uygur Autonomous Region, Xizang Autonomous Region, Enshi Tujia and Miao Autonomous Prefecture in Hubei Province, Xiangxi Tujia and Miao Autonomous Prefecture in Hunan Province, and Yanbian Korean Autonomous Prefecture in Jilin Province.

Since the implementation of the western development, the central government has been increasing its investment, accelerating the economic and social development of the western region, and significantly improving the infrastructure conditions of transportation, water conservancy, power grids and the communications, etc. Since 2000, the state has launched a number of key ecological construction projects in the western region, which have achieved obvious ecological and social benefits as well as better economic benefits.

Extended Text

Five Northwestern Provinces

The five northwestern provinces include Shaanxi, Gansu, Qinghai provinces, Ningxia Hui Autonomous Region, and Xinjiang Uygur Autonomous Region. The five northwestern provinces is a concept based on the administrative divisions of the early founding of the People's Republic of China, and is different from the northwestern region in the physical geographic divisions.

Shaanxi Province, with its capital Xi'an, is located in the hinterland of China's interior and belongs to the middle reaches of the Yellow River and the upper reaches of the Yangtze River. Shaanxi Province is an important hub connecting the eastern and central regions and the northwest and southwest regions of China.

Gansu Province, with its capital Lanzhou, is connected to Shaanxi Province to the east, Xinjiang Uygur Autonomous Region Antonomous Region to the west, Sichuan and Qinghai provinces to the south, Ningxia and Inner Mongolia to the north, and Mongolia to the northwest.

Qinghai Province, with its capital Xining, is named after the largest inland saltwater lake in China, the Qinghai Lake. Qinghai Province is the birthplace of the Yangtze River, the Yellow River and the Lancang River in China, and is known as the "Chinese water tower".

Ningxia Hui Autonomous Region, with its capital Yinchuan, is adjacent to Shaanxi Province to the east, Inner Mongolia Antonomous Region to the west and north, and Gansu Province to the south.

Xinjiang Uygur Autonomous Region, with its capital Urumqi, is located in the middle of Eurasia. Xinjiang Uygur Autonomous Region is the largest province in terms of area, the longest land border and the largest number of neighboring countries in China. Xinjiang Uygur Autonomous Region has extensive deserts and is rich in oil and natural gas. It is the starting point of China's west-east gas transmission and the main position of the western development.

Discussion

> Which cities and attractions do you know about in western China? Describe them briefly.

Chapter 8

Cultural Industry

① Pop Music

Required Reading Text

Pop Music

Pop music, also known as popular music, is a kind of instrumental music and songs with short structure, popular content and lively form, which are loved and widely sung by the masses, compared with serious music and classical music. Pop music is commercial pastime and entertaining music that is market-oriented. Pop music originated in the United States in the late 19th and early 20th centuries.

Pop music emerged in the 1930s in China. After 1949, pop music in Hong Kong and Taiwan gradually developed. In the 21st century, Chinese pop music has formed a state of mutual fusion, penetration and influence between Southeast Asia and China, mainly popular in China, Malaysia, Singapore and other communities where Chinese is spoken. Chinese pop music is also influential outside the Chinese communities such as Korea and Japan.

Shanghai is the center of Chinese pop music. Li Jinhui is known as the "father of Chinese pop music". He is the founder of the musical genre of Chinese pop music. His work *Drizzling*, composed in the 1920s, is considered as the earliest Chinese pop music. The development of Chinese pop music has given rise to many internationally influential Chinese pop stars such as Teresa Teng.

Extended Text

Teresa Teng

Teresa Teng enjoys a very high status in the Chinese pop music. Teresa Teng was born in 1953 in Taiwan, China, and her ancestral home is Hebei Province, China. She is an influential Taiwan singer in Asia and the global Chinese community, and one of the most prestigious stars in the Japanese singing circle of the second half of the 20th century. In 1967, Teresa Teng launched her singing career with the release of her debut album, *Songs of Teresa Teng, Episode I—Fengyang Flower Drums*. In 1969, Teresa Teng became famous by singing the theme song of the Taiwan TV shows *Jingjing*. In 1974, Teresa Teng laid the foundation of her acting career in Japan with the song *Airport*. In 1980, Teresa Teng was elected as the best female singer in the Golden Bell Awards, the highest honor of television production in Taiwan. In the early 1980s, Teresa Teng was successively invited to perform at Lincoln Center in New York, Los Angeles Music Center and Caesar's Palace in Las Vegas.

Teresa Teng's performance footprint have traversed numbers regions in China, Japan, Southeast Asia, the United States, singing more than 1000 songs in Chinese, Japanese, English, Cantonese, Southern Fujia Dialect, Indonesian and other languages, and has had a profound impact on the enlightenment and development of the Chinese music, especially the mainland pop music, and has also made important contributions to the mutual exchange between different pop music cultures in Asia.

Discussion

> What Chinese pop music have you listened to? Briefly talk about your experience.

(2) Films and TV Shows

Required Reading Text

Films and TV Shows

Films and TV shows, a collective term for the visual arts of film and television. In 1905, Ren Qingtai's *The Battle of Mount Dingjun* was the first film in China, marking the birth of Chinese film. In 1958, *A Bite of Vegetable Pancake*, filmed and broadcast by Beijing TV Station, was the first television shows in China's mainland. In the history of Chinese films and TV shows development in the mid-to-late 20th century, films and TV shows made in Taiwan and Hong Kong have been extremely influential in countries around the world.

Taiwan films are characterized by their emphasis on directorial style, their focus on Taiwan history, and their admiration for film as propaganda work. In addition to Hou Hsiao-hsien and Edward Yang, Ang Lee, born in Taiwan, is also a world renown film director. Taiwan TV shows specialize in romantic love stories, with costume TV shows such as *The Legend of White Snake*, *The Legendary Chien Lung* and *Bao Zheng*, idol TV shows such as *The Way We Were*, *Frog Prince* and *Meteor Garden*, and family TV shows such as *Where a Good Man Goes* and *Love Unforgettable*.

The boom of Hong Kong TV shows started in the 1980s with *Shanhai Beach* and *Warrior Fearless*. *At the Threshold of an Era*, filmed in 1999, reached the pinnacle of Hong Kong business TV shows. Hong Kong films can be divided into many categories, such as kung fu films, comedies, police and ganster films, and so on. Hong Kong also has many movie stars, such as Leslie Cheung, Tony Leung, Jackie Chan, Stephen Chow, etc.

Extended Text

Hong Kong Films

Hong Kong films can be divided into different types according to their contents, such as kung fu films, comedies and police and ganster films.

Kung fu films are the biggest feature of Hong Kong and the highest achievement of the Hong Kong film industry. Hong Kong kung fu films have made the world aware of Chinese kung fu. Before Bruce Lee became famous, the Hong Kong film industry had the *Once Upon a Time in China* film series starring Tak-Hing Kwan and

Shih Kien. After Bruce Lee, Hong Kong kung fu film stars include Jackie Chan, Jet Li, Donnie Yen, etc.

Comedies are what Hong Kong movies are good at. There are two comedy kings in Hong Kong. One is Michael Hui and the other is Stephen Chow. Hong Kong Comedies include ordinary comedies like *The Eight Happiness* and *All's Well, Ends Well*, as well as multi-genre comedies like *All for the Winner* and *Kung Fu*, the latter of which incorporates various elements of kung fu and gambling films, making the comedy a richer form of expression.

Police and ganster films highlight the bravery of the police. In the 1980s and 1990s, when Hong Kong films were at its peak, police and ganster films also reached a peak position. John Woo's *The Killer*, Wong Chi Keung's *Crime Story*, and Lau Wai Keung's *Infernal Affairs* series are all classics of the police and ganster genre.

Discussion

What Hong Kong movies have you seen? Briefly talk about your experience.

(3) Animation Films

Required Reading Text

Animation Films

An animation film is a kind of art film that uses drawings drawn by hand or computer to express artistic images. Animation first originated in England in the first half of the 19th century and flourished in the United States.

China's animation business started early. In the 1920s, Chinese animation artists already created works such as *The New Year* and *The Dog Invites Guests*. In 1941, the Wan brothers produced Asia's first animated film *Princess Iron Fan*, whose artistic appeal could be compared to Disney's *Snow White and the Seven Dwarfs* at that time. After the founding of the People's Republic of China, the Shanghai Animation Film Studio reached a high level of artistic creation, producing such exquisite animated films as *The Magical Pen, Little Tadpoles Search for Their Mother, The Monkey King:*

Uproar in Heaven, *The Reed Pipe* and *Prince Nezha's Triumph against Dragon King*.

In the 21st century, with the support and encouragement of national policies, the production units of Chinese animation have been increasing; the production team has been growing; the creation level of animation products has been improved; the construction of animation industrial park has also made promising achievements; Chinese animation has entered a new stage of rapid development. In this period, China's representative original animations include *Pleasant Goat and Big Big Wolf* series, *Boonie Bears* series, *The Legend of Qin* series, *Hua Jianghu* series, *Year Hare Affair* series.

Extended Text

Monkey King: Hero is Back

Monkey King: Hero is Back is a 3D animated film expanded and interpreted based on the traditional Chinese mythological story *Journey to the West*. *Monkey King: Hero is Back* is produced by Beijing Yancheng October Culture Communication Co., Ltd., HG Entertainment Co., Ltd., and Beijing Micro Film and Television Times Technology Co., Ltd., directed by Tian Xiaopeng, and released in July 2015.

The film uses the main characters in *Journey to the West* and re-frames the content, telling the story of Sun Wukong, who has been lonely and suppressed under the Five Elements Mountain for 500 years, and was unsealed mistakenly by the Tang Monk as a child, commonly name of Jiangliu'er, to find his original heart and complete his self-redemption in the adventure of mutual companionship. The film relies on the classic Hollywood narrative model. The story structure is relatively complete, and the production technology level has reached international standards. The most successful aspect of *Monkey King: Hero is Back* is its marketing strategy, which provides a model for the promotion of subsequent animated films.

After the film was released in China in 2015, it was immediately attracted the attention of many audiences and widely reported by the media for its excellent word of mouth. In 2015, the film won the Best Animation Award at the 30th China Golden Rooster Awards and the Outstanding Feature Film Award at the 16th Huabiao Film Awards.

Discussion

> What Chinese animated films have you seen? Briefly talk about your experience.

④ Sports Event

Required Reading Text

Sports Event

Sports event, generally refers to relatively large scale formal competition with levels. China has hosted several world-class sports events, such as the Olympic Games, the Asian Games and various World Championships. The major domestic sports events in China include the Chinese Basketball Association, the Chinese Football Association Super League and the Chinese Table Tennis Club Super League.

Chinese Basketball Association, abbreviated as "CBA", started in 1995 as an inter-year home-and-away basketball league organized by the Chinese Basketball Association. It is the highest level basketball league in China and has produced stars such as Yao Ming, Wang Zhizhi, Yi Jianlian and Zhu Fangyu.

The Chinese Football Association Super League, abbreviated as "CSL", started in 2004, is the highest level professional soccer league in China's mainland organized by the Chinese Football Association (CFA). The lower levels of the CSL are the CFL China League, the CFL Division Two League and the CFL Member Association Champions League.

The Chinese Table Tennis Club Super League, started in 1999, is a boutique tournament jointly organized by the Chinese Table Tennis Association and CCTV. The Chinese Table Tennis Club Super League is held once a year, with men's team and women's team events.

Extended Text

Chinese Women's Volleyball Team

Chinese women's volleyball team is the abbreviation of Chinese women's national volleyball team, which is affiliated with the Chinese Volleyball Association. The Chinese women's volleyball team is one of the sports teams with outstanding achievements among all Chinese sports teams, represented by athlete Jane Lang.

The Chinese women's volleyball team won the World Cup in 1981 and 1985, the World Championships in 1982 and 1986, and the 1984 Olympic Games in Los Angeles, becoming the world's first "five in a row" champion. The Chinese women's volleyball team won the 2003 World Cup, the 2004 Olympics, the 2015 World Cup, the 2016 Olympics and the 2019 World Cup, making them the world champion ten times. In 2020, Peter Chan directed the film *Leap*, which tells the story of the Chinese women's volleyball team that won the championship.

Jane Lang, a female born in Tianjin, China in 1960, entered the junior gymnastic school in 1973. She was selected for the national training team in 1978. In 1981, 1982 and 1984, Jane Lang won three consecutive championships with the Chinese women's volleyball team. In 1985, Jane Lang retired. In October 2002, Jane Lang was inducted into the Volleyball Hall of Fame, becoming the first person in Asia to receive this honor. In 2016, Jane Lang led the Chinese women's volleyball team to win the Olympic champion as the head coach.

Discussion

> What sports events have you watched in China? Briefly talk about your experience.

5 Network Literature

Required Reading Text

Network Literature

Network literature is a style of literature published and read on the Internet. Network literature does not require the intermediary and operation of paper print medium and publishing institutions. It uses the electronic hypertext technology and the network to create and disseminate, with the maximum freedom of publication and personal creative space. Network literature is created with the popularity of the Internet.

Unlike traditional forms of literature, network literature is characterized by diversity, interactivity and the difficulty of protecting intellectual property rights. Compared with traditional literature creation, network literature creation is deeply influenced by readers' preferences. Using the interactive nature of the Internet platform, readers of online literature can interact with authors and other readers, share comments at any time, and continuously enrich the reading experience.

Network literature is mainly novels with a very wide range of topics. Take Baidu novels as an example, its themes for male include urbanity, mysteries, fantasies, histories, science fiction, military, athletics, games, martial arts and suspense, etc., and those for female include modern romance, ancient romance, fantasy romance, youth, games and suspense, etc.

Extended Text

Network Literature Works

Currently, some of the more influential works of network literature in China include *Fights Break Sphere*, *Jade Dynasty* and *Time Raiders*.

Fights Break Sphere, an ancient mystery novel serialized on the Starting Point Chinese net, is written by Tiancan Tudou. The novel tells the story of Xiao Yan, a genius youth who suddenly becomes an invalid after setting an unprecedented cultivation record for his family and finally makes brilliant achievements after hard training. In 2010, the novel was adapted and developed into a web game, and in 2018, the novel was adapted into a TV show.

Jade Dynasty, is a full-length novel written by contemporary author Xiao Ding. The novel tells the story of the growing experience of Zhang Xiaofan, an ordinary teenager living at the foot of the Qingyun Mountain. The whole novel is cleverly conceived and magnificent, opening up a unique and charming world of eastern legend of paladins. In 2007, the novel was adapted and developed into an online game, and in 2016, the novel was adapted into a TV show.

Time Raiders, a series of novels on the theme of tomb raiding, is written by Nanpai Sanshu. The series of novel tells the story of Wu Xie, Zhang Qiling, Wu Sanxing and others who enter the ancient tomb to explore. The series began serializing online in 2006 and was officially published in January 2007. In 2015, the novel was changed into a web series.

Discussion

> What Chinese network literature works have you read? Talk briefly about your experiences.

(6) Book Publishing

Required Reading Text

Book Publishing

Books, one of the main types of modern publications, are discontinuous publications formed by reproducing graphic information on paper, by means of printing, etc. Book publishing refers to the publishing activities of legal entities established in accordance with relevant state regulations. In China, book publishing is subject to a licensing system. Books are published by book publishing houses established by law. The establishment of book publishing houses must be approved by the national publishing authorities and obtain a book publishing license.

Book publishing in China begins with the editor of the book publishing houses proposing the content of the publication through market research. After internal argumentation and validation by the book publishing houses, the selected topic is submitted to the provincial press and publication bureau for approval. After the title is approved by the provincial press and the publication bureau, the publishing business enters the editing process. The main tasks of the editing process include manuscript review and editorial processing. Editorial processing is carried out based on the manuscript review. Subsequently, the book enters the stage of binding design, where the quality of bookbinding and the format directly impact the value of the book. Finally, after the book completes the processes of manuscript typesetting, proofreading, printing, etc., it enters the market.

Since the reform and opening up, China's book publishing industry has achieved rapid development and grown in scale. In the context of strict state control of new book publishing houses, Chinese book publishing has changed from quantitative growth in scale to quality and efficient development. At the same time, a large number of book publishing houses of various central departments and units and local book publishing houses have been largely restructured to become corporate market players.

Extended Text

Book Publishing House

A book publishing house primarily engages in publishing books, audiovisual products, or electronic publications. Some also operate newspapers, periodical publishing, and online publishing businesses. There are over 580 publishing houses in China. In terms of publishing categories, China's book publishing houses can be divided into comprehensive and specialized publishing houses.

The Commercial Press, founded in 1897 in Shanghai, is the oldest publishing organization in China's publishing industry. The founding of the Commercial Press marked the beginning of modern publishing in China. After the establishment of the Commercial Press, a joint-stock company was soon established to develop a variety of businesses centered on publishing, and its strength grew rapidly. In 1954, the Commercial Press was relocated to Beijing.

Zhonghua Book Company, founded in Shanghai on January 1, 1912. Zhonghua Book Company is a Chinese publishing house that integrates editing, printing, publishing and distribution. When Zhonghua Book Company was first established, it mainly published textbooks for primary and secondary schools, and printed ancient books, scientific and literary works and reference books, etc. In May 1954, the headquarter of Zhonghua Book Company was relocated to Beijing.

People's Publishing House, established in Shanghai on September 1, 1921, was founded by the Communist Party of China during the founding of it. The People's Publishing House was the first publishing house founded by the Communist Party of China. After the founding of the People's Republic of China, the People's Publishing House was rebuilt in Beijing in December 1950, with Mao Zedong writing the name of it.

Discussion

What other book publishing houses do you know about in China? Tell us briefly about them.

Chapter 9

Win-Win Cooperation

1 Coastal Opening

Required Reading Text

Coastal Open Cities

Coastal Open cities refer to a series of port cities in China's coastal areas that are open to the outside world and have implemented certain special policies of special economic zones in their foreign economic activities. The coastal open cities are an extension of the special economic zones.

In May 1984, China designated 14 cities, including Dalian, Qinhuangdao, Tianjin, Yantai, Qingdao, Lianyungang, Nantong, Shanghai, Ningbo, Wenzhou, Fuzhou, Guangzhou, Zhanjiang and Beihai, as coastal open cities. In 1985 and 1988, Yingkou and Weihai were successively included as coastal open cities. These coastal open cities have convenient transportation, good industrial base, relatively advanced technologies and good management, relatively developed scientific research, culture and education, experience in conducting foreign trade and information network for internal collaboration, which have better economic efficiency and are relatively developed areas in China.

The basic purpose of opening up coastal cities in China is to give full play to the advantages of natural resources and economic advantages, further develop foreign economic cooperation and technological exchanges, introduce foreign capital and advanced technologies, expand exports and the ability to absorb foreign exchange, and accelerate the construction of socialist modernization.

Extended Text

Special Economic Zones

Special economic zones (SEZs) are areas within a country or region that are set aside to implement special economic policies and economic systems, usually in ports or border cities that are strategically located and easily accessible. In April 1979, Deng Xiaoping first proposed the establishment of export special zones, which were later renamed as special economic zones. The essence of special economic zones is one of the important forms of free port zones in the world. By creating a favorable investment environment, encouraging foreign investment and introducing advanced technology and scientific management methods, special economic zones aim to promote the economic and technological development of the country in which they are located by means of preferential measures such as tariff reductions and exemptions. China's special economic zones implement special economic policies, flexible economic measures and a special economic management system, and insist on an outward-oriented economy as the development goal.

Since September 1979, China has designated certain areas in Shenzhen, Zhuhai and Shantou in Guangdong Province and Xiamen in Fujian Province to set up special economic zones. In April 1988, China established the Hainan special economic zone. After China accelerated its reform and opening up in 1992, it made Pudong in Shanghai a special economic zone. In May 2006, China made Binhai New Area in Tianjin a national comprehensive supporting reform pilot zone. In May 2010, China established special economic zones in Khorgos and Kashgar, Xinjiang.

Discussion

What do you know about China's cities that are open to the outside world? Describe them briefly.

② China's Accession to the World Trade Organization

Required Reading Text

China's Accession to the World Trade Organization

China's accession to the World Trade Organization (WTO) refers to the social event of China entering the World Trade Organization on December 11, 2001. Since China's reform and opening up, especially since it proposed to build a socialist market economy system in 1992, its economic strength has increased significantly and has become capable of participating in international division of labor and competition in many fields.

The negotiations on China's accession to the World Trade Organization have gone through three stages. The first stage, from the early 1980s to 1986, was mainly the preparation stage. The second stage, from 1987 to 1992, was mainly the review of China's economic and trade system. The third phase, from 1992 to 2001, entered substantive negotiations, namely, bilateral market access negotiations and multilateral negotiations around the drafting of legal documents for China's accession. After negotiations, China reached an agreement with all World Trade Organization members on it's accession to the World Trade Organization. On November 11, 2001, in Doha, the capital of Qatar, China signed the protocol of accession to the World Trade Organization.

China's accession to the World Trade Organization in 2001 was a milestone in China's deep participation in economic globalization and marked a new stage in the history of China's reform and opening up.

Extended Text

China's Accession to the Asia-Pacific Economic Cooperation

Asia-Pacific Economic Cooperation (APEC) is an important forum for economic cooperation and the highest level of intergovernmental economic cooperation in the Asia-Pacific region. As the world's largest regional economic organization, Asia-Pacific Economic Cooperation's total economic volume exceeds half of the global economic volume. All menbers are diverse and representative, including developed countries such as the United States and Japan, as well as emerging economies such as China and Mexico.

The first Asia-Pacific Economic Cooperation Ministerial Meeting was held from November 5 to 7, 1989, marking the establishment of Asia-Pacific Economic Cooperation. In November 1991, based on the principles of one China and distinction between sovereign states and regional economies, China joined Asia-Pacific Economic Cooperation as a sovereign state and Chinese Taipei and Hong Kong as regional economies.

Since China joined Asia-Pacific Economic Cooperation, Asia-Pacific Economic Cooperation has become an important stage for China to develop mutually beneficial cooperation, conduct multilateral diplomacy, and showcase China's national image with other economies in the Asia-Pacific region. In October 2001, the 9th Informal Asia-Pacific Economic Cooperation Leaders' Meeting was successfully held in Shanghai, China. The 22nd Informal Asia-Pacific Economic Cooperation Leaders Meeting was successfully held in Beijing, China in November 2014.

Discussion

What international economic organizations does your country belong to? Describe them briefly.

③ Shanghai Cooperation Organization

Required Reading Text

Shanghai Cooperation Organization

The Shanghai Cooperation Organization (SCO), an intergovernmental international organization, is the most extensive and populous comprehensive regional organization in the world. Its predecessor was the "Shanghai Five".

On June 14–15, 2001, the heads of state of "Shanghai Five"—China, Russia, Kazakhstan, Kyrgyzstan, and Tajikistan, along with the head of state of Uzbekistan, held the sixth meeting in Shanghai. Uzbekistan joined the "Shanghai Five" with full equal status. The heads of state of the six countries signed the Declaration on the Establishment of the Shanghai Cooperation Organization and announced the establishment of the SCO. In June 2002, the member states of the SCO held the second summit in St. Petersburg, where the heads of state signed the Charter of the Shanghai Cooperation Organization. The Charter clearly elaborates the SCO's purpose, organizational structure, operational forms, cooperation directions, and principles of external relations. Since 2004, the SCO has initiated an observer mechanism. In 2017, India and Pakistan joined the SCO. In 2022, Iran joined the SCO.

The purpose of the SCO is to strengthen mutual trust and good-neighborly friendship among member states; develop effective cooperation in political, economic, cultural, and other fields among member states; safeguard and ensure regional peace, security, and stability; and promote the establishment of a new international political and economic order that is democratic, fair, and equitable.

Extended Text

Forum on China-Africa Cooperation

The Forum on China-Africa Cooperation (FOCAC), established in 2000, is a collective dialogue mechanism between China and African countries based on equality and mutual benefit. The aim of FOCAC is to conduct equal consultation, enhance understanding, expand consensus, strengthen friendship, and promote cooperation. FOCAC's members include China, 53 African countries that have established diplomatic relations with China, and the African Union Commission. The Ministerial Conference of FOCAC is held every three years, attended by the minister of Foreign Affairs and the minister responsible for international economic cooperation.

In October 2000, to further strengthen the friendly cooperation between China and African countries under new circumstances, jointly address the challenges of economic globalization, and seek common development, the Ministerial Conference of FOCAC—Beijing 2000 was held in Beijing at the joint initiative of China and Africa, leading to the formal establishment of FOCAC. The first Ministerial Conference of FOCAC adopted the Beijing Declaration of FOCAC and the Program for China-Africa Cooperation in Economic and Social Development, setting the direction for China and African countries to develop a new type of partnership featuring long-term stability, equality, and mutual benefit. In November 2000, the Chinese Follow-up Action Committee of FOCAC was established, with its secretariat office located in the African Affairs Department of the Ministry of Foreign Affairs. In September 2018, the FOCAC Beijing Summit was grandly held.

Discussion

> What are the current economic exchanges between China and your country? Please provide a brief description.

④ China-ASEAN Free Trade Area

Required Reading Text

China-ASEAN Free Trade Area

China-ASEAN Free Trade Area (CAFTA), a free trade area formed by China and ten countries of the Association of Southeast Asian Nations (ASEAN), is one of the world's three largest regional economic cooperation areas. In 2010, the China-ASEAN Free Trade Area was officially launched in full swing. Covering 11 countries, the China-ASEAN Free Trade Area is the world's most populous free trade area and the largest free trade area composed of developing countries.

The dialogue between China and Association of Southeast Asian Nations began in 1991. In 1996, China became a full dialogue partner of Association of Southeast Asian Nations. In November 2000, at the 4th China-ASEAN Leaders' Meeting, China first proposed the idea of establishing the China-ASEAN Free Trade Area. In November 2002, at the 6th China-ASEAN Leaders' Meeting, leaders of 11 countries signed the Framework Agreement on Comprehensive Economic Cooperation between China and ASEAN and decided to establish the China-ASEAN Free Trade Area by 2010, marking the official launch of the process of establishing the China-ASEAN Free Trade Area. In November 2004, the two sides signed the Free Trade Area Agreement on Trade in Goods and Agreement on Dispute Settlement Mechanism. In January 2007, China and Association of Southeast Asian Nations signed the Free Trade Area Agreement on Trade in Services. On January 1, 2010, the China-ASEAN Free Trade Area was officially established.

Extended Text

China-Chile Free Trade Area

China-Chile Free Trade Area refers to the free trade area formed by China and Chile. With the development of economic globalization and regional economic integration, countries around the world are actively signing various free trade agreements to achieve the improvement of the overall welfare of the member parties and the world. Chile is the second country to sign a free trade agreement with China after the Association of Southeast Asian Nations and the first Latin American country to sign a free trade agreement with China.

Since the establishment of diplomatic relations between China and Chile in 1970, the two economic and trade relations have entered a phase of normal development. In terms of trade, China's trade with Chile has developed rapidly, with Chile becoming an important trading partner of China in Latin America and China becoming an important trading partner of Chile globally. In the 21st century, bilateral trade between China and Chile has entered a phase of rapid development. In November 2005, after negotiations, the governments of China and Chile formally signed the Free Trade Agreement between the Government of the People's Republic of China and the Government of the Republic of Chile. On October 1, 2006, the China-Chile Free Trade Area was officially established.

The establishment of the China-Chile Free Trade Area provides a broad platform for the development of economic and trade relations between the two countries.

Discussion

> What free trade areas does your country belong to? Describe them briefly

(5) China-Pakistan Economic Corridor

Required Reading Text

China-Pakistan Economic Corridor

The China-Pakistan Economic Corridor (CPEC) is a landmark project of China-Pakistan cooperation in the new era and a significant pilot and model project under the Belt and Road Initiative. The construction of CPEC contributes to promoting cross-border flows of capital, technology, information, and talent between the two countries, achieving mutual benefit and win-win results.

The idea of CPEC was first proposed by the president of Pakistan in an exclusive interview with *China Daily* in February 2006. In May 2013, during the visit of the Chinese Premier to Pakistan, the cooperation initiative for the construction of CPEC was formally proposed. Subsequently, the two governments signed the Memorandum of Understanding on Conducting Long-Term Planning of China-Pakistan Economic Corridor Cooperation. At the end of 2013, with the introduction of China's Belt and Road Initiative, the strategic importance of CPEC, as a beneficial supplement to the Belt and Road Initiative, was further elevated. In February 2014, during the visit of the Pakistani President to China, both sides agreed to accelerate the construction of CPEC. On April 20, 2015, the CPEC project was officially launched.

The CPEC starts from Kashgar and ends at Gwadar Port in Pakistan, spanning a total length of 3,000 kilometers. It connects the Silk Road Economic Belt in the north and the 21st Century Maritime Silk Road in the south, serving as a crucial hub connecting the northern and southern Silk Roads. It is a trade corridor that includes highways, railways, oil and gas pipelines, and optical fiber cables.

Extended Text

Karakoram Highway

The Karakoram Highway, connecting Kashgar in Xinjiang, China, and the northern part of Pakistan, traverses three major mountain ranges—the Karakoram, Himalayas, and Hindukush, as well as the Pamir Plateau, earning it the nickname of "the heavenly road". Built in the 1960s and 1970s with Chinese assistance, it was the only economic lifeline for Pakistan's northern region, making it also known as the "China-Pakistan friendship highway".

In September 1965, Pakistan proposed the idea of constructing a modern highway between China and Pakistan. In March 1966, China and Pakistan signed the Agreement between the Governments of China and Pakistan on the Construction of the Karakoram Highway. The construction of the Karakoram Highway began in 1966 and was completed in 1979, taking 14 years. In May 1983, passenger buses officially opened between the two countries. After the Karakoram Highway was opened to third countries in May 1986, traffic increased significantly, greatly promoting tourism and trade between China and Pakistan. In 2010, the highway was disrupted due to large-scale landslides. However, in September 2015, the Karakoram Highway was reopened.

The Karakoram Highway is a vital transportation artery connecting Pakistan to its capital, Islamabad, and the southern coastal areas. It is also the only land route for China to access Pakistan, its southern port of Karachi, the South Asian subcontinent, and the Middle East.

Discussion

> What friendly exchanges does China have with your country? Please describe briefly.

⑥ Regional Comprehensive Economic Partnership

Required Reading Text

Regional Comprehensive Economic Partnership

Regional Comprehensive Economic Partnership (RCEP), is an agreement initiated by the Association of Southeast Asian Nations in 2012 and developed by a total of 15 members including China, Japan, Korea, Australia, New Zealand.

On November 15th, 2020, the 4th Regional Comprehensive Economic Partnership Leaders' Meeting was held by video, following which the RCEP was formally signed by a total of 15 Asia-Pacific countries, including 10 countries of the

Association of Southeast Asian Nations and China, Japan, Korea, Australia, and New Zealand. The signing of the RCEP marks the official departure of the world's most populous, largest economic and trade scale and most promising free trade area.

On April 15th, 2021, China formally deposited its instrument of ratification of RCEP with the Secretary-General of the Association of Southeast Asian Nations. On November 2nd, the Secretariat of the Association of Southeast Asian Nations, the custodian of RCEP, issued a notification announcing that six ASEAN member countries and four non-ASEAN member countries had formally submitted their instruments of ratification to the Secretary-General of the Association of Southeast Asian Nations, reaching the threshold for the entry into force of the Agreement. Regional Comprehensive Economic Partnership entered into force on January 1st, 2022.

Extended Text

China-Korea Free Trade Area

China-Korea Free Trade Area, refers to the free trade area formed by China and Republic of Korea.

Since the 21st century, China has gradually become the largest trading partner, the largest export recipient and the largest source of imports for Republic of Korea, and Republic of Korea has gradually become the number one source of imports and one of the most important sources of investment for China. In May 2012, China and Republic of Korea officially launched negotiations on the China-Korea Free Trade Area. On November 10, 2014, China and Republic of Korea jointly announced the conclusion of substantive negotiations on the China-Korea Free Trade Area. On February 25, 2015, the negotiations on the China-Korea Free Trade Area were all completed. On June 1st, the China-Korea Free Trade Area was officially signed, marking the implementation phase of the construction of the China-Korea Free Trade Area. On December 9, China and Republic of Korea jointly confirmed that the Free Trade Agreement between the government of People's Republic of China and the government of the Republic of Korea officially entered into force and reduced tariffs for the first time on December 20, 2015, and the second tariff reduction on January 1, 2016.

The China-Korea Free Trade Agreement innovatively introduces local economic cooperation provisions, specifying Weihai City, China and Incheon Free Economic Zone, Republic of Korea as local economic cooperation demonstration zones to play a demonstration and guiding role. The China-Korea Free Trade Area brings a great boost to the development of related industries in both countries.

Discussion

> What economic agreements does your country have with China? Describe them briefly.

Science and Technology Innovation

Chapter 10

Information Network

1 Communication Networks

● Required Reading Text

The 5th Generation Mobile Communication Network

Mobile communication networks refer to the communication medium that enables communication between mobile users and fixed point users or among mobile users. In the field of modern communication, mobile communication is ranked as one of the three most important means of communication along with satellite communication and optical communication. At present, China mainly uses the 5th generation mobile communication network. The 5th generation mobile communication network is a communication network technology developed under the auspices of the Chinese company Huawei. The 5th generation mobile communication network brings a more convenient and fast information lifestyle to Chinese people. Currently, China's 5th generation mobile communication network is in the process of popularization.

Compared with the 4th generation mobile communication network, the 5th generation mobile communication network presents many innovations. First, the transmission rate of the 5th generation mobile communication network is greatly improved. In addition to increasing the transmission speed, the transmission stability of the 5th generation mobile communication network has also been improved. Secondly, the 5th generation mobile communication network can flexibly support different devices, such as cell phones, computers, smart watches, smart home devices, etc. Thirdly, the 5th generation mobile communication network can also extend the battery life of devices.

The 5th generation mobile communication network has been changing the lives of Chinese people and showing Chinese technology to the world.

Extended Text

The 5th Generation Mobile Communication Base Station

The mobile communication base station refers to a radio transceiver station that transmits information among cell phones in a certain radio coverage area through a mobile communication switching center. The mobile communication base station is the interface equipment for mobile devices to access the Internet, and is also a form of radio station. With the development of mobile communication network services in the direction of data and grouping, the development trend of mobile communication base stations is also bound to be broadband and have large coverage construction.

The 5th generation mobile communication base station is the core and foundation of the 5th generation mobile communication network. The 5th generation mobile communication base station can realize wireless coverage and complete wireless signal transmission between wired communication network and wireless terminal. The architecture and form of the 5th generation mobile communication base station directly affects the deployment of the 5th generation mobile communication network. Due to the problem that the higher the frequency of mobile communication networks, the greater the attenuation during signal propagation, the base station density of the 5th generation mobile communication network will be higher.

Mobile operators in China are making great efforts to build the 5th generation mobile communication base station. Currently, all prefecture-level cities in China have built 5th generation mobile communication base station. The large number of the 5th generation mobile communication base station make China the world leader in the number of 5th generation mobile network users.

Discussion

What generation of mobile communication technology is used in your country? Briefly talk about your experience.

② Search Engine

Required Reading Text

Search Engines

A search engine is a retrieval technology that uses a specific strategy to retrieve relevant information from the Internet and feed it back to the user based on the user's needs and certain algorithms. Search engines can improve people's information gathering ability and are a commonly used retrieval technology. Search engines are characterized by high efficiency and speed of information acquisition. In terms of function and principle, search engines are broadly classified into four categories: full-text search engines, metasearch engines, vertical search engines and directory search engines.

Chinese search engine technologies emerged in the early 21st century. When the Internet was just introduced to China, Sohu, Netease and Sina websites began to explore search engine technologies, and the search engines they launched belonged to the 1st generation of directory search engines. In 1999, with the opening of Yahoo China website, Chinese Internet users were able to experience powerful search functions, and could retrieve information on politics, economy, culture, sports and other aspects. In 2000, Robin Li founded Baidu, a 2nd generation search engine, which realized automatic access to information and improved retrieval efficiency. Since then, various search engines have been launched one after another. At present, Chinese people commonly use search engines such as Baidu, 360, Netease and Sogou.

Extended Text

Chinese Search Engines

Chinese search engine technologies have developed rapidly over the past two decades, and the typical search engines in China now include Baidu, 360, Sogou, etc.

Baidu search engine, is a Chinese search engine developed and promoted by Baidu, Inc. It was founded in 2000 by Robin Li. The word "Baidu" comes from the words of Xin Qiji, a lyricist of the Southern Song Dynasty, who said 800 years ago: "in the crowd seeking her for a thousand, hundred times". The emergence of Baidu has made China one of the only four countries in the world that have the core technology of search engine. At present, Baidu is the most commonly used search engine by

Chinese Internet users and has become the main entrance for Chinese Internet users to obtain information.

360 search engine is a full-text search engine developed and promoted by Beijing Qihoo Technology Co., Ltd. Founded in September 2005, Beijing Qihoo Technology Co. Ltd. is China's leading Internet security software and Internet services company. 360 search engine is the 3rd generation search engine, including news search, web search, video search and other functions.

Sogou search engine is the 3rd generation interactive search engine developed by Sohu. Through the intelligent analysis technology, Sogou selectively crawls important information on different websites to ensure that the latest information is available to users in a timely manner.

Discussion

> What kind of search engine do you usually use? Briefly talk about your experience.

③ Communication Platforms

Required Reading Text

Communication Platforms

Communication platforms refer to the platform that unifies the existing communication and contact methods such as cell phones, emails, faxes, etc., and realizes communication and contact on one terminal. The core content of communication platforms is that people can get information at any time and anywhere on any device to realize people's freedom of communication. Communication platforms are based on enterprise organization structure, combined with instant messaging, web conferencing and other systems, making a variety of communication means such as text, voices, videos integrated into one. Representatives of Chinese real-time communication platforms include DingTalk and Tencent Meeting.

DingTalk is a free communication and collaboration multi-terminal platform created by Alibaba Group in 2015, specifically for Chinese enterprises. The core functions of the DingTalk platform include organization online, enterprise communication, and enterprise team office collaboration.

Tencent Meeting is an audio and video conferencing software developed by Tencent in 2019. Tencent Meeting has features of 300 people online meeting, one-click access to all platforms, audio and video intelligent noise reduction, beauty, background defocusing, locked meeting, screen watermark, etc. Tencent Meeting software provides real-time screen sharing and supports online document collaboration.

Softwares such as DingTalk and Tencent Meeting has created a new model for meetings and offices, overcoming geographical restrictions and improving work efficiency.

Extended Text

Instant Messaging Software

In addition to the real-time meeting communication platforms commonly used in offices, Tencent QQ and WeChat are other communication software commonly used by Chinese people.

Tencent QQ, Internet-based instant messaging software, was launched in 1999 and is still the most important communication tool for Chinese people. Tencent QQ supports a variety of functions such as online chatting, video calling, file sharing and email receiving, and can be connected to a variety of communication terminals to form a huge communication network. At present, Tencent QQ covers almost all mainstream intelligent operating platforms.

WeChat, a free application launched by Tencent in 2011, provides instant messaging services for smart terminals. WeChat supports the rapid sending of free voice SMS (short message service), videos, pictures and text across communication carriers and operating system platforms via the Internet. WeChat also provides services such as Moments and message push to meet users' entertainment needs. WeChat also supports friend transfer and QR code payment to promote the circulation of electronic money and facilitate people's lives.

Currently, instant messaging software has gradually replaced cell phone communication and become the main means of communication for young people in China.

Discussion

> What kind of communication software have you used? Briefly talk about your experience.

(4) Online Shopping

Required Reading Text

Online Shopping

Online shopping refers to a shopping method in which buyers search for products and place orders through the Internet, sellers mail the products, and buyers inspect the products and complete the transaction.

Compared with traditional brick-and-mortar shopping, online shopping has great advantages. Consumers can get comprehensive product information through Internet search and get in touch with the seller in time. Online shopping is not restricted by time and place, and can get better goods at a better price, saving both time and effort. Online shopping can expand the consumer market. Merchants only need to send out relevant commodity information on the platform without renting a physical store, saving operating costs.

In 1991, China carried out the application of electronic data interchange. In 1996, China International Electronic Commerce Center was established. In 1997, online bookstores, online shopping and China's commodity ordering system began to emerge. In July 1998, the China Commodity Exchange and Marketplace website officially ran; Beijing and Shanghai launched their e-commerce projects. By the end of 1999, the scale of China's online shopping users kept rising. On March 15th, 2014, the Measures for the Administration of Internet Transactions came into force.

At present, with the popularity of the Internet, online shopping is increasingly becoming an important form of shopping for Chinese people. The Double 11 shopping carnival and Jingdong 618 are representatives of large-scale online shopping promotions.

Extended Text

Online Shopping Platforms

Currently, the main online shopping platforms in China are Taobao, Jingdong and Dangdang.

Taobao, a comprehensive online shopping platform, was founded by Alibaba Group in 2003. In October of the same year, Alibaba launched a new payment tool, Alipay, to improve the online shopping system. Taobao emerged as the most popular way to shop in China, saving people the cost of shopping and ensuring the security of shopping. With the expansion of Taobao and the increase in the number of users, Taobao has transformed from a single online marketplace into a comprehensive retail circle that includes distribution, auction, direct supply, crowdfunding, customization, and other e-commerce models.

Jingdong, also known as Jingdong Mall, is one of the most popular and influential e-commerce sites in China's e-commerce sector. Compared with similar e-commerce sites, Jingdong Mall has a richer product range and has won market share by virtue of its more competitive prices and gradually improved logistics and delivery system.

Dangdang is a well-known comprehensive online shopping mall. At present, Dangdang has expanded from a single shopping platform selling books in the early days to a comprehensive shopping platform selling various departmental goods.

Discussion

> What kind of online shopping platforms have you used? Briefly talk about your experience.

⑤ Mobile Payment

Required Reading Text

Mobile Payment

Mobile payment refers to a payment method in which users use mobile terminals (usually electronic products such as smartphones) to make financial payments for goods or services they consume instead of using bank cards or cash payment. Mobile payment effectively unites the Internet, terminal devices and financial institutions to form a new type of payment system. Mobile payment is a product of the Internet era. Mobile payment has created a new way of payment, leading to the popularization of electronic currency.

Mobile payment breaks the time and space restrictions of traditional cash payment. Users can make payment anytime and anywhere and no longer need to make face-to-face transactions. At the same time, mobile payment supports the functions of inquiry, transfer and recharge of personal accounts, which allows users to understand their consumption information and facilitate the management of personal accounts. In addition, mobile payment is highly secure. Users are required to enter passwords or verify fingerprints when making payment, which protects their privacy.

Currently, mobile payment has penetrated into every aspect of Chinese people's lives. People can make various payment activities such as phone bill recharge, utility bill payment and online shopping through mobile payment, which greatly facilitates people's lives. The commonly used software with payment function in China are Alipay and WeChat.

Extended Text

Alipay

Alipay, a well-known third-party payment platform in China. Alipay Network Technology Co., Ltd. was established in 2004. Today, Alipay has integrated payment, life, government affairs, finance and many other services to become an open life service platform. It not only provides convenient payment, transfer and receipt services, but also supports online activities such as credit card repayment, payment of utility bills and checking logistics information, and its functions cover people's lives comprehensively. Alipay has established strategic partnerships with many banks and international financial institutions at home and abroad, and become the most trusted partner of financial institutions in the field of electronic payment.

In China, Alipay is the leader in mobile payment function. In 2008, Alipay released its mobile e-commerce strategy and launched mobile payment business. In 2009, Alipay launched China's first independent mobile payment client. In 2010, Alipay launched China's first QR code payment technology, which allows users to pay by clicking on the sweep button in the software and identifying the QR code. This new payment method is more convenient and time-saving, further promoting the development of electronic money. Currently, Alipay is the world's largest mobile payment vendor.

Discussion

> What kind of mobile payment software have you used? Briefly talk about your experience.

6 Web Navigation

Required Reading Text

Mobile Navigation

In daily life, with the popularity of smartphones, people mostly use them for navigation. Currently, Amap, Baidu Maps and QQ Map are the most used mobile navigation app in China.

Amap, a mobile navigation app launched in May 2011 by Amap Software Co., Ltd. is a leading provider of digital map content, navigation and location service solutions in China. The company has Class A surveying and mapping qualification for navigation electronic maps and Class A surveying and mapping qualification for Internet map services.

Baidu Maps, a mobile navigation app launched by Beijing Baidu Netcom Technology Co., Ltd. In 2013, Baidu Maps announced that its navigation would be permanently free of charge. In 2019, Baidu Maps launched the world's first map voice customization function.

QQ Map is a cell phone navigation app launched in 2013 by Shenzhen Tencent Computer System Co., Ltd. QQ Map provides users with location and travel-related services including intelligent route planning, accurate navigation, real-time road conditions, aggregated taxi rides, public travel, etc.

Extended Text

Beidou Navigation Satellite System

Beidou navigation satellite system is a global satellite navigation system independently developed by China. The system is built entirely by China and operates independently, providing stable and secure positioning, navigation and timing services for users worldwide. At present, China has applied it in many fields such as transportation, weather forecasting and communication timing.

The Beidou navigation satellite system is a key construction project in China. In 1994, China launched the "double-star navigation and positioning system" and named it "Beidou". In 2000, China successfully launched two Beidou satellites, built China's first generation satellite navigation and positioning system (Beidou-1) and put it into use. In 2004, China launched the construction of the BeiDou satellite navigation system with global navigation capability (Beidou-2). In 2012, China completed the Beidou-2 system, extending its services to the Asia-Pacific region. In 2020, China has basically completed the Beidou-3 system and provided ralated services to the world.

Beidou navigation satellite system is not only a Chinese navigation system, but also a global navigation system. Beidou navigation satellite system has become one of the four major global satellite navigation systems and provides services to people all over the world.

Discussion

> Briefly introduce the mobile navigation software you use.

Chapter 11

Artificial Intelligence

1　Robot

● Required Reading Text

Robots

  A robot, also known as an intelligent robot, is a kind of intelligent machine that can imitate some human activities. Robots can mimic some of the logical thinking activities of human beings and have sensory functions similar to vision, hearing, smell, etc. They can replace human work in environments to which human beings cannot adapt. Robots can assist or replace human beings to complete dangerous and heavy tasks, liberate manpower and further improve work efficiency.

  The earliest robots in Chinese history were puppet robots, named Lingren, created in the Western Zhou Dynasty with the ability to walk, run, sing and dance. In terms of application environment, Chinese robot experts have divided robots into two categories, industrial robots and special robots. China began to develop its own industrial robots in the 1970s. In the 1980s, under the impact of the high technology wave, the development and research of China's robot technology received the government's attention and support. In 1987, China established the first expert group on the subject of intelligent robots. Since the 1990s, China has developed industrial robots for various purposes, implemented a number of industrial robot application projects, and formed a number of robot industrialization bases, laying the foundation for the development of China's robotics industry. In the 21st century, robots are widely used in various industries such as engineering and manufacturing, medical and health care.

Extended Text

Underwater Robots

Underwater robots, also known as unmanned remotely operated vehicles, are a kind of extreme operating robots that work underwater. The underwater environment is harsh and dangerous, and the depth of human diving is limited, so underwater robots have become an important tool for developing the ocean. The research and development of underwater robots is one of the development priorities of China's robot industry. For more than four decades, Chinese scientists have been intensely researching the application of intelligent robots in the ocean, and have achieved certain achievements.

China started to develop remote controlled underwater robots since the early 1980s, and in 1984, the first remote controlled underwater robot Hairen 1 was born in Shenyang Institute of Automation, Chinese Academy of Sciences. In 1987, the first autonomous underwater robot test bed Hairen-2 was built in Shenyang Institute of Automation, Chinese Academy of Sciences. In 1994, China's first autonomous underwater robot Explorer was successfully developed. In the 21st century, with the support of the national 863 program, the China Ocean Mineral Resources R & D Association and the Chinese Academy of Sciences strategic polit project, China has developed the Qianlong series and the Explorer series of autonomous underwater robots for oceanographic investigations. Since 2013, Qianlong-1 has carried out several oceanic survey missions. In 2020, Qianlong-4 carried out its first oceanic survey mission.

Discussion

What movies about robots have you seen? Briefly talk about your experience.

2) Drones

Required Reading Text

Drones

A drone refer to an aircraft and helicopter with no pilot or no pilot (controller) on board, using wireless remote sensing equipment to control the aircraft. Drones can accomplish highly dangerous and difficult missions, and can also be used to perform daily tasks such as aerial photography and terrain mapping. Drones not only have an important strategic position in military warfare, but also gradually enter people's daily lives and work.

China's drone business started in the 1960s. Based on the Soviet La-17 drone, China began to independently manufacture drones in 1966. In the same year, China's first drone, the Changkong 1, made its first flight, and China's independent development of drones began. Since then, China has built the Changhong 1 drone based on the U.S. Firebee drone. It was a high-altitude multi-purpose drone, mainly used for military and scientific research such as military reconnaissance and geological survey. The first flight of this model was successful in 1972, and it was officially equipped with troops in 1980.

At the end of the 20th century, China's drone business entered a rapid development stage. In 2009, the drone square appeared in China's National Day parade to show the world China's strong military power. Since 2012, civilian drones have opened up new markets and explored new functions such as aerial photography and logistics delivery.

Extended Text

Drone Applications

Although China's drone business started late, its development has been highly valued by the national aviation science and technology sector. It has developed rapidly. In recent years, China's more advanced drones mainly include models like Wing Loong UAV, DJI drones, and ASN-206.

The Wing Loong UAV, a dual-purpose multifunctional drone for military and civilian use, is one of the most advanced drones in China. The Wing Loong UAV can perform reconnaissance, surveillance, and attack ground missions for anti-terrorism and border patrol in the military. In addition, Wing Loong UAV can be used in disaster surveillance, atmospheric research, geodestic surveying, etc.

DJI drones are the best civilian drones. DJI drones can be used for aerial photography and for documentaries, commercials or the recording of major events. DJI drones can also be used for environmental monitoring and for air pollution enforcement operations. In addition, DJI drones are used in logistics services to improve logistics efficiency.

ASN-206 is a multi-purpose unmanned aircraft. Its most important feature is that it is equipped with a real-time video reconnaissance system, including vertical and panoramic cameras, infrared detection equipment, etc. It can perform missions like day and night aerial reconnaissance, battlefield surveillance, border patrol, etc.

Discussion

> What drones do you know? Briefly talk about your opinion.

③ The Internet of Things

Required Reading Text

The Internet of Things

The Internet of Things (IoT) is a new generation of network technology based on the Internet and is a new technological revolution. The purpose of IoT is to connect all things to the network for easy identification and management, so as to reach a state of "intelligence".

The early IoT was also called sensor network in China. In 1999, the Chinese Academy of Sciences started the research and development of sensor network. In 2005, the International Telecommunication Union formally proposed the concept of IoT. In 2009, IoT was officially listed as one of the five emerging strategic industries of the country. In the same year, the National Sensor Network Innovation Demonstration Zone was officially approved. By 2012, China has completed the construction of the sensor network demonstration base. In more than a decade of research, China's IoT technologies have matured and the scale of the industry has further expanded.

In China, IoT has a wide range of applications. In terms of protecting the environment, the government uses IoT technologies to monitor the quality of the atmosphere, water quality of lakes, industrial pollution emissions, etc. in real time, which effectively improves the quality of the environment. In the field of transportation, the use of IoT technologies can realize intelligent management of traffic conditions, as well as automatic monitoring and reporting of highway conditions, thereby enhancing traffic management capabilities.

Extended Text

Applications of the Internet of Things

China's IoT has great potential for applications in life, transportation, healthcare, logistics, etc.

In terms of transportation, IoT integrates and connects road traffic information, thus forming a tight transportation network. Currently, many cities in China are already using ITS intelligent transportation systems. For example, Beijing has established a traffic management center. Shanghai has successfully implemented elevated road speed management. Guangzhou has established a sound integrated traffic information platform, relying on the GPS (global positioning) system in the car to upload traffic information to the integrated traffic information platform, enabling the platform to analyze road congestion. Guangzhou also collects communication, monitoring, and road tolling into one system for easy management. In addition, the National Intelligent Transport Systems Center of Engineering and Technology is also actively developing and researching intelligent vehicle systems in an attempt to further improve the intelligent transportation system.

In terms of home life, IoT has created an era of smart homes. Haier Group has developed the Haier smart home system, which takes the U-home system as a platform to connect all devices with the network and realize intelligent management and digital sharing of smart home, security, etc., making users interact with their home appliances through IoT anytime and anywhere.

Discussion

What IoT technologies have you come across? Briefly talk about your experience.

④ Cloud Computing

Required Reading Text

Cloud Computing

Cloud computing, also known as grid computing, refers to the decomposition of huge data processing procedures into countless small programs through a network cloud. These programs are then processed and analyzed by a system of multiple servers to obtain results and return them to the users. Cloud computing is another technological innovation in the information age, which is the coordination and integration of computer resources, allowing users to access unlimited resources on the cloud, without the limitation of time and space. In the past decade, China's cloud computing technology has developed rapidly.

In 2008, IBM established a cloud computing center, IBM Cloud Labs & HiPODS in China. In 2009, Ali Software company established the first domestic E-Commerce Cloud Computing Center in Jiangsu Province. In the same year, China established its first enterprise cloud computing platform: Sinochem's Cloud Computing Platform. In 2010, the Chinese government took the lead in pilot demonstrations of innovative development of cloud computing services in five cities: Beijing, Shanghai, Shenzhen, Hangzhou and Wuxi. In 2011, China built the largest domestic cloud computing pilot zone in Chongqing. In 2018, the China Cloud went out of China and marched towards the world. China has participated in the construction of supermarket chains in Chile and the bicycle sharing system in the UK, providing quality services to users worldwide.

Extended Text

Cloud Computing Companies

China's major cloud computing companies and brands include Huawei Cloud, Aliyun, Tencent Cloud, etc.

Huawei Cloud, a public cloud brand of Huawei, was established in 2005. Huawei Cloud is a browser-based cloud management platform dedicated to providing users with stable, secure and sustainable cloud computing infrastructure services. Huawei Cloud insists on independent innovation and introduces many new Huawei technologies in the research and development process, making Huawei Cloud cost-reducing, elastic and flexible, secure and efficient.

Aliyun, a cloud computing brand of Alibaba Group, was founded in 2009. It is the world's leading technology company for cloud computing and artificial intelligence technologies. Aliyun is committed to providing users with secure and reliable computing and data processing capabilities through online public services. With a wide range of services, Aliyun not only provides high-quality and stable services for large enterprises such as China Unicom, Sinopec and Philips Group, but also serves ordinary users in application scenarios such as the ticketing system of Spring Festival travel rush and the Double Eleven shopping festival.

Tencent Cloud, a product developed by Tencent in 2010, includes cloud servers, cloud security, cloud database, etc., to provide developers and enterprises with one-stop service solutions. Tencent Cloud is committed to building the highest quality and best ecological public cloud service platform for the market.

Discussion

> What cloud computing technologies have you been exposed to? Briefly talk about your experience.

⑤ Big Data

Required Reading Text

Big Data

Big data, a collection of data of enormous scale, has five major characteristics: volume, velocity, diversity, low value density and authenticity. Big data can intelligently process large-scale materials and information to help users obtain higher quality information. Big data is a product of information technology development and represents a new stage in the information age.

With the development and progress of technology, China ushered in the era of big data. In 2014, big data was written into the Chinese government's work report for the first time, and this year was called the first year of big data in China. Since then, big data has started to develop rapidly in China. The development of big data in China is mainly concentrated in Beijing and the eastern coastal region, mainly in developed cities such as Beijing, Shanghai and Guangzhou. Among them, Beijing has the most rapidly growing big data industry. At present, China has made key technological breakthroughs in big data memory computing.

Big data is used in fields like industry, enterprise, transportation, medical treatment, etc. With the support of the central and local governments, Chinese Internet companies have built big data service platforms. On November 15, 2021, the Ministry of Industry and Information Technology officially released the plan for the development of big data industry during the 14th Five-Year Plan period, which clarifies the safeguards to promote the high-quality development of big data industry. With the in-depth development of China's digital construction, the development and application of big data will become the focus of China's technology development.

Extended Text

Big Data Applications

The widespread use of big data will help the government and businesses provide better and more accurate services for the Chinese people.

In 2018, China completed a government-led data sharing and opening platform, breaking down the data barriers between government departments and other institutions. Subsequently, the government further promoted the sharing and integration system of government information resources to realize cross-system, cross-region and cross-business government information linkage, which greatly facilitates people's lives. For example, based on big data applications, Zhejiang Province launched the all-in-one reform to integrate information and greatly improve the efficiency of government departments and institutions.

Taobao Data Cube is a big data application program launched by Taobao platform. Every transaction completed in Taobao will leave information such as transaction time, transaction quantity and commodity price in the big data. At the same time, this information will be matched with personal information features such as the buyer's age, gender, and address. With this information in hand, the Taobao platform can provide buyers with more suitable goods and help them buy better goods at a better price, thus increasing the success rate of the transaction. Merchants can also use big data to understand their business conditions, macro industry conditions, etc., so as to further improve their products, adjust prices, and help them develop better business strategies.

Discussion

> What big data application cases have you come across? Briefly talk about your experience.

6 Face Recognition

Required Reading Text

Face Recognition

Face recognition is a biometric identification technology based on the facial features of a person. Face recognition is mainly used for identity recognition. Face recognition first determines whether a face exists in the input face image or video. If a face exists, the system automatically extracts the facial features of the face and compares them with the face inside the system to identify the user. There are some companies developing face recognition technology in China, and the more successful companies include Hik vision, Iflytek, etc.

Face recognition technology is widely used in China in the fields such as government, security, and bank. In the access control systems, the computer identifies the head of the household by detecting the user's facial features and comparing them with the user's face in the computer. In the field of public transportation, many airports and high-speed railway stations in China use high-definition matching systems between faces and identity documents to help identify users. In the field of public security, China is also applying face recognition technology to criminal investigation cases, using a large database to find and lock the identity of suspects. In the financial sector, face-scanning payment is now a popular payment method in China. People can prevent personal information leakage and improve payment efficiency by scanning their faces to pay.

Face recognition technology in China has been applied in various fields, bringing great convenience to people's lives.

Extended Text

Face-Scanning Payment

Face-scanning payment is a new payment method based on technologies such as artificial intelligence, machine vision, 3D sensing, and big data. Compared with traditional payment methods, face-scanning payment does not require users to enter passwords, so there is no need to worry about password leakage. The face-scanning payment is fast and has the advantages of security, efficiency and convenience.

In 2013, a Finnish company launched the world's first payment platform based on face recognition system. In 2014, Baidu, Chongqing Research Institute of Chinese Academy of Sciences, Ant Financial Services, Alipay, WeChat Pay, etc. took the lead in the technology development and commercial exploration of face-scanning payment. In 2015, known as the first year of face-scanning payment, Alibaba demonstrated Alipay's face-scanning payment technology. In 2018, Alipay announced that its face-scanning payment has been commercialized and planned for large-scale promotion. With the popularity of smart-phones and the introduction of face recognition function, face-scanning payment has started to become popular in China on a large scale. At present, the tools commonly used in China for face-scanning payment has are Alipay and WeChat. In January 2020, in order to regulate the innovation of face recognition offline payment application and prevent the security risk of face-scanning payment, Payment & Clearing Association of China organized the Self-Regulatory Convention for Face Recognition Offline Payment Industry (Trial).

The development and popularity of face-scanning payment is of great value to enhance users' mobile payment experience, improve merchants' operational efficiency and drive the intelligent development of the economy and society.

Discussion

> What face recognition technologies have you come across? Briefly talk about your experience.

Chapter 12

Aerospace

① Fighter Jets

● Required Reading Text

Fighter Jets

  Fighter jets refers to the military aircraft types with basic weapons such as high-altitude missiles and aerial machine guns, and has the ability of air battle. The mainly types are fighter jets and strong attack jets. Fighter jets have good maneuverability, fast flight speed, and strong firepower of on-board weapons, which are suitable for air battle.

  China started to manufacture fighter jets in the mid-1950s. In 1956, China successfully built its first domestic fighter jet, the J-5, which opened a new chapter in Chinese fighter jets manufacturing. While enhancing its own comprehensive national power, China also exported J-5 to Vietnam, Albania, Pakistan and other countries to defend the aviation security of these countries. In 1959, J-6 was successfully tested and then started mass production. In 1966 and 1979, J-7 and J-8 were finalized and put into production. In 1984, J-8 Ⅱ took off for a test flight and soon went into production. In 1998, J-10 made its first flight successful. It is a new type of Chinese self-developed fighter jets with advanced communication equipment and a large combat radius. In 2011, it was the first successful flight of the J-20 developed by China. The J-20 is a fifth generation fighter.

  China is one of the three countries in the world that has five generations of fighter jets. China has defended its airspace by constantly developing its own fighter jets.

Extended Text

J-20

J-20, codenamed Dragon, is a stealthy fifth generation air combat aircraft with high stealth, high situational awareness, and high maneuverability developed by the Chengdu Aircraft Design Institute of China Aviation Industry Corporation (CAIC). J-20 is China's latest generation of twin-engine heavy stealth fighter jet, designed to replace the fourth generation fighter jets like J-10 and J-11. J-20 will be responsible for the future sovereignty maintenance mission of the Chinese Air Force over the air and sea.

In the overall design, J-20 adopts a single-seat, twin-engine, twin-drop tail, duck-type aerodynamic layout with side stripes and strong stealth capability. Among them, the full-motion dual droop tail design of J-20 improves the stability performance of the fighter jets. J-20 is also equipped with radar, large screen LCD information display system and other advanced equipment to facilitate pilots to understand the war situation at all time and provide timely air combat decisions.

On January 11, 2011, the first J-20 was tested. On November 1, 2016, J-20 made its first aerial flight demonstration at the 11th China International Aviation & Aerospace Exihibition. In July 2017, J-20 was presented at the military parade for the 90th anniversary of the founding of the Chinese People's Liberation Army. On February 9, 2018, J-20 began to be installed in the combat units of the Chinese People's Liberation Army Air Force.

China's self-developed J-20 represents the highest level of Chinese fighter jets research, fully demonstrating the strong scientific and technological strength and innovation capability of the Chinese Air Force.

Discussion

> Briefly talk about the fighter jets used in your country.

(2) Transport Aircraft

Required Reading Text

Transport Aircraft

A transport aircraft is an aircraft designed to carry people or materials. Transport aircraft can be divided into military, civilian and general transport aircraft according to their applications.

The earliest military transport aircraft in China was born during the War Against Japanese Aggression. In 1944, China Nanchuan No.2 Aircraft Manufacturing successfully developed the wooden twin-engine medium transport aircraft Zhongyun 1. In 1948, the Chinese transport aircraft Zhongyun-2 flew in Chongqing. In 1957, Y-5 transport aircraft, based on the Soviet An-2 transport aircraft and manufactured by Nanchang Aircraft Manufacturing, made its maiden flight. Y-5 was the first transport aircraft manufactured by China itself. Y-5 is a dual-use transport aircraft for military and civilian, widely used in training, parachuting, sports, transportation and agricultural missions. In 1970, the first flight of Y-7 was successfully carried out by the AVIC Xi'an Aircraft Industry Corporation. In 1984, Y-7 was officially delivered to civil aviation, and in 1986, Y-7 was put into civil air passenger service. Y-8 transport aircraft is a medium-range transport aircraft developed by AVIC Shaanxi Aircraft Manufacturing Company, which can be used to perform airdrop, airborne and maritime operations. Y-12 is a light dual-engine multi-purpose aircraft designed and produced by AVIC Harbin Aircraft Manufacturing Company, has received airworthiness certifications from China, the United Kingdom, the United States and France.

Extended Text

Y-20

Y-20, codenamed Kunpeng, is a new generation of military large transport aircraft developed by China itself. As a large multi-purpose transport aircraft, Y-20 can perform long-distance air transport of various materials and personnel under complex weather conditions. Compared with IL-76 in service with the Chinese Air Force, Y-20 has greatly improved engines and electronic equipment, increased load capacity and excellent short-runway takeoff and landing performance.

For a long time after the founding of the People's Republic of China, China had only small and medium-sized transport aircraft. With the gradual increase in economic development and technological strength, China's aviation industry began to provide new types of aircraft for the aviation military transport force. In 1993, AVIC Xi'an Aircraft Industry Corporation began the preliminary demonstration of a large transport aircraft. In 2007, China launched a large transport aircraft project. In 2013, China's first independently developed Y-20 strategic transport aircraft successfully made its maiden flight, marking the birth of China's large transport aircraft. In 2016, Y-20 completed its test flight and was delivered to troops in bulk. On February 13, 2020, the Chinese Air Force deployed a Y-20 transport aircraft to airlift medical team members and supplies to Wuhan. On January 28, 2022, the Chinese Air Force deployed a Y-20 transport aircraft to deliver disaster relief supplies to Tonga.

Discussion

Briefly describe what you know about transport aircraft.

3 Shipboard Aircraft

Required Reading Text

Carrier-Based Aircraft

Carrier-based aircraft refers to the collective term for naval aircraft and helicopters taking off and landing on aircraft carriers or other surface ships. This type of aircraft has a wide range of roles and can attack targets underwater, on the ground and in the air and perform a variety of missions. The performance of carrier-based aircraft determines the combat capability of aircraft carriers, and the more the number of carrier-based aircraft, the stronger the carrier is. China's carrier-based aircraft started late, and the representative model is J-15.

J-15, codenamed Feisha, is a single-seat, twin-engine heavy naval carrier-based fighter jet developed by China on the basis of the domestic J-11 fighter jet with reference to the Su-33 fighter prototype, and belongs to the fourth generation of fighter improvement. J-15 adds duck wings, two engines, landing gear and boosting gear on the basis of J-11, and has foldable wings to greatly improve the aircraft's performance. In 2009, the first flight of J-15 was successful. In 2012, the first J-15 completed its landing and takeoff tests on the aircraft carrier Liaoning. In 2013, J-15 took off and landed on the Chinese aircraft carrier Liaoning, completing its first flight on board. In 2017, J-15 arrived in the South China Sea with the aircraft carrier Liaoning for training. In 2019, J-15 participated in the military parade to celebrate the 70th anniversary of the founding of the People's Republic of China.

The carrier-based aircraft is an important weapon in naval operations. With the improvement of China's naval strength and technology level, the types and numbers of carrier based aircraft will be further increased.

Extended Text

Aircraft Carrier

An aircraft carrier is a large surface combatant ship that uses aircraft as its primary combat weapon and as its base for maritime activities. The construction of aircraft carriers is the basis for the development of carrier-based aircraft. Aircraft carriers have huge decks and islands to provide takeoff and landing sites for shipboard aircraft.

Since the 1970s, the Chinese People's Liberation Army Navy has been studying aircraft carriers. In 1998, China purchased the Soviet Navy's Varyag aircraft carrier. In 2005, the Varyag entered the Dalian Shipyard and was modified by the Chinese Navy. In September 2012, the Varyag was officially renamed aircraft carrier Liaoning and delivered to the Chinese Navy for research, experiments and training. In November 2013, the Chinese Navy formed an aircraft carrier battle group in the South China Sea with the aircraft carrier Liaoning as the core, marking the beginning of the aircraft carrier Liaoning to form a battle group. In February 2014, the construction of China's first domestically built aircraft carrier began. In April 2017, the aircraft carrier was officially launched. In December 2019, China's first domestically built aircraft carrier, aircraft carrier Shandong, was delivered to the Chinese Navy. The birth and commissioning of the Chinese aircraft carrier has made it possible for China to develop carrier-based aircraft. On June 17, 2022, China's second domestic aircraft carrier, aircraft carrier Fujian, was officially launched.

Discussion

> Briefly introduce what you know about carrier-based aircraft.

④ Carrier Rockets

Required Reading Text

Chinese Rockets

A rocket is a delivery vehicle propelled by a rocket engine that can fly both inside and outside of the atmosphere. Rockets are one of the major inventions of ancient China.

During the Tang Dynasty in China, gunpowder was used in the military, and weapons made from gunpowder were called rockets. During the Northern Song Dynasty, officers Yue Yifang and Feng Jisheng built the world's first gunpowder-powered rocket. This earliest primitive rocket was no different from modern rockets in terms of working principles. In the middle of the 12th century, the primitive rockets were improved and widely used in warfare. In the middle of the 13th century, the Mongols invaded Central Asia, West Asia and Europe and introduced Chinese rocket technologies to Europe and other parts of the world.

After the founding of the People's Republic of China, China launched a number of experimental rockets. In 1956, China's first rocket research institute was established, marking the beginning of China's space industry. In 1960, a sounding rocket designed and manufactured by China was successfully launched. In 1965, China began to develop solid sounding rockets. In 1970, China's Long March 1 rocket successfully launched the Dongfanghong-1 satellite, marking China's first step in developing space technologies and its formal entry into the space age. In 1980, China successfully launched a long-range carrier rocket into the scheduled water of the Pacific Ocean. In 1981, China successfully conquered the "one rocket, three satellites" technology, using one rocket to launch three satellites, becoming the third country in the world to master the technology of launching multiple satellites with one rocket. In 1990, China successfully launched Asiasat-1 communication satellite made by the United States by Long March-3 carrier rocket, becoming the third country in the world to enter the international satellite launch service market.

Extended Text

Long March Series of Carrier Rockets

The Long March series of carrier rockets are China's self-developed space launch vehicles. In the 1960s, China began to develop the Long March series of carrier rockets, and on April 24, 1970, Long March-1 launch vehicle successfully launched Dongfanghong 1 satellite for the first time. On January 26, 2022, China successfully launched Long March-4C carrier rocket from Jiuquan Satellite Launch Center.

Currently, there are four generations of China's Long March series of carrier rockets. The first generation of carrier rockets broke through the bottleneck of China's space technology and completed the leap of China's carrier rockets technology from nothing to something. The second generation of carrier rockets made technical improvements of carrier rockets based on the first generation of rockets and adopted digital control systems. The third generation of carrier rockets is dedicated to improving mission reliability and mission adaptability. The fourth generation of carrier rockets adopts non-toxic and non-polluting propellant to protect the environment. Through continuous technological improvements and innovations, the of carrier rocket of the Long March series of carrier rockets has increased significantly.

Over the years, the Long March series of carrier rockets have strongly supported and guaranteed the successful implementation of a series of major engineering tasks such as China's manned spaceflight, lunar exploration, Beidou navigation satellite system and high-resolution earth observation system, which have laid a solid foundation for promoting the development of related fields and accelerating the construction of a strong science and technology and space power.

Discussion

> Briefly introduce what you know about carrier rockets.

⑤ Manned Space

Required Reading Text

Manned Space

Manned space is a round-trip flight activity in which humans pilot and ride manned spacecraft in space for a variety of exploration, research, experiments, production and military applications. Manned space activities can provide a broader and deeper understanding of the entire universe and make full use of the special environment of space and manned spacecraft to conduct various research and experimental activities and develop the extremely rich resources of space.

The Chinese government recognized early on the importance of manned space in future international competition. After China's first artificial earth satellite went up, Qian Xuesen proposed that China should engage in manned space in 1971. The country named it Project 714 and named the spacecraft Shuguang-1 at that time. In 1975, China successfully launched and recovered the first return satellite, laying a solid foundation for China's research on manned space technology.

In January 1992, China's manned space program was officially included in the national plan, also known as Project 921. In October 2003, China's manned spacecraft Shenzhou-5 was successfully launched. Yang Liwei became the first person to fly in China. This was the first time China completed a manned space mission. China became the third country to master manned space technology after Russia and the United States.

Extended Text

Shenzhou Spacecraft

Shenzhou spacecraft, the first manned spacecraft developed by China on its own with fully independent intellectual property rights, has reached or outperformed the third international generation of manned spacecraft technology.

In November 1999, China successfully launched and recovered the first unmanned test spacecraft Shenzhou-1. In January 2001, China successfully launched Shenzhou-2. In March and December 2002, China successfully launched Shenzhou-3 and Shenzhou-4 unmanned spacecrafts. In October 2003 and October 2005, China successfully launched Shenzhou-5 and Shenzhou-6 manned spacecraft. In 2008,

China's third manned spacecraft, Shenzhou-7, was successfully launched, with astronaut Zhai Zhigang conducting an exit activity. China became the third country in the world to master the technology of space exit activities. In November 2011, Shenzhou-8 spacecraft was successfully launched. In June 2012 and June 2013, Shenzhou-9 and Shenzhou 10 manned spacecrafts were successfully launched and docked with Tiangong-1 target aircraft in space. On October 17, 2016, Shenzhou 11 was successfully launched and successfully docked with Tiangong-2 space lab in space. In 2021, the Shenzhou-12 and Shenzhou-13 manned spacecrafts were launched successfully.

Discussion

> Briefly introduce what you know about spacecraft.

6 Space Exploration

Required Reading Text

Space Exploration

Space exploration refers to the direct detection of physical phenomena, physical processes, and chemical composition of space and celestial bodies using sounding rockets and spacecraft. Space exploration is based on sounding rockets, artificial Earth satellites, artificial planets and spacecraft, and a network of ground observation stations and balloons to form a complete space exploration system.

China's space exploration began in the 1960s. In 1964, China successfully launched a biological rocket. In April 1970, China launched the first artificial Earth satellite Dongfanghong 1. In November 1975, China launched a return artificial satellite. In May 1980, China's long-range carrier rocket was successfully launched. In April 1984, China's first geostationary orbit test communication satellite was successfully launched. In February 1986, China launched an operational communication and broadcasting satellite. In September 1988, China launched an experimental meteorological satellite Fengyun-1. In November 1999, China successfully launched the first Shenzhou-1 test spacecraft. In October 2003, China successfully launched its first manned spacecraft, Shenzhou-5. Astronaut Yang Liwei became the first Chinese man to go into space on a Chinese spacecraft. In January 2004, China started the lunar exploration project. In July 2020, China's first Mars exploration mission, the Tianwen 1 probe, was successfully launched.

Extended Text

Lunar Exploration Project

In January 2004, China's lunar orbiting project was officially launched and named Chang'e Project. In February 2006, China included manned space and lunar exploration project into the 16 national major science and technology projects. China's lunar exploration project has different tasks in different phases: the first phase's mission is to realize the orbiting lunar exploration; the second phase is to realize the lunar soft landing and automatic survey mission; the third phase is to realize the unmanned sample return mission. After the successful conclusion of the third phase of China's lunar exploration project, the fourth phase of lunar exploration has been fully launched.

In October 2007, Chang'e-1 lunar probe was successfully launched from Xichang Satellite Launch Center to explore the composition of lunar materials, the nature of lunar soil and the space environment on the lunar surface. In October 2010, Chang'e-2 lunar probe was successfully launched to obtain clearer images of the lunar surface and more accurate lunar-related data. In December 2013, Chang'e-3 lunar probe was successfully launched. Chang'e-3 carried Jade Rabbit lunar rover for the first time to achieve a soft landing on the moon. Chang'e-3 completed the world's first lunar geological profile using lunar radar, and proved that the moon has no water. In November 2020, the Chang'e-5 lunar probe was successfully launched and returned to Earth with lunar samples.

Discussion

> Briefly describe what you know about space exploration activities.

Cultural Heritage

Chapter 13

Traditional Culture

① Music

● Required Reading Text

Music of China

    Chinese music refers to the folk music of China. The history of Chinese music can be traced back to the time of the Yellow Emperor in the ancient times. Chinese music has had a profound influence on the music of China's neighboring regions. At the same time, Chinese music has been enriched and developed through the process of absorbing foreign music.

    In the Neolithic Age, 6000 years ago, Chinese ancestors were able to make bone whistles. According to documents, ancient Chinese music was characterized by a combination of song, dance and music. In ancient China, poetry and song were indistinguishable, i.e. literature and music were closely linked. The poems in the earliest extant collection of Chinese poetry, *The Book of Songs*, are all orally singable. Tang poems and Song lyrics are all singable, such as Su Shi's *Prelude to Water Melody*, which describes the Mid-Autumn Festival.

    In ancient China, music was very important, and a cultivated person should be proficient in music, cheese, calligraphy and painting. The "music" here is the guqin, which has been handed down until today. In addition to the guqin, ancient Chinese musical instruments include the guzheng, xiao, flute, pipa, erhu, yangqin, bell, and drum. The representative music of ancient China includes *Guangling Verse, High Mountain and Running Water* and *Plum-blossom in Three Movements*. Some of the more representative music from modern China include *The Moon over a Fountain*,

Fishing Junks at Sunset and *The Beauty Lovers*.

Extended Text

Guqin

The guqin, also known as the seven-stringed zither, is a traditional Chinese plucked string instrument, and is the representative instrument of the string group of the "eight tones". The Chinese guqin has a history of over 3000 years.

According to ancient Chinese texts, Shun set the instrument to have five strings; King Wen of Zhou added one string; King Wu conquered Zhou and added another string to make seven strings. The guqin was the most revered instrument in ancient China, ranking at the top of the four arts music, cheese, calligraphy and painting and it is said that the left qin and the right calligraphy. The guqin was regarded by ancient Chinese intellectuals as a representative of elegance, and was also used as an accompaniment to people's chanting. In ancient China, the guqin has always been an essential knowledge and a compulsory subject for intellectuals. The guqin has been featured in Chinese poetry, literature and stories, including the story of Boya and Zhong Ziqi, who became soulmates through *High Mountain and Running Water*. During the Sui and Tang dynasties, the Chinese guqin was introduced to East Asian countries. In modern times, along with the footsteps of the Chinese, the guqin has spread around the world and become a symbol of Chinese culture.

On November 7, 2003, the UNESCO World Heritage Committee announced that the Chinese guqin was selected as a World Intangible Cultural Heritage. In 2006, China inscribed the guqin on the first list of China's Intangible Cultural Heritage.

Discussion

> What Chinese classical music have you listened to? Briefly talk about your experience.

② Poetry

Required Reading Text

Poetry of China

Poetry is one of the major styles of literature. In ancient China, it was called poetry when it was not music, and song when it was music, but now it is generally referred to as poetry. Poetry is a literary genre that uses highly condensed language to express the author's rich emotions in a vivid way, reflecting social lives in a concentrated manner and having a certain rhythm and rhyme. Poetry was one of the first literary genres to emerge in China. It originated from the ancient social life, as a rhythmic and emotional form of language arising from labor and production, love between the sexes, and primitive religion. Poetry vividly reflects the living conditions and inner prayers of the Chinese ancestors, and also expresses the power of the Chinese national language in a short, vivid form. *The Book of Songs* is the first collection of Chinese poetry. Chinese Han poetry has gone through the stages of development of Han, Wei and Six Dynasties music, Tang poetry, Song lyrics, Yuan operas, Ming and Qing poetry and modern poetry.

Ancient Chinese poetry, also called old poetry, is poetry composed in literary language and traditional metre. Ancient Chinese poetry in a broad sense include various ancient Chinese rhymes, such as narrative, lyric and song. In a narrow sense, it only includes ancient poems and modern poems. The creation of ancient poetry was one of the ways for Chinese writers to express their thoughts. Modern Chinese poetry, also known as new style poetry, is the poetry that has been written since the May Fourth Movement. Modern Chinese poetry is characterized by writing in vernacular language, expressing the new contemporary content of science and democracy, breaking the shackles of the old poetic meter, and being flexible and free in form.

Extended Text

Tang Poetry

Tang poetry, the general term for poetry of the Tang Dynasty, is one of the precious cultural heritages of the Chinese nation and a pearl in the treasure house of Chinese culture. Tang poetry has greatly influenced the cultural development of many countries in the world and is an important reference for future generations to study the politics, public sentiment, customs and culture of the Tang Dynasty. Tang poetry was the most prosperous and glorious period in the history of ancient Chinese poetry.

The forms of Tang poetry are diverse. The ancient poetry of the Tang Dynasty had no fixed number of stanzas or words, but mainly consisted of five lines, seven lines and miscellaneous words. There were two types of poetry in the modern style, namely, the quatrain and the rhyme, each with five-character and seven-character lines.

The poets of the Tang Dynasty were divided into many schools. The representative figures of the idyllic poetry were Wang Wei and Meng Haoran, whose representative works included *Remembering My Brothers in Shandong on the Ninth of September* and *To an Old Friend's Cottage*. The representative figures of the frontier poetry were Gao Shi, Cen Shen, Wang Changling and Wang Zhiwan, whose representative works included *A Song from Yan*, *A Song of White Snow in Farewell to Field-Clerk Wu Going Home*, *To the Border* and *Liangzhou Song*. The representative figure of the romantic poetry was Li Bai, whose representative works included *Dreaming of a Trip to Tianmu and Staying Behind* and *The Sichuan Road*. The representative figure of the realistic poetry was Du Fu, whose representative works included *Three Officials* and *Tree Parewells*.

Discussion

> Which ancient Chinese poems have you read? Briefly talk about your experience.

③ Opera

Required Reading Text

Opera of China

Chinese opera is a traditional Chinese theatrical form, which includes literature, music, dance, art, acrobatics and other factors. Chinese opera was formed in the Han and Tang dynasties, and only in the Song and Jin dynasties it gradually become a more complete opera art. According to the statistics in 1985, there were about 340 kinds of opera plays in various ethnic groups and regions in China.

Chinese opera is characterized by the aggregation of many art forms in one standard, reflecting their individuality in a common nature. Opera music is the musical part of Chinese Han opera, including the vocal part of singing and rhyming, and the instrumental part of accompaniment, opening and passing music. Opera music is mainly based on singing, with solo, antiphonal style, unison and helper singing forms, and is the main means of expression for developing the plot and portraying the characters.

Chinese opera, Greek tragedy and comedy, and Indian Sanskrit drama, are known as the three oldest theatrical cultures in the world. After a long period of development and evolution, Chinese opera has gradually formed into five major opera genres: Beijing opera, Yue opera, Huangmei opera, Ping opera, and Yu opera.

Extended Text

Yue Opera

Yue opera is the second largest opera genre in China and is known abroad as Chinese Opera. It is one of the five major opera genres in China and is known as the second national opera. It originated in Shengzhou, Zhejiang Province, was born in Shanghai, flourished throughout the country, and spread throughout the world. In its development, it has drawn on the strengths of such distinctive genres as Kun opera, drama and Shao opera, and has undergone a historical evolution from male to female Yue opera.

Yue opera is a lyrical drama, based on singing, with a beautiful voice, touching, beautiful and elegant performances, and a strong sense of Jiangnan's spirituality. It has a variety of artistic genres, with the talented and beautiful women being the main theme. Yue opera is popular in southern regions of China, such as Shanghai, Zhejiang, Jiangsu, Fujian, Jiangxi and Anhui provinces. The representative works of Yue opera include *The Butterfly Lovers*, *The Romance of the West Chamber*, *The Emerald Hairpin*, *Chasing Fish*, *Love Detective*, *The Pearl Tower*, *Liu Yi Delivers the Letter*, *Five Daughters offering Felicitation* and *The Desert Prince*.

In 1953, Shanghai Film Studio produced *The Butterfly Lovers*, the first large-scale color opera film after the founding of the People's Republic of China. In 2006, Yue opera was included in the first batch of national intangible cultural heritage list.

Discussion

> Which Chinese operas have you seen or heard? Briefly talk about your experience.

④ Painting

Required Reading Text

Chinese Painting

Chinese painting, abbreviated as guohua, refers to the Chinese national painting with a long history and fine tradition, which is a unique system in the world of art. The tools and materials used in Chinese painting include brushes, ink, Chinese paints, rice paper and silk. The subjects of Chinese painting can be divided into figures, landscapes, boundary paintings, flowers, birds, animals, insects and fishes.

There is a saying in China that painting and calligraphy have the same origin, that is, both writing and painting in ancient China originated from early pictographs. Various decorative paintings were painted on pottery and bronze vessels in the Neoithic Period. During the Warring States Period, paintings painted on silk fabrics—silk paintings—appeared in China. During the Han Dynasty and the Northern and Southern Dynasties, Chinese paintings were mainly religious paintings. During the Sui and Tang dynasties, Chinese landscape and flower and bird paintings had matured, and religious paintings reached their peak. During the Five Dynasties, Nothern Song and Southern Song dynasties, figure painting shifted to depicting secular life, and landscape painting and flower and bird painting jumped to the mainstream of the painting circles. During the Yuan, Ming and Qing dynasties, Chinese ink and landscape painting and freehand flower and bird painting developed prominently.

With the gradual stabilization of social economy, many great painters who loved life and revered art emerged from various periods of Chinese history, among which the representative ones were Gu Kaizhi, Yan Liben, Zhang Zeduan, Tang Yin, Zheng Banqiao, Xu Beihong and Pan Tianshou.

Extended Text

Landscape Painting

Landscape painting, or shanshui for short, is a type of Chinese painting that focuses on depicting natural scenery of mountains and rivers, evolving from the background of geographic situation maps and figure painting. Chinese landscape painting is divided into blue-green landscape, ink landscape, gold-blue landscape light-red landscape, light blue-green landscape and boneless landscape. The representative painters of Chinese landscape painting include Zhan Ziqian, Wang Wei, Fan Kuan and Zhang Hong.

Chinese landscape painting emerged in the Qin and Han dynasties. During North and South Dynasties, Chinese landscape painting gradually developed, but was still attached to figure painting. During the Sui and Tang dynasties, landscape painting gradually matured and became an independent school of painting. During this period, numerous landscape painting schools and painters emerged in China, such as Zhan Ziqian's colorful landscapes, Li Sixun's gold and blue landscapes, Wang Wei's ink and wash landscapes, and Wang Qia's splashed ink landscapes. During the Song Dynasty, Chinese landscape painting was already very prosperous and a large number of painters appeared, such as Jing Hao, Li Cheng, Dong Yuan, Fan Kuan, Xu Daoning, Song Di, Mi Fu, etc. During the Yuan Dynasty, landscape painting tended to be more realistic, with a focus on the real things with the imaginary and a new style of brushwork and ink. Since the Ming and Qing dynasties, landscape painting has evolved, focusing on the management of position and expression of mood.

Representative landscape paintings from various periods of Chinese history included Zhan Ziqian's *Spring Journey* from the Sui Dynasty, Li Sixun's *Pavilion with River Sails* from the Tang Dynasty, Fan Kuan's *Travelling amid Mountains and Streams*, and Huang Gongwang's *Dwelling in the Fuchun Mountains* from the Yuan Dynasty.

Discussion

> Have you ever seen a traditional Chinese painting? Briefly talk about your experience.

5 Calligraphy

Required Reading Text

Calligraphy of China

Calligraphy, an art form of written expression, one of the traditional Chinese arts, refers to the law of writing Chinese characters with a Chinese style conical brush. Chinese calligraphy was created and developed within Chinese culture. Chinese characters are an important element of Chinese calligraphy. Chinese calligraphy is known as poetry without words, dance without movements, painting without pictures, music without sound, etc.

The art of Chinese calligraphy began at the stage when Chinese characters were created. The first works of calligraphic art were not words, but some pictographs or pictorial characters. From the Xia, Shang and Zhou dynasties to the Qin and Han dynasties, various Chinese calligraphic styles appeared one after another, among which five scripts—seal script, official script, cursive script, running script and regular script—gradually became established and the art of calligraphy began to develop in an orderly manner. The prosperous period of the art of calligraphy began in the Eastern Han Dynasty. During the Eastern Han Dynasty, specialized works on calligraphy theory appeared in China, and the earliest calligraphy theory was proposed by Yang Xiong. During the Jin Dynasty, the most influential calligrapher in the history of calligraphy was Wang Xizhi. During the Tang Dynasty, regular script, running script, and cursive script developed to a new level, influencing future generations far more than any previous era. Ouyang Xun, Yu Shinan, Chu Suiliang, Yan Zhenqing, and Liu Gongquan were among the great calligraphers of this period. During the Qing Dynasty, Chinese calligraphy was divided into two major periods of development: the study of rubbings and the study of monuments.

Extended Text

The Four Treasures of the Study

The Four Treasures of the Study refers to the unique Chinese tools of calligraphy and painting, namely, pen, ink, paper, and inkstone. The name of the Four Treasures of the Study originated during the Northern and Southern Dynasties.

The pen is a brush. The brush holder is usually made of bamboo, but it is also made of rhinoceros horns, ivories or gold and silver. Good brushes have four advantages: sharpness, flushness, roundness and flexibility. Since the Yuan Dynasty, brushes produced in Huzhou, Zhejiang Province, is the most famous variety of brush in China. Ink is the color material for writing and painting. Before the invention of artificial ink, natural ink or semi-natural ink was generally used as the writing material. Depending on the raw materials, ink can be divided into oil smoke ink, lacquer smoke ink, pine-soot ink, ect. Paper is one of the four major inventions of ancient China. Rice paper is a unique handmade paper for brush painting and calligraphy. Rice paper is flexible, white and smooth, with durable color and strong water absorption. The inkstone is a tool for writing and painting in China to grind color. The inkstone is known as the first of the Four Treasures of the Study by the ancient Chinese. During the Han Dynasty, inkstones were already very popular. In the Song Dynasty, inkstones were commonly used.

The Four Treasures of the Study are unique, showing the customs of the Chinese people that are different from those of other peoples, and contributing to the progress and development of the world culture and national culture.

Discussion

Have you ever seen Chinese calligraphy? Briefly compare the similarities and differences between the Chinese characters you write and Chinese calligraphy.

6 Handicrafts

Required Reading Text

Handicrafts of China

China has a wide variety of handicrafts, among which the more representative ones are ceramics, jade carving, wood carving, bamboo weaving and paper cutting.

Ceramics, a collective term for pottery and porcelain, is made from a mixture of two raw materials: clay and porcelain. During the Tang Dynasty, Chinese ceramics reached a high level of production technology and artistic creation. Chinese pottery was exported to Japan, India, Persia and Egypt, and played an important role in international cultural exchange.

Jade carving, which refers to the processing and carving of jade into exquisite crafts, is one of the oldest varieties of carving in China. In the process of production, the craftsmen carefully design and repeatedly refine the jade according to the natural color and natural shape of different jade materials in order to carve the jade into a beautiful craft.

Wood carving, a type of sculpture, is a separate type of work from woodworking. Wood carving is often referred to as a folk craft in China. Wood carving is complex, with a wide range of genres, of which Zhejiang's Dongyang wood carving is renowned nationwide.

Bamboo weaving is a handicraft that uses bamboo in the mountains to weave various utensils and crafts. Bamboo weaving not only has great practical value, but also has a deep historical background. At present, the main products of bamboo weaving in China are hats and bamboo baskets, etc.

Extended Text

Chinese Paper Cutting

Chinese paper cutting is a folk art that uses scissors or a carving knife to cut patterns on paper to decorate life or to complement other folk activities. In China, paper cutting is interwoven into the social life of people of all ethnic groups and is an important part of various folklore activities. Paper cutting was most prevalent in the Tang Dynasty and developed into a profession during the Southern Song Dynasty. Paper cutting is one of the most popular folk arts in China, as it has been a part of Chinese history and culture for thousands of years.

Window flowers are paper cutouts used to paste on windows for decoration. They are most common in northern China. In the past, Northern farmhouse windows were mostly wooden lattice windows, vertical, square or with geometric lattice, with a layer of white paper glued on top, which would be replaced on New Year's Day and pasted with new window flowers to show that the old was gone to welcome the new. The forms of window flowers include corner flowers that decorate the corners of the window panes, picked flowers, and window flowers used to display continuous sets of operas or legends.

Paper cutting contains rich cultural and historical information, expresses the social cognition, moral concepts, practical experience, life ideals and aesthetic interests of the general public, and has multiple social values such as cognition, edification, expression, emotion, entertainment and communication. In 2006, paper cutting art heritage was included in the first batch of national intangible cultural heritage list.

Discussion

What traditional Chinese handicrafts can you do? Briefly talk about your experience.

Chapter 14

Food Culture

1. Seasoning

Required Reading Text

Seasoning of China

Seasoning is an auxiliary product that people use to make food. As the saying goes, "five spices blend with a hundred flavors", seasoning plays an important role in Chinese food culture. Good seasoning can remove the raw material odor, increase the flavor of food, give the dish color, sterilization, etc. In Chinese food culture, seasoning can be roughly divided into five types: savory seasoning, sweet seasoning, sour seasoning, spicy seasoning, and fresh seasoning.

Most of the dishes are inseparable from the savory taste. Savory taste is the base flavor of most compound flavors and is the main flavor in culinary applications. According to the literature, the first use of salt in China was about 5000 years ago during the time of the Yellow Emperor. Savory seasoning includes soy sauce, salt and sauce. Sweet seasoning can make food sweet and tasty, and can also be used to remove bitterness and fishy. In Chinese cooking, sweet seasoning is used more in the south. In China, sugar made from sugar cane juice can be traces back to the Eastern Han Dynasty. Sweet seasoning includes honey, sugar, etc. Sour seasoning is also widely used in cooking, with the effect of keeping astringency, can help the digestion of the stomach and intestines, but also remove the fishy taste and greasy taste. Sour seasoning includes vinegar, ketchup, etc. Spicy seasoning can remove the taste tension, enhance appetite. Spicy seasoning includes pepper, chili, ginger, scallion, garlic, etc. Fresh seasoning includes fish sauce, monosodium glutamate, oyster sauce, etc.

Extended Text

Soy Sauce

Soy sauce is made from soybeans or black beans, wheat or bran, and salt through the process of making oil and fermentation. Soy sauce is a traditional Chinese liquid condiment. Soy sauce is reddish-brown in color, has a unique soy aroma, tastes delicious and helps to promote appetite. Soy sauce is generally divided into dark and light soy sauce. Light soy sauce is used to enhance freshness and dark soy sauce is used to enhance color. The composition of soy sauce is complex. In addition to salt, there are many amino acids, carbohydrate, organic acids, pigments and spices, etc. It is mainly salty, but also fresh and fragrant. Soy sauce can increase and improve the flavor of dishes, and can also add or change the color of dishes.

Soy sauce evolved from sauce, and China was the first country in the world to manufacture and consume sauce. As early as 3000 years ago, the making of sauce was recorded in China during the Zhou Dynasty. Originally, soy sauce was an ancient Chinese imperial condiment made from fresh meat by marinating, similar to the process used to make today's fish sauce. Because of its excellent flavor, soy sauce gradually spread to the people. It was later discovered that soy sauce was made from soybeans with a similar flavor and was cheap, so it became widely available for consumption. With the development of China's foreign cultural exchange, soy sauce gradually spread to Japan, Korea and Southeast Asia.

Discussion

> Briefly describe the seasoning used in your national cuisine. Talk about the similarities and differences with Chinese one.

② Cuisines

Required Reading Text

Cuisines of China

China is a country with profuse food culture, and different cuisines have been formed in a certain region for a long time due to the influence of geography, climate and products, cultural traditions and ethnic customs. In China, Shandong, Sichuan, Guangdong, Fujian, Jiangsu, Zhejiang, Hunan and Anhui cuisine are known as the eight major cuisines.

Shandong cuisine is known for its fragrant, crispy, thick and pure taste, and it is especially good at making pure and turbid soup.

Sichuan cuisine pays attention to color, fragrance, taste and shape, and especially works hard on taste, which is famous for its many, wide and thick flavors.

Guangdong cuisine refers to Cantonese cuisine. The characteristics of Guangdong cuisine are rich and fine selection of materials and light taste.

Jiangsu cuisine is mainly seafood and is known for its delicate preparation, beautiful color and fresh flavoring.

Suzhou cuisine tends to be sweet, with fine knife work, delicate fire, fresh hues and chic shapes. Jiangsu cuisine is famous for its main ingredients, its original taste, its lightness, especially for its soup making.

Zhejiang cuisine is light, fresh, tender and tasty.

Hunan cuisine is mostly served with chili peppers as the main dish.

Anhui cuisine is traditionally seasoned with ham and is characterized by heavy color, oil and fire.

Extended Text

Zhejiang Cuisine

Zhejiang cuisine is a regional cuisine of Zhejiang Province. Zhejiang cuisine has a wide range of ingredients, and the main ingredients are seasonal and varied. Zhejiang cuisine is characterized by fine knife work and exquisite dishes. Zhejiang cuisine is seasoned with fire, and is fresh, tender and tasty. Zhejiang cuisine is mainly composed of four local flavor dishes from Hangzhou, Ningbo, Shaoxing and Wenzhou.

Hangzhou cuisine is very delicate and uses quick-frying, stir-frying, stewing, frying and other cooking techniques commonly. The dishes are cooked with freshness, tenderness, delicacy and mellowness. The famous dishes of Hangzhou cuisine include West Lake Carpin Sweet and Sour Sauce, Dongpo Pork, Shelled Shrimps with Dragon Well Green Tea leaves, and Braised Spring Bamboo Shoots. Ningbo cuisine has a lot of seafood, and stewing, grilling and steaming are the common cooking methods. The taste of Ningbo cuisine is fresh and salty in a moderate range, and the dishes are fresh, tender and smooth, with emphasis on the original taste. The famous dishes of Ningbo cuisine include Yellow Fish in Pickled Cabbage Soup, Steamed Turtle in Crystal Sugar, Pot-Roasted Eel, Slippery Yellow Green Crab, Ningbo Roast Goose, etc. The ingredients of Shaoxing cuisine are mainly fish, shrimp, river food, chicken, duck, poultry, beans and bamboo shoots. Shaoxing cuisine is crispy and glutinous, with thick soup and mellow taste. The famous dishes of Shaoxing cuisine include Fried Shrimps, Dried Vegetable Stew Meat, Dinegar-Flavored Fish Head and Belly, Steamed Mandarin Fish, etc. Wenzhou cuisine is also known as "ou cuisine", with mainly seafood dishes and fresh light but not thin taste. The famous dishes of Wenzhou cuisine include Three Silk Knocking Fish, Fish Brain with Tangerine Pith, Garlic Fish Skin and so on.

Discussion

> Briefly introduce the cuisines of your country.

③ Tableware

Required Reading Text

Tableware of China

Tableware refers to non-edible tools that come into direct contact with food during meals, utensils and appliances used to assist in food distribution or ingestion. Tableware in daily use in China includes metal utensils, ceramic tableware, tea and wine utensils, glassware, paper utensils, plastic utensils, and a wide variety of containers and hand-held utensils for different purposes. At the table, chopsticks, spoons, bowls and dishes are the most frequently used tableware by Chinese people.

Chopsticks, the most common tableware used by Chinese, are used directly to hold food. The time when Chinese started using chopsticks is uncertain, but they have been used for at least 3000 years.

Spoons are a tool used for serving soup and rice. Spoons are the oldest tableware used in China, roughly 7000 years old. There are many different kinds of spoons, including spoons for soup and frying spoons with a handle for stir-fry.

Compared to the plates commonly used in the West, most Chinese people prefer to use bowls. Bowls can be divided into large bowls and small bowls. Rice bowls are small bowls, which are used to serve rice. Soup bowls belong to large bowls, which are used to serve communal soup. The soup bowl has a communal spoon to serve soup.

The dish is a small and shallow vessel for serving food or condiments. Dishes are smaller than plates and are mostly round. Dishes also have other shapes, such as oval and rectangular dishes.

Extended Text

Chopsticks

Chopsticks, known as zhu in ancient times, are usually made of materials such as bamboo, wood, bone, porcelain, metal, and plastic. Chopsticks are one of the hallmarks of Chinese food culture and one of the most commonly used tableware in the world. Chopsticks were invented in China and later spread to other countries like Korea, Japan, and Vietnam. Serving chopsticks also originated in China. Both the sharing of meals and the use of serving chopsticks have a long history in China.

There are many folk legends about chopsticks. One legend is that Jiang Ziya was inspired by a sacred bird to invent silk and bamboo chopsticks. One legend is that Daji invented jade hairpins as chopsticks to please King Zhou, and another legend is that Yu invented chopsticks to save time by fishing for hot food with tree branches when he was taming the flood. Ordinary chopsticks are about 22–24 cm in length, thick at the top and thin at the bottom, and round at the top and rectangular bottom. The advantage of this shape is that they are easy to hold and do not turn easily. The smooth and rounded end of the chopsticks that holds the food at the entrance will not hurt the lips and tongue.

In China, there are many rules for using chopsticks. When placing chopsticks, they must be placed in pairs. When eating with chopsticks, the chopsticks should not touch people nearby. When talking to someone, you should put down your chopsticks as a sign of courtesy. Chopsticks should not be licked or inserted vertically into the bowl.

Discussion

> Which tableware is used in your country? What are the customs of using tableware?

4 Seasonal Food

Required Reading Text

Seasonal Food

Eating according to the seasons throughout the year is another characteristic of Chinese food culture. Since ancient times, China has been seasoning and serving dishes according to seasonal changes.

In spring, it is especially suitable to eat some warm and tonic food, and leeks are a very good choice. It is also the most beautiful time to eat spinach as it is the most tender season. This is the time when spinach is called "spring spinach" and is particularly tasty with its red roots and green leaves and freshness. The spring bamboo shoots are also particularly delicious, and this is the most suitable day of the year to eat bamboo shoots.

Summer is the season to taste freshness. Plums, cherries, fragrant plums, broad beans and new tea are all seasonal delicacies. In the hot summer, people will have a bowl of chilled and sour plum syrup or cold and sweet mung bean soup to relieve the heat. In summer, it is appropriate to eat some bitter food, such as bitter melons, bitter vegetables, bitter bamboo shoots and lettuces.

Autumn, the season of harvest, have the most abundant food. For example, hairy crabs are fattest in autumn. And in autumn, it is the time when fresh lotus roots should be marketed, and pork rib and lotus roots soup is also delicious in autumn.

In winter, dumplings are still eaten on the Winter Solstice in the north. On the 8th day of the Lunar New Year, everyone sits together to drink Laba porridge, and in many places, there are also customs such as soaking Laba garlic and eating Laba beans. Other dishes such as hot pot and raw rolled porridge are also good for warming up in winter.

Extended Text

Qingming Seasonal Food

Qingming is one of the 24 Chinese solar terms, which falls on April 5 or 4 every year. At this time of year, one should pay attention to health care.

One of the most suitable seasonal vegetables to eat around Qingming is shepherd's purse. Shepherd's purse helps to strengthen immune function and is suitable for consumption during the Qingming Festival. Snail is also a delicacy during this time of year. Around Qingming, the earth recovers from the warmth of spring, and snails that have lain dormant in the mud crawl out of the soil. This is the best time to eat snails because of their fatty flesh. Qingming is also a good time to eat shrimp. During this time, river food is fat and delicious. Toon, also known as cedrela sinensis bud, is known as vegetables on the tree. The toon is usually sprouted during the Qingming season and picked around the Grain Rain. The young shoots of toon can be used to make various dishes such as scrambled eggs with toon, toon and bamboo shoots, and toon with tofu. It is not only nutritious, but also has high medicinal value, with anti-inflammatory, detoxifying and insecticidal effects.

In addition, there are also snacks such as green rice balls and mugwort ban that are suitable for eating around Qingming. During the Qingming Festival, it is customary to eat green rice balls in the south of the Yangtze River. Green rice balls are made of mugwort juice mixed with glutinous rice flour and then wrapped in bean paste or lotus seed paste, which are not too sweet but not greasy and have a light but long fragrance. Mugwort ban is a special snack for the Qingming in the Hakka region of Guangdong Province.

Discussion

> What are the specialties of your country in different seasons? What are the differences and similarities with the Chinese ones?

(5) Tea

Required Reading Text

Tea of China

Tea, generally includes the leaves and buds of the tea tree. Tea originated in China. China is the origin of the tea tree and is the first country to discover tea and develop it into a culture.

The Bashu region is the cradle of Chinese tea. As early as the Warring States Period, the Bashu region has formed a large-scale tea area, with tea as a tribute. After Qin unified China, tea drinking gradually spread to other parts of China. In the Western Han Dynasty, tea developed into a high-grade drink in the court and became specialized appliances. During the Jin Dynasty, tea trees were planted in the middle and lower reaches of the Yangtze River. With the establishment of the Eastern Jin dynasty in the south, the tea cultivation and tea drinking in the southern region gradually expanded to Ningbo and Wenzhou coastal area in eastern Zhejiang. By the Tang Dynasty, the middle and lower reaches of the Yangtze River had become the center of tea production and technology in China. During the Song Dynasty, the center of gravity of tea in China shifted from the east to the south, and tea gradually developed in the area around Lingnan. For example, Jian'an, Fujian Province became the main technical center for the production of Chinese dough tea and cake-shaped tea. After the Ming and Qing dynasties, the Chinese tea producing areas were basically stable and the development of tea was mainly reflected in the improvement of tea production methods.

Extended Text

The Chinese Tea Ceremony

The tea ceremony refers to the procedures and techniques for preparing and drinking tea. The tea ceremony originated in China and flourished in southern China as well as Japan. China has a unique spirit of the tea ceremony, namely "harmony, quiet, joy (yi) and truth (zhen)".

Harmony is a common philosophical concept of Confucianism, Buddhism and Taoism, which means the organic unity and harmony of the universe and all things, and therefore the beauty of harmony after the realization of the unity of heaven and man emerged.

Quiet is the necessary way for Chinese tea ceremony to cultivate self-cultivation and self-pursuit. Only through the "calmness", we can taste the true meaning of the life through the light tea soup, understand the heart and see the nature in tea activities, understand the mysteries of the universe through a small teapot, exercise personality and go beyond the self through the tea ceremony.

Joy means happy and pleasant. In the process of drinking tea, we either recite poems and make pairs, cultivate our bodies, send sentiments, make friends; or refresh the mind, assist in mediation and enlightenment; or enhance physical fitness and prolong life by using the medicinal value of tea.

Truth means verity, authenticity and sincerity. Verity refers to the comprehension of the "Tao" to get the spiritual sublimation in tea tasting. Authenticity refers to the expression of one's true self in tea tasting, unrestrained and free to think about the sea and sky. Sincerity means being honest in tea tasting, exchanging feelings, and communicating ideas.

Discussion

> Do you have a custom of tea tasting in your country? Briefly introduce it.

6 Wine

Required Reading Text

Wine of China

Wine refers to a beverage made from fermented sorghum, barley, rice, grapes or other fruits, and is one of the main beverages in human life. China has a long history of making wine, and there are many varieties. From literary and artistic creation, cultural entertainment to food and cooking and health care, wine plays an important role in the daily life of Chinese people.

Chinese wine making first originated in the early Xia Dynasty or before, with a history of more than 4000 years. In the 5000-year history of the Chinese people, wine and wine culture have always occupied an important position. Wine is a special kind of food that belongs to the material, but at the same time is integrated into people's spiritual life. There are many stories about wine in Chinese history, such as Tao Yuanming, a poet of the Jin Dynasty, who could not live without wine for a day, Li Bai, a great poet of the Tang Dynasty, who wrote better poems the more he drank, and Wu Song, a hero of the Liang Mountain in the Song Dynasty, who drank 18 bowls of wine in one breath and killed a fierce tiger with his bare hands. In China, wine has been widely integrated into people's lives, and the wine culture has been enriched and developed as never before. Birthday banquets, wedding banquets, funeral banquets and other related wine customs and rituals have become an important part of Chinese people's lives.

Chinese wine is divided into baijiu, huangjiu, fruit wine, prepared wine and beer. There are many famous Chinese wines, Moutai, Wuliangye, Fenjiu, Zhuyeqing, Luzhoulaojiao, Gujing Gongjiu, Shaoxing Jiafan, Changyu wine, Great Wall dry red wine, etc., all of which are world-famous.

Extended Text

Huangjiu

Huangjiu, also known as old wine, is a variety of low-alcohol juice wine made from glutinous rice, millet, black rice, corn and wheat, which is steamed, mixed with wheat bent, rice bent or wine medicine, and sweetened and fermented. Huangjiu, originating from China, is known as one of the world's three most ancient wines, along with beer and wine. Huangjiu, a Han Chinese specialty, is a low-alcohol brewing wine. The Chinese began making huangjiu in large quantities about 3000 years ago during the Shang and Zhou dynasties.

Chinese huangjiu has a wide range of origins and many varieties. Some of the more famous ones are Fangxian huangjiu, Shaoxing old wine, Longyan sinking jar wine, Jiujiang sealing jar wine, Fujian old wine, Wuxi Huiquan wine, Jiangyin Heidu wine, Shaoxing Zhuyuanhong and Nüerhong. Depending on the production process, huangjiu can be divided into glutinous rice huangjiu, millet huangjiu, rice huangjiu and monascus huangjiu. Glutinous rice huangjiu uses liquor and wheat bran as saccharifying and fermenting agents and is mainly produced in southern China. Millet huangjiu is produced mainly in northern China, using branquill made from rice mold as saccharifying and fermenting agents. Rice huangjiu is a modified huangjiu, produced mainly in Jilin Province, Shandong Province and Fanxian in Hubei Province, China, with rice quill and yeast as saccharifying and fermenting agents. Monascus huangjiu is made from glutinous rice with red yeast as saccharifying and fermenting agents, and is mainly produced in Fujian and Zhejiang provinces, China.

Discussion

> Do you have a drinking habit in your country? Tell us briefly about it.

Chapter 15

Differences Between China and Foreign Countries

1 Greeting and Communication

Required Reading Text

Greeting and Communication

China has a unique culture of communication. For example, when greeting each other, Chinese people usually look for a topic and make small talk with each other as a sign of friendship and politeness. For example, "Have you eaten?", "What are you doing?" and "Where are you going?" and so on. It is worth noting that the above greetings can only be carried out between the more familiar people. If you don't say anything when you meet someone you know, it will lead to suspicion: "Why is this person so cold to me?" This is the Chinese unique mentality. Westerners are very individualistic and private, and may think that what I'm doing, where I'm going, whether I've eaten or not are all personal and have nothing to do with greeting each other.

In the process of communication, salutation is the first message conveyed to the other party. Different names reflect the differences in role identity, social status and closeness of the two parties. Therefore, the name should not be exported freely, and some details should be paid attention to. For example, you cannot mispronounce a person's name or call an unmarried woman as "madam". In addition, in contemporary

China, the name "xiaojie" has a derogatory connotation, so women should not be addressed as "xiaojie".

When meeting and talking about the weather, Westerners limit themselves to making objective comments about the weather, while Chinese people often talk about the weather as if they are family members and show their concern.

Extended Text

Meeting Etiquette

Meeting etiquette refers to the most commonly used and basic etiquette of daily social etiquette. Shaking hands is a very common etiquette in China, generally used when meeting each other, parting, congratulations, condolences, etc.

Fist-and-palm salute, also known as the bowing salute, is one of the traditional Chinese manners that has been used for more than 2000 years and is often used when people meet each other. Fist-and-palm salute means that both hands are held together in front of the chest. When saluting, regardless of respect, we should arch our hands until they are flush with our eyebrows and shake them up and down in a weighted manner a few times. If it is a heavy salute, you may bow after making a fist-and-palm salute with hands folded in the front.

Bowing, meaning to bend over and salute, is a courtesy to show respect for others. Three bows is called the most respectful salute. In China, bowing is often used for subordinates to superiors, students to teachers, juniors to elders, as well as for service personnel to greet guests and actors to thank the audience with applause.

It is worth noting that meeting etiquette varies among different ethnic groups in China. For example, Heilongjiang Manchu traditional etiquette is reflected in all aspects such as clothing, food, housing, words and behaviors. According to the different generations and gender, the Manchu rituals are divided into kneeling, waist-hugging, shoulder-brushing, hand-shaking, sideburn stroking and so on.

Discussion

What is the meeting etiquette in your country? What are the differences from China?

② Lifestyle

Required Reading Text

Lifestyle

Lifestyle refers to the activities of daily life of individuals and their families, including clothing, food, housing, transportation, and the use of leisure time. The differences between Chinese and Western lifestyle are mainly in the areas of language, food, education, and architecture.

Language. Chinese characters are pictographs and square characters. Chinese is subtle, elegant and flamboyant. Western languages are straightforward, frank, and somewhat spirited.

Food. There is a huge difference between China and the West in the way of eating. Chinese people like to be lively and gather around for a meal. Westerners like to dine in a quiet, elegant environment, where everyone has their own plate, all assigned in advance. Chinese staple foods are dominated by grains, followed by vegetables and dominated by plants. Westerners' staple food is predominantly meat.

Education. Western education is dominated by the idea that everyone is a special talent and all students are given the opportunity to excel. Chinese education emphasizes the collective, group consciousness and hardly focus on individual differences.

Architecture. The difference between Chinese and Western architectural styles is essentially due to the difference in culture. Chinese culture values people, while Western culture values things. Chinese culture values morality and art, while the Western culture values science and religion.

Extended Text

Diet Style

In terms of food, Chinese people's staple food is mainly cereals and their products, such as noodles, and their side dishes are mainly vegetables, supplemented by meat. In the West, meat and dairy are the main staples. In the drink, Chinese people are used to drinking tea; Westerners like to drink coffee.

In the way of eating, in China, in any banquet, there will only be one form, that is, everyone sitting around in a group and sharing a seat. Chinese banquets have to use round tables, which formally creates an atmosphere of unity, courtesy and common interest. In the West, the meal system is divided, so that each person orders his or her own food, and orders what he or she wants to eat, which also shows the West's respect for individuality. In most Chinese banquets, seating is based on orderly and respect for the elders, while in the West, seating is based on ladies first and respect for women. Chinese people also like to share food and drink together, and the atmosphere is harmonious and interesting. Westerners are less enthusiastic and less polite between guests and hosts, focusing more on personal independence.

Discussion

> Talk briefly about lifestyle in your country. Compare the similarities and differences with that of China.

③ Aesthetic Thinking

Required Reading Text

Aesthetic Thinking

Aesthetic thinking is the general, indirect, and dynamic reflection of the world's objects in aesthetics. Chinese embody the spirit of humanism in aesthetic thinking, while Westerns embodies more the spirit of scientism.

The biggest difference between Chinese and Westerners in their aesthetic way of thinking is wholeness versus individuality. Chinese emphasize wholeness and comprehensiveness, and advocate that when grasping the aesthetic object, not in isolation, static view of a particular aspect, but in systematical and holistic view to grasp the object. The characteristics of holistic thinking is focused on the unity of heaven and man, the harmony of heaven and man. In modern philosophical language, it is the unity of man and nature, the unity of subject and object, the unity of subjective and objective, etc. Westerners think locally and individually, analytically and empirically, favoring specialized and precise studies and examinations of a particular part or sector of the world. Analysis, diversity and divergence are its basic characteristics. "Golden ratio" "unity of diversity" "distinguish manking from heaven" and other cultural concepts of form are the specific performance of this kind of thinking. The logical character of Western thinking makes people like to compare art to natural science in aesthetic activities, emphasizing rational analysis of aesthetic categories.

Extended Text

Architectural Style

In architecture, Chinese people pay attention to subtlety and seclusion, and it is better to have a winding path. This place has a rockery; that place has a bamboo forest and flowers; everywhere you go, there are different scenes. People artificially make lakes, hills, small bridges and flowing water at homes, pursuing the unity of heaven and man. Chinese gardening is concerned with the implications but not exposition. Unlike Westerners, Chinese know things more by direct experience. They believe that intuition is not a direct response of the senses, but a mental activity, a sublimation of inner experience, which cannot be sought by reasoning. Garden landscape draws on poetry, painting, and strive to be subtle, deep, illusory, so as to see small in large, large in small, real in the virtual, virtual in the real, or hidden or revealed, or shallow or deep, so that many completely opposing factors intertwined and blended into one. Suzhou gardens are a typical representative of Chinese architecture.

Discussion

> Briefly talk about the traditional architecture of your country. What are the similarities and differences with Chinese traditional architecture?

④ Concept of Time

Required Reading Text

Concept of Time

The concept of time is the natural or physical time perceived by human observation. The differences between Chinese and foreign concepts of time are mainly reflected in the following points.

The first is the pluralistic view of time and the unitary view of time. Chinese is a typical nation with a pluralistic view of time, emphasizing the adaptation to time. People are more concerned about timing and degree, and are more flexible but less planned. On the contrary, Westerners have a typical unitary view of time, which emphasizes the arrangement of time.

The second is circular and linear view of time. In the Chinese concept, time is cyclical, meaning that time changes in coordination with the state of nature, such as the alternation of day and night, the reciprocation of seasons, and the cyclical growth of plants. Western culture, on the contary, is deeply influenced by Christianity. Westerners look to the future, leading people to hold a linear view of time, believing that time is a linear one-way continuous movement.

The third is continuity and immediacy of time. In Chinese culture, people traditionally focus on the continuity of time and do things in a steady manner. The longer something takes, the more important it becomes. Westerners value the immediacy of time and emphasize efficiency in getting things done in the shortest possible time.

Extended Text

Time Orientation

Time is an important aspect of environmental language, and different cultures breed different concepts of time and time behavior. Many cultural differences are reflected in the differences between the past time orientation and future time orientation in China and the West.

Chinese people just take a backward-looking or past orientation in their time orientation. Chinese people like to look back in history and show respect to their parents and elders in terms of social ethics. The Chinese care deeply about the rules of the old ancestors and successful experiences and lessons of failures. The past is often the standard by which the present is measured and is an important reference for the success or failure of today's things. Thus there are Chinese idioms such as "learn from the past" "remembering the past is the teacher of the future" and "learn from the past, grow from the past". The Chinese are not as interested in the future as they are in the past, because it is unknowable and unpredictable.

In contrast to the Chinese time orientation, Westerners are time oriented by the future. They emphasize the future, expecting it to be more exciting than the present world. The Chinese terms "elder" and "big", which are often used to express respect, has no such meaning in the West. Because in the Western mind, "elder" means that youth has passed away, and is a synonym for bad. If we really want to address them, we must use "respected" or "senior".

Discussion

> Briefly talk about the similarities and differences between concept of time and China's?

5 Thinking Patterns

Required Reading Text

Thinking Patterns

Chinese prefer figurative thinking, while Westerners prefer abstract thinking. Figurative thinking involves a process of imagination. This way of thinking is perceptual and intuitive. Abstract thinking is a thinking activity that uses concepts to make judgments and reasoning.

Chinese prefer integrative thinking and Westerners prefer analytic thinking Chinese tend to think holistically and prioritize the whole. When Chinese observe and analyze things, they do not talk about as they are, do not divide and analyze things, but look at things as a whole and pay full attention to the connection of that thing with other things. Westerners favor an analytic mode of thinking. For Westerners, to understand one thing, it must first be divided and taken apart in order to figure out the internal structure.

Chinese prefer to think alike, while Westerners prefer to think differently. Both Chinese and Western cultures notice the contradiction and opposition of things. Chinese culture emphasizes more on unity and the way of thinking of seeking common ground, emphasizing the harmony and coexistence of all things. Ethically, in order to take care of the overall situation and the whole, Chinese are willing to sacrifice individual or local interests when necessary to protect the interests of the whole. In Western culture, thinking mode of seeking differences is more common, pursuing the meaning of individual survival.

Extended Text

Integrative Thinking

Integrative thinking emphasizes the whole. For example, traditional Chinese medicine views the human body as a whole, using the science of yin and yang and the five elements to illustrate the dependency and constraint relationships among the five organs. Analytic thinking emphasizes the parts or the individual. Thus, Western medicine is based on human anatomy and explains pathological phenomena based on the physiological structure of the nine systems of the human body.

The Chinese emphasis on the whole is also reflected in the classification of artistic disciplines. For example, Peking opera, as Chinese national art, is a comprehensive performance that emphasizes singing, chanting, acting and fighting. This type of performance can be broken down into opera, dance drama, and modern drama in the West. Another example is that in Chinese paintings, there are not only paintings, but also often accompanied by poems, calligraphy and seal engraving. In Western paintings, there is usually only the painting, and at most the name of the painter is signed on the painting. As a result, the classification of Chinese art disciplines is often less clear-cut, and people are more accustomed to the aesthetic sensibility of comprehensive categories.

On the linguistic level, it is also expressed in this way. For example, in the expression of time, the Chinese order is year-month-day-hour-minute-second. Westerners, especially the British, express it as minute-hour-day-month-year. Chinese are used to express space in the order from big to small, from whole to part, while Westerners do the opposite.

Discussion

Talk briefly about the similarities and differences between your country's thinking patterns and China's.

⑥ Gathering Style

● Required Reading Text

Gathering Style

A gathering is a gathering of many people at a specific time and place to communicate. There are major differences between the Chinese and Western ways of gathering.

The first is the time of the gatherings. Chinese gatherings usually take place during the day, or if it is an evening gathering, the gathering starts very early. The host has to get busy even earlier, because the primary purpose of the party is often to gather for a meal. The end of the gatherings is also basically earlier, and will not end until the next day. Western gatherings, on the contary, start very late and often do not end until the next day.

The second is the location of the gatherings. Most Chinese gatherings are at home. For example, A dinner party is when the invitee prepares a good meal at home and waits for the invited person to visit. In contrast, Westerners tend to choose restaurants and bars for their gatherings.

The last is the people who attend the gatherings. Chinese gatherings are generally composed of people who know each other, and it is considered rude to bring people to the gatherings who are not familiar with the host. Western gatherings will have many unfamiliar faces.

It is worth noting that food is important in Chinese gatherings. The dinner is the highlight of the gatherings. People tend to talk and laugh at the table. In contrast, food does not play a major role in Westerners' gatherings.

● Extended Text

Chinese Gatherings

There is a Chinese proverb that says "Food is the first necessity of the people". This shows that eating is a very important thing in Chinese people's daily life.

There is a lot more behind the Chinese dinner than just eating for the sake of eating. For example, "Hongmen banquet" "defining a hero while warming the wine", and "cup of wine to release military power", which have gone down in Chinese history, reflect the importance of Chinese gatherings. In China, there are many different kinds of dinner parties. Whether it is a holiday, a wedding, a funeral, a birthday celebration, a negotiation, or a move, there will be a gathering. It is evident that it is not simply dining gathering, but carries many social connotations.

In addition, Chinese are also very particular about the etiquette of their meals. From seating arrangement to the order of serving, from the person who is the first the pick up food to the time to leave the table, there are clear rules that explain the concept of "China is a nation of manners" to the fullest. In a Chinese meal, the seat in the middle of the table is for the most honored person, and the food is served in the order of cooling first, then hotting, simplifying first and then complicating.

In China, most interpersonal communication takes place at the dinner table. At the table, Chinese people drink wine, eat and communicate at the same time.

Discussion

Briefly talk about the similarities and differences between the way of gatherings in your country and China's.